Hello, and welcome.
And thanks for reading this book, howe
Amazon, stolen off a friend, or the barg
your local charity shop.
It was the charity shop I reckon.

Anyway, this is my weighty review of Manchester City's 2018/19 season. A season that almost finished me off.

Relive the highs, the lows, and the staggering stress levels one more time as Pep Guardiola guided his team to an unprecedented domestic treble. A treble without applause, as the vultures circled above perhaps the country's greatest ever club side.
For the first time in their history, Manchester City FC retained a football trophy. And they did it twice.

I'll be looking back at every game in a blockbuster season: the controversies, the debates, and of course all of the action. I'll be looking at the defining moments that shaped the season and the defining players too. It's a story of how the world's greatest manager wove his magic in a little part of east Manchester. It's a story that thankfully has a happy ending, but a bittersweet one as we waved goodbye to one of the club's greatest servants. Most of this book was written at the time of events, with me filling in a few gaps in recent weeks and adding a bit more insight. So some of my predictions, concerns and rants may seem embarrassing now, but so be it.
And don't worry, there was time left over to have a few digs at Liverpool and Manchester United too.

So sit back and enjoy, as I review the greatest of nine months.

Drink it in.

So before we look at the season, there were the summer months to enjoy after the Centurions cemented their place in football history. Here's what happened as the UK sweltered in a rare but welcome heatwave that lasted for many a month.

Manchester City pretty much exist in the modern age to boil the urine of rival fans, and that was shown to good effect as Pep Guardiola won Manager Of The Year after the season ended, somehow edging out the genius that is Sean Dyche. Needless to say, Dyche was not in the running the following season, though blinkered cheerleaders such as Alistair Campbell probably think he should have been.

Anyway, we will all have different ideas on how you decide on who is the best manager. The one who wins the league, or the one who performs above expectations? The problem with the latter, and let's not forget Alan Pardew has won this award, is that there is always a manager who exceeds expectations. If that is always your criteria, then the league-winning manager will never get the award, unless he is Claudio Ranieri. Pep got 100 points. He's the don. Accept it.

There was other good news – in fact it flooded in during the summer, as England melted. David Silva's son Mateo was deemed well enough to go home, and has prospered ever since. The fact David played through such a harrowing period of his life says more about the guy than I can put into words.

And then Pep signed a contract extension! The deal sees him through to the end of the 2020-21, and is obviously great news. More so because the man is still something of an enigma. He is clearly a stress ball in human form, and the job must take a lot out of him. To have him commit at this early stage is great news. Part of me expected the three year cycle to be his life-span at City, so for every year beyond that I am truly grateful. Get that statue sorted.

Preferably of him in a large cardigan on the touchline.

The giggles just kept on coming in. A lethargic Manchester United lost the cup final to Chelsea. That was just a warm-up to the main event, which of course was Liverpool losing the Champions League final.

Now I make no apologies here. Laughing at Liverpool is THE definition of karma. How can you not take some satisfaction at the deluded cult proclaiming how they were the greatest, assuming the trophy was already theirs, lording it over all and sundry, defeat and then the inevitable recriminations, death threats against their own keeper and naturally the Ramos campaign to have him hung, drawn and quartered. And all they are left with at the end of it all is one League Cup trophy in twelve years and a rusting trophy parade bus.

They had their excuse though, this one quite novel – the keeper was concussed, hence why he threw the ball in his own net. They should stop complaining – over the coming season, they seemed to come up against a lot of concussed goalkeepers.

The Kippax

The most excellent writer Ste Tudor asked me for my thoughts on the Kippax for an article he was writing. I include my thoughts below, as only a few lines made it to the final piece. This may have been related to me sending it a week after the deadline.

Talking about the Kippax feels like talking about a past-life, a distant era of football Pinks, pay-on-the-gate, season-ticket stubs and outside urinals. An all too distant memory in a world of sanitised stadia, match day "experiences" and billion dollar deals.

I was 20 when the Kippax hosted its final match as a terrace. After that Maine Road was home to the white elephant that was the new, sparkly seated stand, for just nine years. It may have kept the name, but it wasn't the same. Nothing was the same again.

The Kippax was different not just because it was the place where City fans forged their footballing experiences, but because it ran down the side of the pitch, not behind a goal, like most of the hard core terracing areas did at the time. I liked that. I liked the freedom to pick a spot down most of the touchline, the challenge of finding that perfect placement, of avoiding a pillar, of avoiding the more manic elements of our support, an option sadly missing in the modern game.

And I liked standing. Standing leant itself to a better atmosphere, to surges that seemed innocent and fun at the time, to heaving masses of humanity that are seared in your memory and probably helped you fall in love with the beautiful game. Not that every game was a seething mass of humanity of course. In the 1980s, at most grounds, there was room for a picnic, but you tend to hold on to the memories that make you smile most.

And the Kippax was where the noise came from. As a youngster I sat in all parts of the ground, as I didn't have a season ticket, but when I was in the Main Stand or the Platt Lane end, I always felt like I was missing out, gazing lovingly at the stand I should be in, every match. A stand full of exotic smells, exotic to me as a kid at least – beer, fags, humanity. As a kid it was the most exciting place in the world –I felt cool, I felt like I was an adult, and despite what may have been occurring on the pitch, there was nowhere else I would rather be. Going to a match and standing on the Kippax was an adventure, something modern football rarely is anymore. This is where you came of age as a child. Young football fans across the world were going through the same experience.

But hey, that's nostalgia for you – the experience was often miserable, the weather terrible, the football worse, the stand half-empty.

Still miss it all though.

Adventures In Kiev

But back to Liverpool – by the end of this book, you'll think it was actually about them. They had a profound effect on us all. After Liverpool's defeat to Real Madrid, I read one of those laughable pieces that their fans do so well. It was almost beyond parody, but I had a go, as you can see below. The gist of the original article was predictable – they didn't really lose, morally, they are the best fan base ever, and everyone loved them. You get the idea.

This was my version.

LIVERPOOL IN KYIV: A PLACE AND EXPERIENCE ALL LIVERPOOL FANS WILL REMEMBER FOR ALL TIME MORE THAN FANS OF ANY OTHER CLUB COULD POSSIBLY EXPERIENCE OR EVEN IMAGINE IN THEIR WILDEST DREAMS

We're different. We just are. Wiser, sometimes older, often better, but always different. Other fans will deny it, but deep down they know it. They ache with longing, envy, jealousy. From the estuaries of the Wirral to the steep ascent to the Hawthorns, from the banks of the Seine to the far-flung bars of Rome. Yes we've been to all of them, and more. Pioneers in every sense of the word.

Some say that as gold-seekers prospected in the Wild West and England saw the dawn of the industrial revolution, there were already Liverpool fans planning their first trip to see their beloved red-shirted heroes in action. Yes it was 1840, but Liverpool fans have never been restricted by schedules, fixture lists or the actual existence of a football club when conquering foreign lands. We're a family. It's what we do. #YNWA

And that's how it was in Kyiv (note the spelling). We came from all corners of the earth. From Liverpool, obviously, but also Paris, Dubai, Ireland, the Galapagos Islands, Aberdeen, Ireland, Helsinki, Ireland, and beyond. Epic journeys across continents, the likes of which had never been seen before.

Pioneers.

We've sung about conquering Europe but the reality is — just like the Shankster prophesied himself — we've only gone and conquered the bloody world. Just by turning up and drinking beer in bars and making our own flags. It was that simple, apparently.

Liverpool have torn through Europe like never before, a trail of glory that we will tell our grandchildren about. And your grandchildren too. Whoever you support, this was a tale for the ages. Beating one of the world's best teams and a few other teams too.

Take Dave, who had travelled from Cork, In Ireland. Dave had had a terrible year. He lost both his legs in a combine harvester tragedy in January, the use of both arms after holding up a Liverpool scarf for 17 hours consecutively, and his wife left him in March for a fax machine salesman from Limerick.

I asked him about his injuries. "Tis merely a scratch" he bellowed, and we all laughed at his ingenious quoting of The Holy Grail. On a nearby table, a Ukrainian woman laughed too. She did not speak English, but she understood.

She understood Scouse.

A common language, spread across the globe. She got it. We shook hands, and over an ice cold Carlsberg, stories were told, bonds formed, and memories forged like never before in the history of humanity.

Pioneers.

Dave had hopped to Dublin, before stowing away on a ferry, hitching to Folkestone, getting a job as a plate washer on a ship to Tallinn, before hot air ballooning to Moscow, then unicycling to Kyiv (note the spelling). He set off last November.

Commitment to the cause unique to the Redmen tribe.

The city of Kyiv (note the spelling) had never seen an invasion like this before, and was ill-prepared for such numbers, such passion, such wit. Hotels were full, and alternative plans had to be made. Me, Micky, Shagger, Dobbsy and Smithy stayed in the apartment of a Ukranian family. I think perhaps at first they were somewhat overawed by our passion for football and coarse humour, but by the end of our three day stay, we had friends for life.

We broke the ice with stories about Avaline, Joey, Freddie and the other Boswells. "Gotta get up, gotta get out, grab the world by the throat and shout allez allez allez!" sang the young girl in the corner with glee. Ten minutes previously she didn't know a word of English, but now she was one of us. We sang yellow submarine until dawn, regaled our hosts with tales of other epic journeys and even discussed Fred Talbot's derelict weather map in Albert Dock.

Elena asked us about Liverpool's proud history. About John Aldridge's moustache, and why he called everyone nuggets. King Kenny, and those t-shirts for Luis Suarez. We explained that human flesh was a delicacy in Uruguay, and she nodded with complete comprehension. She pretended to bite my arm and we laughed until we could barely breathe. We talked about the Klopp philosophy and why other teams do not understand the bond we have with him. I explained, with just a tin of beans and the Cyrillic alphabet, how Bertrand Russell once said that science is what you know. Philosophy is what you don't know. I felt it was then that Elena had her life "eureka!" moment. Naturally, you'll want to know about the match, but that was not the point of the trip. Yes, the scoreboard said 3-1 at the end. Some who fail to see the romance in football will point at that and say Liverpool lost that match. So naïve. But at 5am the following morning, as the party continued unabated, and I told a transfixed Sergei, son of our host Elena, about the time Liverpool swept past Cardiff in the League Cup final on penalties, it transpired to me that Liverpool did not lose the Champions League final. No. They just weren't victorious in traditional terms. Nor did they draw. But they didn't lose. Perhaps there's an argument that two Champions League trophies should be handed out this season to acknowledge the brilliance of Liverpool's performances? A re-match would be fairer, but I can't see that happening.

Any proper Real Madrid fan will acknowledge though that this was a match that was, to all intents and purposes, except for the actual score and the record books, a draw. A match where Liverpool once more failed to get the decisions, as seen throughout this remarkable cup run. An arm lock not out of place in WWF, a vicious elbow, a goal scored with a high foot (dangerous play)and a goalkeeper allowed to play on with concussion by the corrupt UEFA despots. No matter. I had always said the result was not important, and so it proved. We carried on singing long after the full-time whistle, saluting our Redmen heroes. It is said that our flags could be seen from space. Wouldn't surprise me.

You don't get relevance from trophies alone. If anything, they distract from relevance. They make you *less* relevant. Relevance is earned not bought. It's gained organically, in the bars of Kyiv (note the spelling), in the journeys of guys like Dave, in historic success in the 70s and 80s only, in having the biggest flags and in YNWA hashtags. Things money cannot buy. In a way, perhaps Liverpool are almost *too* relevant now. It would certainly explain the bitterness and rancid glee from rival fans with little to look forward or back to. They can't create what we have – nobody comes close (*you can say that again – Ed*).

What we did win was the hearts of a city and a country that will no doubt now adopt Liverpool as their second, or maybe even their first team to support. A red invasion we can all get on board with. In fact, it may be best to disband all local clubs, now that their support will be pretty much non-existent. Might as well be Manchester City.

By the time we left the apartment of Elena and her family, they were now part of our family. The Liverpool family. Elena had painted the whole apartment red, 4 Liverpool flags hung out of the front window (BOOZING WITH THE BIRD WE'RE CHOOSING, SALAH MAKING REAL CHICKEN IN KIEV, 70% OF THE WORLD IS COVERED BY WATER, THE OTHER 30% BY JAMES MILINER, and JURGEN'S GOT A HUGE DIJK), and Elena had quit her job to travel the world with only a flag, hope and 50,000 Ukrainian hryvnia to sustain her.

As we left to head home to our spiritual home, I hugged Elena. To both our surprise, a solitary tear rolled down her rosy cheek, and dropped to the floor. We both stared at the floor, in shock. Then we both cried like never before. Literal goose bumps. You may think a solitary tear means very little, but to us, it meant so much more. It was a symbol. A symbol of unity, of never walking alone (unless you're in goal for Liverpool), of conquering the world, of new friendships, of pioneers. All the stuff I've already mentioned basically. We came, we saw, we conquered Kyiv (note the spelling).

The trip had one more surprise to throw at us though. It took four hours to get the airport. Not because of traffic or a broken down car. No, everywhere we went, locals would fling themselves at our feet hysterical with emotion. One man with no teeth showed me his new Liverpool tattoo, and tried to pair me up with his daughter. A woman ran alongside our car singing "you'll never walk alone" for over two miles. You'd think this was all a dream or over-sentimental tosh if I hadn't witnessed it for myself. One man even pleaded with us to take him back to Liverpool. We politely declined, but not before donating a flag emblazoned with "WE DID IT SIX TIMES. LIVERPOOL ARE BOSS" to him by way of an apology.

Late that night I finally returned home. It seemed like I had been away for years. I had changed, the people of Kyiv (note the spelling) had changed, we were all different people now. Older, wiser, happier. The draw with Real Madrid would go down in history. Books would be written. And the poetry. The endless poetry.

Last night I phoned Elena to catch up and reminisce. Her number seems to be temporarily out of action, which is a shame, but we'll no doubt catch up properly soon. Perhaps Elena and her family will come over to Liverpool to see their new favourite team. Perhaps they'll never leave. It wouldn't surprise me.

I sat down, and re-watched the match. How unlucky. But never mind. Next year is our year. And then I started to whistle, and a little song fell out.....

Gotta find it

get us a share

makin' bread out
of nothin' but air
Ridin' high but
hittin' the ground
catchin' the penny
but missin' the pound
Doesn't matter 'cause
we'll soon turn it around
soon as we get home
it's why we're tryin', home
instead of cryin', home
YNWA Carla Lane.

Raheem Sterling – And So It Began

Raheem Sterling was in the news again, when certain odious members of our press decided to be outraged at a tattoo Sterling had inked a year previously. That outrage was delayed until just before a World Cup, because trying to scupper the team's chances at major tournaments is what our press do best. Sterling had already given a full explanation as to why he had such a tattoo, containing a gun – his father was murdered by such a weapon when he was just a young child. He didn't have to explain, and other footballers with similar tattoos received no media attention whatsoever.

But the tide was turning. Eventually Sterling would speak out, and many footballers of colour decided enough was enough, disgusted by the blatant and covert racism they encountered on a daily basis. By the end of the season, Raheem would become a focal figure in the fight for a brighter future.

And as sure as night follows day, the journalists that had spent years criticising him changed their tune quicker than a DJ who inadvertently plays a Jimmy Saville number. Hypocrites to a man.

Because it would always be a man – a middle-aged, white, privileged one.

Elsewhere, the shock news emerged that Leroy Sane had not made the Germany squad. The reasons were never made clear, but rumours abounded about attitude and the like. It must be some squad to omit him. As it turned out, it wasn't, and with hindsight the decision looked even more foolish.

The 2018 World Cup

And so onwards and upwards, and a summer of feeling good about your national side, for a change. In a tournament that did not have a single 0-0 draw in first two rounds, it was a competition that was always fun to watch. Everyone had suddenly abandoned their high moral ground and were happy to enjoy Russian hospitality and watch loads of football. Funny that. VAR was used, successfully, which was more than could be said for the subsequent nine months, and the best team won. Sterling was of course still the fall guy in a system that restricted the talents of him, and also the likes of Kane and Alli. England did not really play that well, relying on set pieces to travel deep into the tournament, but Southgate helped restore some pride on and off the pitch.

Still, the press still tried their hardest to ruin it all, with leaked England team sheets and tattoo faux outrage. Things change, and yet they stay the same. I wrote more after the tournament, after the greatest trip of my life, a great two weeks in Sri Lanka. Saw elephants, water buffalo, monkeys and even a chipmunk. Marvellous. I wrote the brief summary that follows at some point after returning.

The 2018 World Cup (again)

As I was away for the second half of the World Cup, I thought I would collate my thoughts on the entire tournament into one piece, a tournament that did not disappoint.

The initial point to raise naturally is whether the tournament should be held in a country such as Russia. Human rights and all that, but is it any more acceptable for it to be held in a country that sells arms to Saudi Arabia, and does its executions on the quiet, such as the UK? Or perhaps the USA – I mean where do I start with that country right now? I don't have the answers, I just know a winter World Cup in Qatar is definitely beyond the pale. Not surprisingly anyway, Russia was on its best behaviour for the watching world, the World Cup always a PR opportunity for the host country. Putin warned off the hooligans and there were few incidents of note. Of course the country is hardly the wild west that some would have you believe. I visited St Petersburg just a few years ago and it is a beautiful, modern city, though it has its problem with pickpockets like most major cities. What visiting fans experienced was pretty much what the country is like, I imagine. There are other issues naturally, and away from the cameras life is rather different for many, but as already mentioned, that is the case in any country. The bidding process was rotten to the core, but there are worse places to host a World Cup, as we will soon discover. In four years' time, the football crowds will merge in pubs around the country with the Xmas drinkers and carnage will no doubt ensue. Imagine cheering on your country at a World Cup with a novelty jumper on – it's not right, on many levels.

(I was forced to wear the jumper, honest).

Still, no doubt all the United, Liverpool and other clubs' fans that suddenly expressed an interest in middle-eastern human rights policies during the previous season boycotted the tournament on moral grounds. No? Thought not.

England and Southgate

But when push comes to shove, the England team was average, and little more. I'm happy they got favourable coverage, and a semi-final can never be sniffed at for a country with such a wretched finals record, but this is a side far from dominating any competition. A side that relied on players "doing a job" not always natural to them and taking advantage of set-piece prowess.

My City season card arrived in its customary tin, and needless to say annoyed some City fans as per, as this time around there was a bag of confetti included in the package. Obviously fat, middle-aged balding men who think the club is essentially them in body and spirit will not be throwing confetti in the air, but if you don't like it, put it in the bin. The club is not run according to your individual needs and specifications, and we are not still in 1982, things have changed. The club could avoid such debates by keeping things simple. But I really don't have the energy to get wound up about something given to me for free. At least they try stuff. If confetti is winding you up, then I suggest you seek help. I also suggest plenty of kids will appreciate the gift. And don't get wound up because SCOTT OF MANKUNIA things it's sooooo embarrassing. His club is such a shambles, what else has he got to have a go at?

Grumpy old man rant over. Another one will no doubt be along shortly.

places bag of confetti in bin

Elsewhere, what I believed to be our primary transfer target Jorginho went to Chelsea, which was frustrating and disappointing, as I thought he would be a great addition to the squad. I had never seen him actually play football, but still. The worry was that a Premier League winning side was once more failing to strengthen from a strong position. But the squad is already magnificent, so time will tell. In the end, it seemed City dodged another bullet.

And so with the World Cup done and truly dusted, thoughts turn back to domestic squabbles. Empty seats, net spend, history. It was nice to take a break from it all, but you can't escape for long. A truncated transfer window has got fans of most teams panicking, except Liverpool, who have committed significant funds as they attempt to win the Premier League for the 1st time. They're allowed to, naturally.

And for Pep Guardiola and his centurions, who made the league resemble a walk in the park last season, a new challenge – the rather significant one of defending a league title. In recent years at least, it is a challenge that has defeated all who have tried. The last team to retain a Premier League title was Manchester United in the 2008/09 season, so City will need to overturn a decade-long trend to do likewise. Not surprisingly United under Ferguson were quite adept at defending titles, but the only other team to do so was Mourinho's Chelsea in the 2005/06 season. It seems that success does not automatically attract further success. The title has been successfully defended 7 times in 26 attempts.

But why is that? One reason springs to mind immediately.

You see, there has to be a psychological aspect to this. Winning football matches after all is not about which team has the best players. It would be rather boring if that was always the case. A title-winning team is not just a collection of great players, it is driven, and hungry for success. Alex Ferguson used to change his number 2 on a regular basis to keep things fresh, to stop staleness creeping in – because a key question will always be at the front of a manager's mind after winning a title. Can the same players keep the intensity and drive to keep on winning? It is difficult to maintain year after year after year. Vincent Kompany alluded to this way back in April: "My team-mates might roll their eyes when I say this: I want to see how the reaction is going to be now," he said. "I've never been able to retain the title and want to see if this team has got it to carry on and be even more successful."

There's other factors too. A recent explanation must surely be found in the summer recruitment of title winners. Recruitment that has frankly been disastrous. I'm sure many will agree that you should build on success and reinforce not when just when you are at your weakest, but also when at your strongest – squads can be driven further not just by the desire for silverware, but also by fresh faces and competition. A look at post-title purchases by the likes of City, United, Chelsea and Leicester paints a sorry picture.

The obvious starting point to reinforce this argument is City's activity in the summer of 2012. City were on a high following THAT goal, and Mancini was a god, a deity in human form. A first title in 44 years, having played some of the best football the Premier League had ever seen. City were finally top dogs, and this was a chance to dominate the league for years to come. Unfortunately, that's not quite how it panned out. Mancini himself had ideas on who needed to come in, but those ideas bore precious little resemblance to what then transpired. The summer of 2012 saw Jack Rodwell, Scott Sinclair, Maicon, Javi Garcia and Matija Nastastic arrive, and whilst Nastastic looked a superb prospect and Maicon made some sense at the time as cheap backup, this was a disastrous recruitment drive. Mancini never got over the lack of support he got that summer, spent the next season starting fights in empty rooms, and within a year was gone as City never recaptured the form of the previous season.

City are not alone in this respect however. The following season saw Alex Ferguson's swansong, and the biggest recruitment of all was to announce his successor as David Moyes. How we laughed. Joining David was the one and only Marouane Fellaini, and a certain Jesse Lingard. This was not the recruitment to take United forward, especially as Ferguson's will to win and drive had papered over the cracks of the squad he left behind. Moyes didn't last the season.

And so back to City. Contrary to popular belief, it was the Cityzens who ultimately triumphed during the 2013/14 season, and were once more pronounced champions. Time to learn from past mistakes and really turn the screw on our competitors. Except that Pellegrini was always just passing through, and there seemed a lack of conviction to give him the tools to dominate further. And so in came Mangala, Sagna and Caballero. It's hard to comprehend when you look back. City became the latest in a string of teams who failed to strengthen and paid the price the following season.

And still the trend persisted. Chelsea brought in Pedro, Rahman and Falcao on loan, amongst other underwhelming arrivals. Leicester seemed unsure of how to act as champions and how bold to be in the transfer market, and their 2016 summer acquisitions have largely faded away. They spent more than £60 million on Islam Slimani, Ahmed Musa, Nampalys Mendy, Ron-Robert Zieler and Bartosz Kapustka. And so to Chelsea once more, who brought in Bakayoko, Danny Drinkwater, Rudiger and Morata. Big outlays for once, but mixed results, and Chelsea ended the season outside the Top 4.

And amongst the frothing and fretting on the internet right now is the genuine concern that City are repeating the pattern, once Jorginho slipped through their grasp. Mahrez is an excellent addition, but if the PR being put out by City is true, namely that there is no great desire to sign another midfielder, then you hope Txiki, Pep and the rest of the gang know what they are doing. I can't imagine Pep being particularly satisfied at such a scenario. This squad is good enough to not need major strengthening, but still there are concerns about cover, especially for ageing players – and there is always room for improvement.

As for this upcoming title defence, there are specific factors that will not help City in the following weeks. With more players at the World Cup than any other team, it's hard to predict which eleven players will walk out for the opening game at the Emirates. The pointless 3rd/4th place play off has hardly helped either, with a spate of City players involved in the tournament for longer than was necessary. These players need total rest now, as any attempt to bring them back early could have disastrous consequences down the line. City dropped points in their second game last season and hardly set the world alight in the opening few weeks of the season, but if they start sluggishly this season, the vultures will need little invitation to circle.

This is a different world however from the days of Ferguson and Wenger. The game has never been more awash with money, and no club has been able to dominate the domestic game. The football media love a narrative about how a team might be on the cusp of dominating for years to come, and of course City are the latest team to fit this narrative. But until they have won title after title, it's a pointless debate.

And there's plenty more to factor in. There is the downside to being champions – the effect it has on opposition teams. It is probably fair to say that many a team will raise their game when the champions are in town. It is the biggest scalp of all for any team, to beat the best in the land and all the world. Also, champions have to adapt – opposition teams have a greater idea of their strengths, of how they achieved their success. Guardiola himself has had to adapt throughout his brief two year reign due to opposition teams changing their set-up to counterbalance the City team's strengths, so it will hardly be new to him.

But for me, it still comes back to the mental aspect above all else. Even without additional recruitment, you are still left with a squad that was good enough to win the title the previous season, subject to no major sales. The key is to want it just as much the second-time round. To have a squad that wants to keep winning, rather than rest on its laurels – the 3rd season of Pep's reign will tell him more about how many of his squad possess such a mentality. Unless you have been there, done it, got the T shirt, it's probably hard for us to comprehend. But league campaigns stretch over 9 months, and they require a relentless dedication to winning football matches and overcoming obstacles. A title winning squad needs mental strength at that "business end" of the season, and need to be led by a manager who knows how to deal with pressure and take that pressure off the players. If Pep can summon another title-winning team out of the current squad, then we will know for sure that this squad is one of the greats.

Riyad Mahrez

And so in the end City made one solitary major signing in the summer of 2018, and by selling off a few youngsters and fringe players pretty much made a net profit on sales, not that I care. Killing football indeed. The signing of Mahrez as we approached the middle of July was not a great surprise. City had been linked with him for quite a while, and the pursuit of Alexis Sanchez showed that Pep saw the need for an extra attacking player in the squad.

At £60m the signing became City's record one. It is not a signing that blows me away, but I am fine with it. He adds another option to an already scintillating attacking roster, and we are taking about someone who has won Footballer Of The Year, the season Leicester won the league. He was often unplayable that season, including against City. The question is how he fits into a very different environment to what he will be used to. Time will tell.

The other concern is not who City signed, but who they did not. Fernandinho is not getting any younger, and Benjamin Mendy's injury worries mean that the left-back area could be very problematic.

The History Of The Community Shield

It's close. Not long now. Yes, just a week to go until Premier League fans get to see some proper football (feel free to check out some wonderful league football in the meantime). Of course before Manchester United v Leicester City and more, there's the small matter of the 2018 Community Shield. And small is the correct word. The most glorified of friendlies is a chance for returning players to regain match fitness, and for fans of the victorious side to claim the first trophy of the season, whilst fooling no one. Pep Guardiola has described the match as the first final of the season, and whilst, technically, he is correct, he's fooling no one either.

Nevertheless, the season showpiece has quite a rich history. Below is a truncated history of a game that has had many formats and many names.

1898 – The Sheriff of London Charity Shield (or Dewar Shield) is established. The match was played annually between the best amateur and best professional club in England, though Scottish amateur side Queens Park also took part in 1899, a dangerous precedent that eventually led to Welsh teams doing whatever they wanted.

1904 – Corinthians 10 Bury 3. Seems Bury showed a lack of spirit on the day #taxi.

1908 – amateur clubs fall out with the FA ("The FA seem stuck in the 19th century" – Charles Charlie Charles, Woolwich Arsenal, 1907) and the schism sees the birth of the Charity Shield, whereby the football league 1st division champions would play the southern league champions. The first game saw Manchester United beat Queens Park Rangers in a replay, the only time the match has required a 2nd match.

The match is played at Stamford Bridge. The ground has hosted the most Charity Shield games outside Wembley (10).

1911- the highest scoring game in the shield's history, as Manchester United defeat Swindon Town 8-4. United have won the shield more than anyone else (17 victories).

1912 – some of the Shield proceeds are donated to the Lord Mayor of London's "Titanic" disaster fund.

1913 – the format that decided who played who was a fluid concept for much of the shield's history. In 1913 the Shield was contested between Amateurs and Professionals XIs. In 1921 the Shield was contested between the Football League and FA Cup winners for the first time. The format continued to vary in the 1920s but in **1930** the Football League winner v FA Cup winner format returned, and with a few exceptions, this format has remained to the present day.

1950 – this year's game involved the England world cup team against an FA team that had toured Canada that summer. England win 4-2, banishing forever painful memories of losing to the USA 1-0 in the world cup that year. Bizarrely, the English touring team, that contained such luminaries as Nat Lofthouse and Stanley Matthews, carried out their goodwill visit to Canada at the same time as the world cup, so a poor performance by the world cup squad is not that surprising, with hindsight. Matthews had actually been part of both squads at one time or another that year.

1959 – this was the year the game was first moved to the start of the season.

1961 – Spurs win the double, so play a Football Association XI, at their own ground. They win 3-2.

1967 - Spurs goalkeeper Pat Jennings scores a goal from his own penalty area against Manchester United at Old Trafford. Alex Stepney was the embarrassed keeper at the other end and the match finished 3-3.

1971 – grumblings continue through the 1960s as to who should play this game. In 1971, Arsenal win the double, and because of pre-season friendly commitments (lucrative US tour?), decline to take part in the Charity Shield. Leicester City are invited to take part as Division 2 Champions, and they go on to beat FA Cup defeated finalists Liverpool.

1972 – it seems the Charity Shield is not much of a pull for top teams any more. Derby and Leeds both decline to play (League and FA Cup winners), so the honourable, classy Manchester City step in to save the day, despite the fact they finished 4th in the league. City heroically beat 3rd division champions Aston Villa 1-0, against all odds.

City unfairly lose the following season's shield, despite having home advantage. Maine Road had hosted the game for the 5th and final time.

1974 – the game moves to Wembley, and the modern format is established.

1984-87 – Everton win 4 Charity Shields in a row (though that includes sharing 1 with Liverpool in 1986)

1993 – penalties are introduced. Past draws meant both teams holding the trophy for 6 months each.

1998-2001 – Manchester United lose 4 Charity Shields in a row.

2002 – the trophy is re-named the Community Shield, because the FA cannot be trusted. An investigation posed serious doubts over the FA's allocation of income from the game to various charities. The inquiry also concluded that there were unacceptable delays in making donations to the charities nominated by the participating clubs.

The present day – like the myth of the curse of the Manager Of The month award, there is a similar conspiracy theory that winning the Community Shield leads to an unsuccessful league campaign thereafter. Only seven of its 26 winners in the Premier League era went on to be champions the following May, including a particularly inglorious period of eight clubs in a row between 1997 and 2004.

This means nothing though, because as we may well see this Sunday, the approach to the game and the players picked tells us virtually nothing. What's more, only 7 of 26 title-winning teams, and 2 managers, have successfully defended a Premier League title, so the difficulties of doing that may, just may, be more relevant than a curse from a pre-season friendly victory.

2018 - City will be making their 11th appearance in the season curtain-raiser, their first being in 1934, when the FA Cup holders were thumped 4-0 by Arsenal.

2018 - @simplymartial69 mocks the empty seats at Wembley, calling Manchester City a "small club". He gets 800 retweets.

The 2018 Community Shield: Manchester City 2 Chelsea 0.

It was time. Time for the game whose importance can only be decided at full-time. So with that in mind, well done City for winning their first trophy of the season!*

A glorious sunny day in London, global warming posing a clear threat to the health of Kevin De Bruyne as he reddened on the City bench. It's not a perfect ground, but it still looks good in the sun, and a day out at Wembley should never be sniffed at, irrelevant of the importance. No trip down for me though, with 2 weeks in Sri Lanka ensuring I will be eating little more than stale bread for a few weeks at least.

And Pep certainly talked the talk, declaring it the first final of the season. I don't truly agree, but his joy at the opening goal showed this meant something to him, City's first Charity/Community Shield win at Wembley.

It is still a friendly though, and the crowd was perfectly satisfactory with that in mind. Much bigger battles will follow, but naturally when the side is this good, what else can rival fans pick at? The pre-match training shirt perhaps, with just cause. Predicting the starting XI was nigh on impossible, but the side picked was stronger than I expected. In fact, I looked at both teams and thought they were fairly strong, then considered the absentees for both clubs and realised there is serious strength in depth for Chelsea and City. It should be obvious to me for City of course, but sometimes it needs to be laid out in front of you to remind you of the ridiculous squad that City have now. A team of absent players would probably finish in the top 6.

Anyway, good to see Foden, always good to see Sergio, and good to see Mr Mendy. Bravo in goal was disappointing as it suggests he might remain there next week. More on him later. Bolton had cruelly picked up a small knock during the week, so Walker was in too, and it would be interesting to see the Bernardo/Foden axis in central midfield, many convinced that is where Bernardo's future lies. Stones and Laporte were the central defensive pairing, which was of little surprise to anyone.

They hopefully are the future.

And for a game that I insisted did not matter, I was still so, so keen to see a good performance. Keen for signs that nothing has changed, and this group of players was as hungry as ever, and committed to securing the first trophy of the season.**

And they were. They were excellent. Simple as that. From the first minute, the application and attitude was equal to that seen in a league or cup match. And none were better than Bernardo Silva and Foden. They dominated the midfield, and were the liveliest players on the pitch from the get-go. Silva looks really up for the season ahead, and Foden looked like he had come of age. Long may it continue.

City as a whole were pressing impressively, putting in the hard yards and giving off the impression of being weeks ahead in their preparation for the coming season. There was real concern after the World Cup and looking at the teams put out in previous friendlies*** that City would be woefully short of first-teamers once the Arsenal game came around, but this game put most of the doubts firmly to bed, with a cup of cocoa, a nice bedtime story and a pint of Night Nurse.

Mendy was bursting forward in the early stages and the gaps were there for City players to exploit. Sane shot wide when he could have laid it off to Mendy instead and Bernardo Silva wriggled free in the area but his cross eluded Aguero.

It was no surprise therefore when City opened the scoring after 13 minutes, and what a lovely goal it was. Foden surged forward, laid it off to Aguero, and the rest was history. And this was one of those rare moments when I knew it would be a goal as soon as he swung his foot. I know I know, I could not have known, and yet weirdly it seemed inevitable to me at the time. As soon as he used his studs to shift the ball left, it was a done deal. Rudiger made it so, shifting out the way as if expecting a through ball, and within a second the ball had nutmegged him and it was 1-0. Caballero had no chance. Goal number 200 in City colours for the club's greatest ever striker.

Just reward, and City continued to threaten. However, if there was one section of the game when City were least dominant it was probably the second quarter. Chelsea eased their way back into it, but without really threatening. Bravo was proactive for once and scooped away an in-swinging free kick, Morata fired over as did Hudson Odoi, one hell of a prospect, who gave Walker plenty of food for thought in the early stages. Walker's pace won that particular duel in the end.

Naturally there was time too for a "Bravo moment", as an innocuous ball forward from Alonso bounced over him before he scrambled back to claim the ball close to the goal line. Not his greatest moment, and sadly not his worst either.

But Bravo was ok – his greatest weakness for me, that led to so many shots hitting the back of the net, was his tendency to be rooted to his line. He seems more proactive when I have seen him in recent times, and even if the odd error results from this, it can only be a good thing. Chelsea's one shot on target that first half, from Hudson Odoi, was hit powerfully and bounced just in front of him, so I can excuse the fumble, just. His second half interception of a dangerous cross was excellent, and he was then undone by a viciously spinning ball that completely changed direction. Again, no blame from me, and as you'd expect his distribution was calm and composed.

The second half was one of quiet domination, ending with total domination where multiple chances were spurned. Sane was off at half-time, and whilst it is reported that he suffered a knock, he was very ineffective, so the change made sense anyway. On came the phantom of the opera, Gundogan, and he helped exert further control of the midfield. Shame that Bernardo had to change his role somewhat, but he is excelling wherever he plays right now.

City had so many chances though. Aguero shot tamely wise, and then missed a much better chance. Released on goal, he rounded Caballero but sliced the ball into the side-netting. With hindsight, from my comfy seat he should have shot when through on goal, and with an exquisite through ball Foden should have got his 2nd assist of the game.

Instead, the assist went to Bernardo Silva soon after, following another beautiful move. A great interception from Stones in defence, Gundogan took it forward, passed to Silva on the right, a cute through ball to Aguero and it was 2-0 as he slotted it inside the near post. Game over too, as Chelsea were not coming back from this.

Mahrez then shot wide from distance, and Aguero almost had his hat-trick as a Walker cross found him at the far post, his shot into the ground parried away by Caballero. Diaz came on and was extremely lively.

And so a comprehensive victory for City, and nothing less than they deserved, a promising snapshot I hope of what lies ahead. 18 shots to 5 tells its own story. And always nice to see Vincent Kompany climbing the Wembley steps to lift up a trophy.****. This was not the strongest side for either club, but it was still two strong sides. It was a helpful barometer of where the clubs are. Maybe.
Having said that, Chelsea have lost the last 5 Community Shields they have appeared in, so they shouldn't lose too much sleep over the defeat. Sarri is not going to impose his methods on the squad in just a few weeks, And whilst we can all have a giggle at Jorginho's error-strewn appearance, we should conclude very little from that too.

Man of the Match? Yes, Aguero scored two, and with a successful knee operation behind him the sky's the limit for him, and Foden just oozed class and should have had two assists, but I feel Bernardo Silva just shades it ahead of some stiff competition. He's just playing at the top of his game right now. He has grown at City with every passing month.

Mendy had a solid game, but for me that wasn't even the most important aspect of the day for him. It's just great to see him fit and healthy and happy (no change there). More should come with playing time, though there was little wrong with the performance at Wembley. Early bursts forward were not repeated throughout the match, but he was solid enough, and clearly gives City an extra dimension. Opposing full-backs will be wary of his threat in the coming years. And what a life he leads – every time he steps on a football pitch, someone gives him a medal at full-time.

*Not a trophy
**Not a trophy
***Not a trophy
****Not a trophy

Manchester City 2 Chelsea 0 – Community Shield Player Ratings

Claudio Bravo – 7
Hear me out. Yes, he let a ball bounce over his head, and another ball span away from him 2nd half, but he was proactive and generally efficient, not that he was over-worked on an afternoon where City mostly dominated. His one shot saved was spooned out, but it bounced just in front of him and was hit with power. A satisfactory performance if nothing more.

Kyle Walker – 7
Given plenty to think about by the exciting young Hudson Odoi in the early stages of the game, but he won that duel eventually and put in an unassuming, consistent display.

Benjamin Mendy – 7.5
His barnstorming runs of the early stages were not replicated throughout the match, but that was not all his fault. He still surged forwards, not always receiving the ball, but such runs opened up spaces for other, especially in the latter stages. Crisp passing, effective distribution and neutered opposition down that side fairly well. Most importantly, he is fit and raring to go.

Aymeric Laporte – 7.5
Not his most difficult of afternoons, but coped with any Chelsea forays up field comfortably enough. As you'd expect, classy on the ball, and always looking for an option.

John Stones – 7.5
See above. Also, his interception led to the 2nd goal. Hopefully a defensive partnership is beginning to form that could serve City well for a long, long time. Stones had a generally excellent World Cup, and that should be a big boon to City after he had mixed fortunes last season.

Fernandinho – 7
Good to see him back – put in a typical performance with little fuss. Helped keep Chelsea at bay with relative ease, and provided platform for Bernardo Silva and Foden to dominate.

Riyad Mahrez – 6.5

Always available, but things really didn't come off for him on the day, most notably when he mis-controlled when almost through on goal. The best is yet to come.

Leroy Sane – 6.

Another wide player who struggled to make an impact on the game, in the 45 minutes he got. Shot wide early, then was on the periphery for much of the half. Hopefully his summer freedom has not carried over into this season.

Phil Foden – 8.5

Brilliant. Just brilliant. The best compliment I can pay is that he belonged on the pitch, and looked like a first teamer doing his usual stuff. Partnership with Bernardo Silva worked excellently, a constant threat. One assist, could have had two, and was a joy to watch.

123 passes, with a 94.5% success rate. 3 shots on target, and dispossessed a Chelsea player 7 times.

I've picked the wrong man of the match, haven't I?

Bernardo Silva – 9

My man of the match, just. One of those rare players where the ball seems to be glued to his feet. Sparkled in a central role and has been City's stand-out player in pre-season. Growing month by month, am excited to see him in action this season. At the heart of much of the good things City did, and got an assist too with a delicate through ball to Aguero.

Sergio Aguero – 8.5

Goals 200 and 201 for City – he's back! Saw some criticism of him at half-time from Michael Cox (Zonal Marking) that apart from the goal he had been fairly poor, with some underwhelming link-up play, and of course he missed a great opportunity in the 2nd half, and had shot tamely wide just prior to that. But hey, he got 2 goals, and you can't ask for much more than that.

Well you could ask for 3 goals, but he had a shot saved from Caballero, a tough chance that he did well to get a strike on goal from. Anyway, it was the Aguero we know and love, and with his knee blessed by Dr Cugat during the summer, the world is his oyster.

Ilkay Gundogan – on at 45 minutes – 7
Did a job, maintaining City's domination in the midfield, with little fanfare. Wears a face mask with aplomb.
Gabriel Jesus – on at 68 minutes – 7
Not sufficient time to rate a performance, but looked lively enough, fresh from his contract extension. Forced one save from Caballero after skinning Sideshow Bob.
Brahim Diaz – on at 76 minutes – 8
Again I can't really give a proper rating, but thought he was electric in his short time on the pitch, as the game got stretched. A real threat every time he went forward, the highlight being a beautiful through ball to Gundogan.
Kompany and Otamendi – too little time on pitch to rate
Claudio Gomes – 10
Didn't put a foot wrong the whole time he was on the pitch. Flawless performance.

In other news, Joe Hart leaves for good, to Burnley. Good luck to him. There's little left to say that has not already been said. Hart's fall from grace has been dramatic, but I hope he can find some redemption over at Turf Moor. He will have plenty of competition there though, and could still find himself exiled for large parts of the season. We will see. An integral part of our past success, but he has a mountain to climb to rediscover his old form. I wish him all the best.

Random Thoughts

It's been a while, a while since Jesus popped that ball into the back of the net and I decided that reaching 100 points was important after all. A long time since I've had to moan about something, if we ignore the incompetence of Manchester airport, and an even longer time since I've had chance to rant at the media, with them even being nice to the England football team during the summer. Of course there was the curious case of Raheem Sterling, but I don't have the energy for that, and we'll all hate him too when he leaves on a free in 2 years, engineering a move to Real Madrid. Maybe.

But whilst there has been a steady stream of football, much of it interesting, since the end of last season, it's good to be back to domestic duties, and the stress levels can rise once more, the hairs grey further, and the crocodile tears of Jose Mourinho will keep this pleasant land green. Liverpool fans will be unbearable, and that's in relation to previous levels of being unbearable, so it could be a long nine months, especially if they win some games or one of their players scores a nice goal, but we wouldn't have it any other way. Well we would, but we've no choice. Imagine what flags they'll be parading about nearly winning something last season.

Still, the very short transfer window gave us all a temporary distraction, and there was something to raise the odd eyebrow occurring this week as the deadline approached . You'll have noticed it for sure, and I need little excuse to rally against the media narrative. A year ago we bought a certain goalkeeper named Ederson. You may know him. Looks like a Bond villain, transformed our play, and was so good he got a new 7 year contract before he'd seen a year out at the Etihad. He cost £35m it seemed, and at the time of the signing, the fee caused people to faint in the streets, commentators to wonder what had happened to our once beautiful game, and consider why City persisted in destroying football, throwing money around like Wayne Rooney on a Saga holiday.

This is how it is now of course, though the net spenders have had to have a summer off as City sold more players than we signed, and thus might get close to breaking even by the time the rest of Europe catches up and close their transfer windows. We no longer have the most expensive goalkeeper, but we'll always have the award for most expensive right back from Yorkshire, most expensive central defender named John, and we've cornered the market in turning Silvas into gold.

Anyway, it's different now, of course. It's just the market, stupid, the market City probably created, no doubt. It's the normal price. You know, £71m for an uncapped goalkeeper is normal a year after £35m a year ago was obscene. This market moves in mysterious ways. Normalising a fee for a goalkeeper that is greater than City have ever spent on any player. It was ever thus. After all, Mourinho moaned last summer about how United could not compete with City as we spend on full backs what they spend on strikers. Then Woodward spent this summer desperately trying to spend striker-level sums on defenders. But Mourinho was proved right – United can't spend on full backs what we do, cos no player in their right mind wants to go there. I can't think why – after all, players go to City to make money, and to United to make history, remember? Little wonder Paul Pogba is on the verge of a hunger strike to get out of there.

Whatever. City haven't been too adept at signing players either. The season ahead will be tougher for City than the previous one, I have little doubt about that. Previous champions have suffered badly by not strengthening after a title win, and it seems City are now repeating this pattern. There are some differences this time around – this squad is super strong and needed competition for Fernandinho and nothing more, once Mahrez was on board, so if he stays mainly fit during the season, it's not a disaster, whilst Mendy of course feels like a new player – on the proviso he too stays fit of course, Foden may have his breakthrough season, hopefully, whilst Bernardo Silva has moved up another gear if the early signs are to be believed. All in all, we're not in a bad position, when all is said and done, and by the time you listen to this maybe a late bid for Nzonzi will have changed matters. No Pjanic.

It will be interesting to see just how much criticism flies Klopp's way if Liverpool do not mount a serious title challenge this season. Net spend is irrelevant, a smokescreen to protect against potential failure, to dampen expectations, reduce pressure. It does not matter how you constructed a team for £300m – through sales, a bond scheme, or adult nappy partners in Uzbekistan – a £300m team should still be challenging for a title, in any country, at any time. Simple as that.

But why should it be harder for City? Well there's the clear psychological issue of defending a title – players find it hard to maintain the desire once a prize has been won once, but with Pep overlooking everything, this should not be a problem – after all, just look at how he celebrated a goal in the Community Shield, which is a glorified friendly whatever anyone says – he never rests, and never will. Little wonder he burns out occasionally. And there's the lack of strengthening already mentioned, the fact I don't think 100 points will be achieved again, because it's just so hard to be that relentless for so long, especially in a league awash with money where promoted sides spend £40m.

To be honest, Liverpool do look good, though they may struggle like City used to against teams with a low block just looking to defend. And with any successful team, other managers slowly work out the secret to their success they adapt, and the methods become less successful. Pep will have to adapt yet again to keep ahead of the chasing pack, though obviously he doesn't need to be told that.

Never mind. Even the youth players seem ingrained into our possession football now, and the football just seems on a higher plain with each passing month. Unless when we're playing Liverpool, obviously. Almost worth that extra £10 on my season ticket. Not sure about the confetti though. Let's hope for another special seasons from our very own centurions.

THE 2018/19 SEASON

Premier League: Arsenal 0 Manchester City 2

And so we're back, properly this time. After the delight of last week's glorified friendly victory, this was the real deal, and quite the test to open up for the defending champions. What happened to the nice, easy fixture to allow us to ease ourselves into the season? If only David Gill was a blue.
Still, in the end, it turned out to be a blessing. City have three points, and have a tough fixture out the way, with Huddersfield, Wolves and Newcastle on the horizon. Marvellous.

Anyway, a new Premier League season started just 26 days after the World Cup final, and it seemed like no time at all. Not good to have the pre-match nerves back either. I don't miss them.

Before every game I try and pick a side, and tend to get it horribly wrong. That's what happens when you can't read the mind of your manager, the squad has real depth, and you throw in the lottery this time of an opening game of the season. Whilst the back six was called fine, plus the inclusion of Mahrez, Sterling and Aguero, I did not see the inclusion of Gundogan. Still, I wasn't far off, which makes a change.
Kevin De Bruyne remained on the bench then and David Silva was not to be risked after a minor injury. Laporte and Stones were picked for central defensive duties when some thought Kompany may be chosen to deal with Aubameyang, and Ederson went straight back into the side despite no match practice. A strong side, despite the bench overflowing with talent.

It was difficult to know what to expect for so many reasons. New season, new players, lack of match practice, and no Arsene Wenger fiddling with his oversized coat on the touchline whilst whinging to the 4th official. A new dawn. Unai Emery has rarely beat Guardiola, perhaps never, but he has often tested him back in Spain, and this would be an interesting tactical battle.

The crowd certainly seemed up for it, for a short while at least. A new season always brings new hope for any fan, and with a new manager this was only exacerbated after the staleness of the twilight years of the Wenger era. There was determination in the play from Arsenal, but the fact is that whilst both teams gave away the ball too much, City soon began to exert a level of domination on the game.

Key to this was more tactical tinkering from Pep. He had spoken over the summer about adapting more methods in the coming season, including the difficulty of overcoming low blocks and 5-4-1 formations. Arsenal were not going to sit back and defend all match of course, but Guardiola used the inclusion of Mendy to showcase another approach – him and Walker got forward regularly, overlapping Mahrez and Sterling, and as Mendy showed regularly, underlapping too, going wide when Sterling cut in and going inside when Sterling went wide. It certainly opened up Arsenal and their defenders did not know how to deal with it. More precise final balls and better decision making could have wreaked havoc on their back line.

Still, it did not take long for City to take the lead, 14 minutes to be precise, and Raheem Sterling once more demonstrated that scrutiny of his play has little effect on his club form. Mendy laid the ball off to him, he dribbled inside, past at least two Arsenal players and sweetly struck the ball into the back of the net from just outside the area. Cech made scant effort to save it, suggesting he may have been at least partially unsighted, or perhaps caught unawares by the shot and the minimum back lift.

After a delicious Aguero lay-off, Sterling had already tested Cech prior to the goal, and City were creating chances. Aguero sliced a shot into the side-netting whilst Cech made a great double save from a Mahrez free kick and Laporte's follow up from just two yards out. There was rare danger at the other end however as Mendy over-committed himself and allowed Bellerin to get free in the area, Ederson thankfully beating away his fierce shot. Mahrez then curled a shot just wide, and Aubameyang hit one much wider. There was also time for Cech to almost stroke the ball into his own net from a back-pass.

Arsenal rallied in the second half once more, but to little effect. In fact, it was sloppiness from City players that granted them most of their opportunities. They were severely lacking any killer instinct however. Ozil and Aubameyang regularly wandered offside, and Lacazette, on as a substitute in the 54th minute, shot wide when in an excellent position. It was their only true chance of the half, though casual play from Ederson should have led to at least once more opportunity, but Ozil's ball control was woeful.

And so in the 64th minute, having already started time wasting for some reason with a lengthy substitution, City put the game to bed. Just moments before, Aguero missed a one on one, when perhaps he should have squared to Kevin De Bruyne, but we cannot be surprised at a striker being selfish. It didn't cost City anyway, as Mendy surged down the left, his cross into the centre was not perfect but Bernardo Silva anticipated it and swept home with aplomb. Cech was nowhere near the ball once more. City saw out the game with ease after that, and the likes of De Bruyne, Sane and Jesus got some minutes on the pitch too, without really affecting the score.

Job done then, and that's all you can ask for on the opening weekend of the season. City were sloppy at times, but controlled swathes of the match and had two beautiful finishes to secure three points. As Pep said after the match, the team will improve, which is chilling news for City's competitors, whoever they may be. Don't forget last season, where City did not start well, not really getting going until after the third game. It is normal to be rusty at this stage. It is football.

Stones and Laporte were at the heart of all that was good. Laporte especially can be pleased with his efforts, and his raking balls forward can be a potent weapon for the team in the coming years. Sterling was a menace throughout and Bernardo Silva grew into the game and scored another beauty at the Emirates.

Mendy has received criticism for his performance, including some careful words from his manager, but he was one of many who were sloppy with their distribution at times. I'm hardly overly concerned on day one of the season. He allowed Bellerin past him too easily in the first half, but rustiness from him is understandable, more than any other player. He will need time to get used to what is expected of him, and as long as he takes on board what Pep tells him, he will be fine. He was naturally a huge threat going forward dovetailing with Sterling well. Sadly just the two assists for him on the day.

On the other side, Walker and Mahrez combined well too. 23 sprints from Kyle Walker, the most by any Premier League player at the weekend. He was great. Mahrez has not set the world alight yet, not made the headlines, but had a good performance, and together the two gave Maitland-Niles a tough 35 minutes.
Gundogan has once more attracted criticism, as he tends to do. It was partly merited as it was not his best game. Maybe playing with a mask is tough. Anyway, he was not terrible, but his distribution fell short of what we'd expect. Again, opening day and all that....

Ederson after all was just as sloppy, but his reputation is of course much higher. I discussed last week how it may be difficult for a goalkeeper to go straight into the side for a big game after no real pre-season, and he seemed to pay the price. Fewer casual passes next week please.

Man of the Match? For me Sterling edges it. His wonderful finish settled the nerves early on, and allowed City to quietly dominate the match with considerable ease.

And so with this potential banana skin avoided, City are in a good position already, with games against Huddersfield, Wolves and Newcastle coming up. There is no room for complacency though. Huddersfield drew at the Etihad last season, though it was a day for celebration, and the performance suffered as a result. Wolves will certainly be a test however. No time for rest.

Arsenal 0-2 Manchester City: 5 things we learned as City emerge victorious once more

In the biggest game of the opening weekend of the Premier League, new Arsenal manager Unai Emery saw his side lose 2-0 to Manchester City with goals from Raheem Sterling and Bernardo Silva. It was a stark reminder of the task ahead for Emery, whilst for Manchester City it was business as usual as they look to become the first team to successfully defend a league title for a decade. They were not at their best but still had too much for Arsenal on the day.

A changing of the guard, but the same old problems for Arsenal
For Arsenal, some things never change. After 22 years the manager has, but for the fourth successive time Arsenal succumbed to a Manchester City side who were simply better on the day. It's the first time City have beaten Arsenal four times on the row since 1937. Unai Emery was never going to arrive, wave a magic wand and make everything better overnight. He needs time, and multiple transfer windows to return Arsenal back to where they believe they belong. With a fairly modest budget at his disposal, it will not be easy. Against City, there was a distinct lack of control or goal threat form the whole side, though there are new signings and injured players that can help in future. This is a club that has been sleepwalking for a good few years though and will require a change of direction and a change of mentality. Emery, who seems better

suited to Arsenal than massaging egos at PSG, will have to turn a set of players into winners again, and that may be his biggest challenge of all.

Manchester City can prosper without David Silva

It is a thought that sends shivers down the spine of every Manchester City fan. One day, and that day may be approaching fast, David Silva will say his goodbyes and finally leave Manchester City, retiring back to Gran Canaria, leaving behind a legacy of being one of City's greatest players. For many fans he seems irreplaceable, and the fear is that the team will lose something special without him in it.

However, there are signs emerging that a natural heir might already be at the club, one who even shares the same surname. David Silva was not considered fit enough to star against Arsenal, but Bernardo Silva carried on his preseason form by starring once more in a central role. In his debut season at City, it seemed that Bernardo was destined to feature on the right side of midfield, but his recent conversion to a central role has been a revelation. He has not yet reached the heights of David Silva in his pomp, but his ball control, guile and movement puts him not far behind. What's more, he has one asset that David Silva has struggled to master whilst at The Etihad – a genuine goal threat. Bernardo Silva might just make the exit of his namesake that little bit easier to deal with.

Pep Guardiola never rests

A new season, and not a moment's rest for Pep Guardiola. He had spoken in the summer about how he had been trying new ideas, especially against teams with a low bock who looked just to defend. Arsenal certainly don't fit this criteria, but it was clear from the off that Pep had new ideas on how to beat the opposition. On this occasion he flipped the wide men, putting a left-footer on the right side and a right-footer on the left, and with their propensity to cut in onto their stronger foot, it allowed both full backs to not only overlap but underlap too. For much of the match it caused confusion in the Arsenal defence, and was a key factor in deciding the outcome of the match. Pep has had to constantly adapt during his two years at City as opposition managers come up with new ways to restrict his free-flowing side, and it seems he will continue to adapt in the next 12 months.

Raheem Sterling never hides

There has rarely been a player under the scrutiny to the level of Raheem Sterling in the past couple of years. His England performances were pulled to pieces by all and sundry, and there are many who still think he is little more than a speed merchant. However, with a new season it seems little has changed at club level. In the 2017/18 season, he scored 18 goals and 11 assists and against Arsenal he took a mere 14 minutes to pick up where he left off. He was one of the best players on the pitch, and continues to revel in his role at City, hence the pressing desire by the City hierarchy for him to sign a new contract.

Many have questioned why Sterling struggles to transfer his club form to international games, but he is hardly the first player to struggle for England. Greater support would probably help, and an understanding of what he offers to every manager that has consistently picked him. At City he is surrounded with better players than at national level, and has taken on board the clear and precise instructions passed to him from Guardiola. There is no reason why he cannot do the same for his country in the future.

A deep squad despite a solitary summer signing

One of the more impressive trends of recent years at Manchester City has been the lack of 1st team players leaving the club. Players have tended to leave only when the club wished them to do so, and the likes of Sergio Aguero, David Silva and Yaya Toure stayed for longer than many initially anticipated. Thus, the failure to sign their key target Jorginho in the summer should not have serious repercussions. With Riyad Mahrez coming in, this is the deepest squad the club has ever had. City fielded a strong side that was too good for the home side, yet could still pack the bench with talent. It is a worrying thought for City's title rivals that the side that walked out at the Emirates was missing David Silva, Kevin De Bruyne, Vincent Kompany, Gabriel Jesus, Nicolas Otamendi, Leroy Sane, Phil Foden and more. Fabian Delph did not even make the squad. This is a squad well equipped to fight for multiple trophies season after season.

De Bruyne Injury (a recurrent theme)

It's the type of news every football fan fears the most. Rumours emerge that your star player has picked up an injury, and it might be a bad one. That was how Wednesday afternoon panned out for Manchester City fans.

The rumour was true, as confirmed when De Bruyne hobbled into a Manchester cinema that night for the premiere of a City documentary that debuts this week. Manchester City have sent the player to be examined by the trusted Dr Cugat in Barcelona but the assumption is two to three months out, having torn his lateral ligament in his knee on the training ground.

Losing a player who was locked in a two-way tussle for the PFA Player Of The Year award last season is naturally a massive blow to the Citizens. De Bruyne is central to much of City's attacking intent, a master of decision-making, efficiency and pinpoint passing. A player with no weak foot who can operate across wide areas of the pitch. In a team of stars, he still stands out. Any team would miss him.

Good Timing?

But just how much will City miss him? It might be clutching at straws, but there are mitigating circumstances that might alleviate the damage for City and their fans. If De Bruyne is out for a couple of months, he's picked the best time to do it. With a succession of winnable games and the impending International breaks, better now to pick up an injury than at the key stages of the season in March and April. City host Huddersfield for their first home game of the season this weekend, then travel to Wolverhampton Wanderers, before playing Newcastle United, Fulham, Cardiff City and Brighton. City should win them all, whichever team they field, though football does not always work like that. The loss from a 2-3 month injury would be most profoundly felt when City travel to Anfield in October, but they tend to lose there anyway. A tough Champions League draw could also pose problems, but as champions, City are in Pot 1. Last season De Bruyne admitted suffering from fatigue from January onwards. With a full recovery from injury, hopefully he can see the remainder of the season out without such concerns. And whilst it seems illogical to say, De Bruyne is not in the top five of biggest losses even if he is potentially the best player in the squad. This is because there is an abundance of talent ready to take his place even if they do not possess his unique skill set. Losing a player like Fernandinho or Ederson could potentially be far more destructive for City's season, because there is no player of the same quality to step in.

Guardiola's Options

For Pep Guardiola, he will already be formulating alternatives during De Bruyne's absence. The player did not start for City's Community Shield victory nor their league opener at the Emirates, so his absence is nothing new. Bernardo Silva and Phil Foden starred in the first game, but Guardiola turned to experience for the Arsenal match, preferring Ilkay Gundogan, with mixed results. With David Silva hopefully over his niggling injury, the question for Guardiola is whether a pairing of the "two Silvas" weakens the midfield due to their similar attributes. Against defensive teams in the coming weeks, that may not be much of a hindrance. The alternative silver lining that Guardiola trusts Phil Foden against teams he considers weaker than Arsenal. All football fans love to see a locally born academy player break through, and if De Bruyne's lengthy absence helps aid Foden's development in the first team squad, that would be a significant consolation.

Fluidity In Attack

The final issue to consider is the effect on City's wide players and their second forward, Gabriel Jesus. Raheem Sterling, Riyad Mahrez and Leroy Sane would naturally have expected plenty of playing time this season, but De Bruyne's injury may increase further their time on the pitch. Three players comfortable out wide are not obvious replacements for a player like De Bruyne who revels in a central role, but Guardiola has shown repeatedly in his two years at the Etihad that he does not operate with players in fixed positions, and all three could move centrally either during matches as a tactical switch or even operate there from the start. For Gabriel Jesus, who was relegated to the bench against Arsenal, the opportunity may arise for playing time if Guardiola wheels out his 3-5-2 formation for the games ahead, especially if he sees potential in that formation breaking down stubborn, defensive sides.

A moderate injury is not a disaster
With Kevin De Bruyne pencilled in to return to the starting side for City's next game at home to Huddersfield, his injury is naturally bad news for him and the team as a whole. In a team packed with top class players, he was still something of a talisman, a player that could be devastating from central and wide players, a player who could be the key difference in tight games.
But City can cope without him. The football calendar is not only kind in the coming weeks but the squad is possibly the deepest it has ever been in the club's history. City lost their left back last season for over six months and it made little difference to their relentless pursuit of league glory, even without recognised back up. With De Bruyne there is an embarrassment of riches for Pep to utilise as an alternative, and if De Bruyne can return within two or three months his absence should not be too costly.

All Or Nothing Review

"If you hate me, hate me guys. Some of you guys play better when you are angry with me. You have to be friends – teammates. With me, it doesn't matter. Hate me if you want, criticise me. No problem at all. But when the referee starts the game, show me your value guys. Every single training session, every single game."

And so the moment all City fans had been waiting for – except that moment came a few hours earlier than originally anticipated. On Thursday evening, Amazon Prime released their eight-part behind the scenes documentary on Manchester City's 2017/18 season. Their timing was impeccable, and you probably know how it ends. The trailers had everyone salivating, but it was now time for the main course. And what a feast it was. Under the guiding hand of Salford-raised narrator Ben Kingsley, the series looks back at the 57 games played by City during another eventful season. No spoilers naturally, but I'll cut to the chase. It's bloody brilliant.

The worry with such a programme is not just that it paints the club in a bad light, but individuals too, delves too deep into areas we do not need to know about do not concern us. After all, some things are best left behind closed doors, and airing dirty laundry in public is never a good idea. Thankfully the documentary maintains a delicate balancing act and handles events with great skill throughout. Just as importantly, the club is well run now, and full of winners, and thus there is not the sort of laundry that was exposed the last time City tried this, namely in 1981, and the release of City! a six-part documentary from Granada following Peter Swales around from one mishap to another.

The club is slick now, the documentary too. Beautifully filmed, including some dreamy drone shots of Manchester, which is nice. Naturally the shots avoid Piccadilly Gardens and Mary D's. Above all though, there is no drop in quality or interest, every minute informing and entertaining. It's hard to take your eyes off the screen, for six hours, and it will be even harder for rival fans to pretend it's amateurish and embarrasses the club, though naturally they will try. It's a programme fans of any other club would kill to see made about their own side.

And it filled in loads of details from an amazing season. Details I didn't realise needed filling in. It's the minutiae that really struck me, not just about the team, but about how a club operates and how it functions. The details about the low points as well as the highs. I feel I know Pep a bit better, a bit more. I feel the same about the players. Hey, I feel it about the kit manager and Sergio's son Ben. What's more, you will learn things about individual events and players that may well change your opinions and shatter misconceptions. And the programme is well-paced, taking time-outs to focus on individual players, and looking at all aspects of the club's operations, not just the manager, players and executives. I still can't comprehend how much Fabian Delph's shin pads cost, and I worry Sergio Aguero still gets lonely.

But naturally, the series revolves around City's manager, City's figurehead. And Pep is as fascinating as you'd expect, a different person from the persona presented at press conferences, but also in many respects especially as you'd expect him.

It will not surprise you to learn that Pep is intense. Almost permanently intense. You get the impression that he wheels his tactics board around with him wherever he goes. His talks are not jam-packed with tactical insights. Often they serve nothing more than to inspire the players, with encouragement, criticism and to be honest words that meant little to me and will not have been taken on board by a group of players with mixed abilities when understanding English. He clearly has the respect of the players though. They know not to err, and any words from him are relayed to an attentive audience.

Pep confesses similar things in the first episode. As he says, "the locker room is the nicest place to be", but admits he does not have all the answers but acts in front of the players as if he does, to give them confidence - and that he must adopt the role of a father, brother or son and give the best advice you'd hope to receive in your own life. Occasionally we see the man not obsessed with every precise detail of his role. After the penalty shoot-out at Leicester we see him drop his guard, his joy at the victory clear to see, his role changed to that of a bantering boss buying in a round for everyone at a works do.

There are two areas that interested me most behind the scenes. Firstly, it was fascinating to see the discussions between Txiki, Khaldoon, Sorriano and other executives that give a proper insight into how transfer targets are identified and how decisions are made. If it makes sense for the club, they will do it. If not, then they won't. Quite simple when you break it down. Intelligent, driven men who operate with reason, and soon quash laughable claims of incompetence in their roles.

But the key area of fascination is in the changing room. The preparation, the reactions, the camaraderie, the "pep" talks, the interaction between manager, players and staff, and the symbiotic relationships that are a huge factor in success. All life can be found here, all the emotions of a season, compressed, packaged and on display in one enclosed area. The changing room footage is the beating heart of the documentary.

And what comes across is the camaraderie. This is clearly a well-bonded unit, and that is clearly a factor in the team's success. There was no clearer example of this than when David Silva's teammates rallied round him during the most difficult of times. We know football players are humans, that they make mistakes, that they feel what we do, but it sometimes helps to be reminded of this.

There's so much more, as you will have discovered, or will do in the future. The role of Vincent Kompany as a leader, diplomat, conduit, is clear, for example. "His speeches are so good, he could go for president," said Bernardo Silva. It digs deep into player's emotions, and their struggles, their mistakes. It's not always easy viewing, but it's never boring. It's just a shame that United refused permission for the cameras to record the Old Trafford derby. All the series lacked was footage of Jose Mourinho covered in milk.

Drink it all in, this unique footage of a unique season. It was everything I had hoped it would be. What a time to follow the team.

Premier League: Manchester City 6 Huddersfield Town 1

It felt like I hadn't been away. New card, but same ground, people, trainers, lucky socks and queues. Nice to be back, but it felt like I had barely had a break with the World Cup keeping everyone occupied for a while.

Same superstitions too, and not just the socks. Always enter left turnstile, always walk up steps one at a time, always keep valuables in left pocket – wallet, phone, keys, confetti. And what thanks do I get from the club for maintaining this winning streak? None.

Anyway, by the time I was in the ground (1:30 prompt), the team sheets were long out, yet still made little sense to me. What was Pep doing? What formation was it? Was he taking risks that did not need to be taken?

No. No, he wasn't. Anyway, it was clearly a back three as Vincent returned, and Bernardo seemed to be tasked with occasionally performing basic right-back functions, but he wasn't called on much. Having said that, the Guardian minute-by-minute called it as a back four after 10 minutes, but neither "wing back" spent much time in their own half, and Fernandinho floated about, doing what he always does, conducting the orchestra.

And with the return of Benjamin Mendy to full fitness, comes the pairing once more of Sergio Aguero and Gabriel Jesus. Obviously Pep Guardiola was considering dropping Sergio Aguero, Jamie Jackson said so and his contacts are flawless, but it seemed he had a late change of heart, perhaps when it dawned on him that Sergio is the dog's testicles.

The formation didn't matter anyway. It worked, whatever it was. Guardiola had talked in the summer about the challenge of defeating a low block and a 4-5-1, and this seemed to be his

answer. David Wagner's plans, probably designed to combat two side players and Aguero, went out the window, even more so when Aaron Mooy's wife went into labour, and he must have scratched his head with the rest of us when all of City's wide players were left on the world's most expensive bench.
And it didn't matter! What a time to be alive...

Perhaps the only negative can be dealt with early doors. Gabriel Jesus was in many respects wonderful, but also extremely wasteful. I guess we can excuse the shot saved by Hamer, and perhaps he was caught by surprise at the far post soon after, but the shot wide in the second half was admittedly terrible. He got his goal, but there was plenty of rustiness to buff away in future games.

From the first second, there was little to worry about though. David Silva, his beautiful son watching on, was unplayable. Huddersfield could not keep possession of the ball, and when they did, at least two City players harried them until they got it back. Mendy was a whirlwind down the left, Bernardo was Bernardo and the front two were full of energy and movement.

And then there was the distribution of Ederson. Wagner seemed to be caught between a rock and a hard place, his principles demanding a high press, his head saying just to defend deep. And despite City's chances, his team was doing ok for the first quarter. But it couldn't last. Ederson had already tested Huddersfield's deepest lying defender Schindler with long balls towards Aguero, and eventually it paid dividend. Aguero could not be offside from a goal kick as he stood behind Schindler, curved his run, and the Huddersfield goal keeper Hamer made a fatal error, rushing out to block Aguero when Schindler probably could have held him up. I thought the instant lob was coming, so was shouting abuse as Aguero held up the ball and didn't then lay it off to 2 onrushing City players. The rest is history – pure class once more from the main man.

That was the first ever Premier League assist by a City keeper. And probably won't be the last this season either.

And with that goal, the floodgates opened. Jesus may have been hovering offside before finishing off Mendy's surging run, but such details are quickly forgotten in routs. The third was of course down to Hamer once more, but still credit should be sent Mendy's way, whose early low crosses are just deadly. Not impressed by the goal celebration though.
Game over. Surely? Well it was, but not before City made us sweat for a short while. Huddersfield made a rare incursion up field, and scored, the goal far too simple. Throw-in, flick-on, prod home. No doubt this will have left Guardiola furious at half-time, and no wonder when you consider Gabriel Jesus was marking Mounie. A mis-match, and the result was a goal conceded.

When City play with such dominance, we can let such things slide however. Within three minutes of the restart, the game was definitely over. A beautiful free kick from our Spanish magician and Hamer was motionless in net. No jump from the wall either if memory serves me right, perhaps wary of a De Bruyne type shot under their feet.

Have we under-used Silva in such situations? I don't think our record from free kicks recently has been great, but there always seems to be someone ahead of Silva in the queue to take them. With the arrival of Mahrez, that won't change any time soon. A shame, as he seems rather good at them.
The rest of the match was a stroll. City have a tendency to see out games like this without going for the jugular, instead choosing to conserve energy. And whilst the temp did slow down for a short while, the last ten minutes resembled a siege, and you feel that if more goals had been needed, they would have been scored. Of course two more were, the highlight being Mendy's beautiful cross (one of 12 he put in during the match,

one short of the record under Pep) and Aguero's delightful improvised finish.

His 9th hat-trick in the Premier League, his 13th in all competitions. Into the top ten of Premier League all-time top scorers, alongside Robin Van Persie. And if this is a new and improved Aguero, free of injury after five years of pain in his knee, god help opposition defence this season. Keep this up and he is surely a shoe-in for PFA Player of the Year runner up spot behind *insert name of Liverpool player*.

As for Mendy, that is four assists in two games. Walker was brilliant last season and he got five, but Mendy is clearly a different type of player to all other full backs we have had. Please stay fit.
Manchester City have now scored 104 goals in 39 games at home under Pep Guardiola in the Premier League.

Regarding the confetti, the kids clearly loved it. And some adults to be fair. Stop whinging about every little thing the club does, they don't do it just for your benefit. That's my job!
You can't buy class, it is true. Only one team from Manchester displayed it on Sunday however, as per. I've never more felt like singing the blues. Keep counting those empty seats. It's all you've got…

Ratings:
Ederson – 8
Stones – 8
Laporte – 8
Kompany – 8
Mendy – 9.5
Bernardo Silva – 8
Fernandinho – 8
Gundogan – 8
David Silva – 9
Gabriel Jesus – 8

Aguero – 10
(Mahrez – 7, Sane -7, Foden – N/A)

Pep – 11

Bernardo Silva

After Manchester City's 2-0 win over Chelsea in the Community Shield, Pep Guardiola was effusive in his praise for one player. "Right now it's Bernardo and 10 more, but it's about what you do over the season," Guardiola claimed. "In this moment Bernardo is far above the other guys. Today the performance [of Bernardo] was a masterpiece."
Naturally this was a statement that needed to be taken in context, a statement as much about the fitness of players in pre-season after various levels of exertion during the summer, than a statement about how much Pep rates the Portuguese maestro.
He certainly does rate him though, especially after Silva's gradual integration into the title-winning side saw him improve month-by-month. Apart from Ederson and Kevin De Bruyne, Silva was involved in more games than any other City squad member, but many of his early appearances were off the bench. That's rarely the case now, for a player Pep Guardiola admires for his character and fight. What's also interesting however is that the praise from Pep in pre-season was directed towards a player who had spent most of the friendly games playing in central midfield, raising talk of whether he could become the natural heir to his namesake David Silva, who at 32 is approaching the twilight years of his career, even if his performance levels are as good as ever.

Bernardo Silva is not the first player to find himself in this position. The aforementioned David Silva has spent plenty of time out on the flank during his City career, before finding a home in the centre. It is understandable. City have at times been blessed with too many playmakers who naturally levitate towards the centre. It is no surprise that to crowbar such talent into teams managers have at times resorted to playing them in wider positions. However, now that City have invested heavily in natural wide talent, the likes of Bernardo Silva can flourish in what may well be their natural habitat.

This shift may not have been immediately apparent when Bernardo Silva moved to City. He had spent much of his time wide at Monaco too, so on the surface it seemed this was where Guardiola intended to play him too.

He is not a natural wide player, though his skill with a football has allowed him to adapt and flourish near the touchline. We see wide players traditionally as pacey with the need in the modern game to work the whole of their side of the pitch, pitching in with defensive duties when required, covering the full back, especially ones that like to maraud forward. This is not really Bernardo's game, and I doubt Pep Guardiola would expect it of him. He certainly does not have the pace to skin a full-back, and thus can often be found cutting back inside towards a crowded penalty area. Acentral berth certainly suits his skill-set perfectly, and whilst he may not have yet reached the heights of David Silva (nor be expected to), he has one asset that perhaps David Silva lacks, namely a constant goal threat. Thus, playing centrally allows him to utilize such a skill, and his goals during City's last two visits to the Emirates prove his innate ability on the ball and an eye for goal.

And yet against Huddersfield Town, Silva was back in a wide position, with no right back behind him, as Guardiola unveiled a new experimental formation to combat teams who look only to defend against City, a formation devoid of natural attacking wide players. Silva had little defending to do as City predictably dominated the match, City's defence shifting across the pitch when required, but it seems his career as a central midfielder is not guaranteed just yet. After all, there is still stiff competition for the central midfield positions at City, and you feel that the hierarchy in the squad suggests that in a team containing the likes of Kevin De Bruyne and the two Silvas, it would be Bernardo that would shift wide. Or perhaps it suggests that he can maintain his performance levels wherever he operates. Positions are so fluid under Guardiola, and sometimes it's hard to define where players are asked to operate. Against Arsenal, Bernardo Silva may have played centrally, but drifted wider

wider at times. This is the beauty of City's attacking talent. He, like Sane, Sterling, David Silva or Kevin De Bruyne can function comfortably across the line. Hence, in the 90th minute against Huddersfield, it was Bernardo Silva who scuffed a shot right in front of the goal, the keeper palming the tame shot away. There's little doubt that Bernardo Silva is ready to take centre stage.

Elsewhere, news broke of a serious injury to Claudio Bravo. An Achilles tendon snapped meaning his season was effectively over before it had begun. Most City fans may shrug their shoulders at losing a player who has struggled to adapt to the English game, but apart from the human element of a player having to go through that, it is potentially problematic if anything happens to Ederson this season, Muric presumably the next in line. He may prove to be a revelation, but it is not ideal. I guess we'll get to see what Muric is made of in the cups, at the very least.

Ten Years Of Vincent Kompany

I'm not sure who "they" are, but "they" say a week is a long time in politics. It can be in football too, no more so than at the start of a season, when a solitary defeat sends a club into meltdown, leads to riots in the street or results in Jose Mourinho calling Luke Shaw fatty bum bum in a pre-match press conference,before retiring to his hotel room to binge on chicken and mushroom pot noodles. Let's be honest, it's only a matter of time.

With that in mind, ten years is a ridiculous length of time. Look at our lives. Ten years ago I had black hair and had no idea what gout was. Nor Twitter, Instagram or best of all, memes. Katy

Perry topped the charts with tales of kissing a solitary girl. What's more, she liked it.

City were owned by a soon-to-be fugitive, whose main gift to fans was free curry in Albert Square. Thankfully before his exile, Thaksin Shinawatra had a couple more gifts to hand out. One was selling up and sodding off, the other was Vincent Kompany, signed 10 years to the day that I write these words.

Ten years. Quite a lot has happened at City since then, all things considered, but the main man is still here.

It seems strange to consider that Hamburg were quite happy to get rid of him. He arrived back late from the Olympics, had other niggling issues with management and was known even then as the glass man, prone as he was to the occasional injury. £6m was all it took to secure his transfer which today wouldn't even pay for Fabian Delph's shin pads, or Bebe.

But credit where credit is due for Mark Hughes, who had shown an interest in the player for a while, though credit removed for seeing him as a defensive midfielder. To be fair, Vincent saw himself as one too. Thankfully Roberto Mancini saw something else in him, and the rest is history.

I don't need to run you through his career, you'll know it all. So many awesome performances, so many highs, 7 trophies(not 9), THAT header against United, so, so many injuries. At one time he was so good he made the PFA team of the year, though obviously individual awards were to elude him because at that time Liverpool had a player who was doing quite well.

The fact is, there is no better sight than seeing Vincent Kompany lifting a trophy. None. OK, maybe no queue at N1 turnstile, but that apart, none, and the latter is yet to happen, so in a way it's hard to judge. But seriously, all my favourite City moments can be linked to that sight, one way or another.

The true regret with Kompany is naturally that his body let him down on too many occasions. I've expected him to leave the club for this reason for the past 4 years, but despite the incredible damage his repeated breakdowns must have on a player mentally and physically, he never gave up, and on Sunday played his 336th game for the club. Signing just before the 2008 takeover, Vinny has shared the journey with us bitter berts, even marrying a Mancunian for added effect. With rumours he is part of a consortium planning to take over Stockport County, a moustache is surely the next natural step.

Kompany was the sort of player City missed during the dark times. Successful clubs, especially down the road, could keep players, wanted to keep players, the players wanted to stay. They had club legends who were there for a period of continued success, whose deeds will live on in the fans' memories for many decades to come. City had club legends too of course, the definition does not depend on trophies won, but the term is elevated when they are part of something bigger, something better, when they are there for a change in the balance of power for the first time in over a generation, there to celebrate with us days we never thought we'd see. When they climb those Wembley steps time after time with a smile on their face. And throughout, our captain did it with a level of skill, determination and grace that we've rarely seen before, or will again. He was the player fans of other clubs respected even if they were wired to hate his club, the player they had to dig really deep to find fault with.

Kompany is more than a great footballer though. So much more. You'll have seen a glimpse of the during the All Or Nothing documentary. Bernardo Silva commented that he could be president his speeches are that good. I'll assume he wasn't referring to the USA. He is a conduit between all branches of the club, a connector and an expert communicator. When Pep Guardiola gives one of his half-time talks that no doubt falls on untrained ears, you'd expect Kompany to be the translator. A footballer, captain, leader, diplomat and ambassador for our club. A man from whom I gain almost as much satisfaction from hearing him talk as I do watching him play football. Almost.

So how do we reward such a stalwart, a club legend? A statue for starters, his goal celebration pose a possibility but perhaps not fitting for a defender. City need more statues, though the bees will do for now. A decade usually signifies a testimonial, and an all stars game for charity would work, though God help us if it doesn't sell out. The seat sniffers' heads will explode. Anyway, whatever it is, I hope it is more than a lifelong season ticket, especially as Yaya Toure's is probably available anyway. Whatever it is, it won't be enough. It can't be.

My hope now is that he can stay generally fit and lift at least one more trophy, ideally the biggest two of all. I hope too that when his body finally decides enough is enough, he been be involved with City in some way or another. He won't be short of offers. He may not even stay in football, but whatever he does, you kinda get the feeling he'll be pretty good at it.

Sadly this was not the last eulogy I would write this season to the big man.

Premier League: Wolves 1 Manchester City 1

It seems every time I go away for the weekend and watch City in some foreign (Buxton) pub, City falter. I take full responsibility for this one. Remember City losing to Cardiff City 3-2? Yep, was camping near Cartmel that weekend. Burnley 1 City 1 last season? Yep, in the Lake District that day. City 1 Everton 1 last season? On holiday in Turkey.
I'll stay at home in future.
To be fair, when I saw the fixture list for the first time, this game worried me as much as the opener against Arsenal. My fears were well-founded for once.

But I'm not going to dissect the match – you've probably seen it, read stuff, dissected it yourself.
Ok, just briefly then. I didn't really understand Stones dropping out, though Pep clearly thought Vincent would be better dealing with the likes of Jimenez. It shouldn't have mattered either way. But it's clear Wolves mean business in this division. Good players, well-drilled and like their opposition on Saturday they all seem to know what their job is, and how to perform it well. Last season's Carabao Cup game seems a lifetime ago, but it still gave us pointers that Nuno Espírito Santo was putting together a good side, and a squad that all played the same way.

And yes, Wolves were disciplined, kept the pitch narrow when necessary and blocked Mendy and Walker, but City were partly the architects of their own downfall too. Pep had warned against complacency, and I don't think this result was a by-product of being complacent, but it was sloppy throughout, with far too many misplaced passes, even when not under huge pressure.
Perhaps, like last season, City haven't got going fully yet, and results have been deceptive, the previous two games played against compliant sides that played into our hands? We shall see I guess.

Hardly a time to panic though is it, or throw players under the bus. City have 7 points after 3 games, the same as last season.

Still, Kompany had one of "those" days, though he calmed down after half an hour or so, and Fernandinho too, who Pep had said had not reacted perfectly (physically) after the Huddersfield game showed that we will need back up for him during the season ahead.
These games happen – they have happened every single season of the club's existence, including when we have been the best team. Let's not forget, City simply drew a football game, nothing more, nothing less. Things didn't pan out the way we had hoped on the day, and that's why we love the sport because it is not predictable, and if everything ever became easy for City, it would get quite boring too.

The greater worry is that this City team has revealed its weakness, first exploited by Liverpool (repeatedly), now mirrored by teams playing in a similar fashion. That the Wolves formation, that blocked our full-backs and utilised skilful counter attackers to put City's defence under pressure, is the way forward. The home side knew when to press and when to drop, and the defence and midfield seemed perfectly in tune with each other. Not easy to implement of course, but Pep will have to continue to adapt as rival managers adapt to him.

The last thing you want to read is another debate on VAR, but as it emerges that City voted for its introduction this season, but too many other teams didn't, it seems ridiculous that goals like Boly's can be allowed to stand in the biggest league of the biggest sport in the world. But here we are, another season, and another spate of ridiculous decisions against City, which of course opens me up to accusations of being bitter, blinkered and selective in my judgement. Whatever. Wolves fans will naturally point out that Kompany could easily have been sent off in the first half, but then I would counter that if he had been cautioned for an early shirt pull, he may not have been so negligent with his later foul. We will never know.

As for the penalty appeal – against us it would be given etc, hashtag bitterblue, hashtag paranoia. I don't blame the referee for not seeing it at normal speed, I mean he can't spot Ashley Young scything down Sergio Aguero, so he ain't gonna see that, but it was a penalty. As always though, the game rolls out differently if it had been given, so it is not an argument for saying we should have won 2-1, as the equaliser may never have happened.

Mendy needs to work on the defensive side of his game, that much is clear, but then I don't expect our players to win every duel. Traore is frustratingly inconsistent, but at his best almost unplayable. Costa looks like a cracking player too. Our players will fail to block crosses now and then, or get turned, or slip, or not mark an opposition player. Having said that, I doubt Pep is so forgiving.

But let's be honest, we can slate the passing, various players and more, but on most days City would still have won that game. It was, as the old cliché goes, one of those days. Well hopefully anyway.

As for Sane, it should be noted that he was a substitute for 5 of the first 6 games last season, and it turned out quite well for him, but you can't help suspect something is not right at the moment. His cameo was one of the worst I have seen, though Aguero did not help by blocking his one good run. Perhaps there is an argument that he should start the next couple of games to get his season going, but Pep will of course be privy to information I do not possess. I suspected a slow start to the season post-World Cup, and perhaps we have got ahead of ourselves in thinking that the whole squad was fit and raring to go. One disappointing result and a different narrative emerges. And despite City's wealth of options, Kevin De Bruyne was missed. He is one of those special players that makes a difference on a day like this. Let's hope there aren't too many days like this in the next three months.

Onwards and upwards – the quadruple and the invincibles tag is still on!

The Lesser Of Two Evils: A Story About Manchester City

Imagine the following scenario, if you can.....

Everything began to change in early September, as the first leaves float gently to the ground.
At the Etihad, things unravel quickly. The signs have been there – a Rafa Benitez defensive masterclass whereby eight Newcastle players never shifted from their own goal line sees Newcastle leave Manchester with a point. Pep Guardiola had started scratching his head with increased frequency and intensity, causing bleeding and a head lice problem. Benjamin Mendy succumbed to another injury whilst dressed in a shark suit at the City Store. No official reason is given for why he was there, or what he was doing. He was out for three months.
Results falter, not helped by a Fulham goal scored when Mitrovic was allowed to carry the ball under his shirt from the half-way line. Paddy Barclay points out on Twitter there was nothing in the rules prohibiting this.
Then it was time to go to Anfield once more. Once off the blazing bus, the City players succumb to a 7-0 defeat and David Silva is sent off after getting in the way of a Sadio Mane scissor kick, Martin Atkinson brandishing the red card as he is stretchered off unconscious. By now Pep is wearing trackie bottoms and loose-fitting Diadora tops to matches, and Duncan Castles ponders whether the end is near. Pep can ill-afford another Jose Mourinho beasting, and by now eats alone in the City canteen.
Across the city, a remarkable transformation takes place. Manchester United started September in 12th place in the league. By the end of October, they are top. Jose Mourinho leaves his hotel room only to take pizza deliveries and for matches, but his methods start to work.
Jose's media team of Duncan Castles, Neil Custis and Gary Neville work tirelessly to deflect criticism away from the manager, so that he is free to concentrate on his job. Custis is almost sacked in early January after a late-night, obscene

Twitter tirade after Edinburgh Airport lose his golf clubs, but Mourinho stands by his man. The golf clubs are never recovered, but Custis laughs off the incident during an episode of Sunday Supplement. The episode is heated, and at one point Custis rips Ollie Holt's alice band off his head and stamps on it after Holt questions Mourinho's methods. The remainder of the day sees some hilarious banter between the two on social media.

Seven consecutive 1-0 wins see United climb up the table, and they never look back. Team after team are bored into submission by Mourinho's pragmatic football. Phil Jones is recalled to the England team, and made captain.

The good times are back at Old Trafford. Stephen Howson's pub tours are booked up until late 2020, Boylie's songbook enters into its 14th reprint, and Mark Goldbridge's joy burst over so much during one game that he inadvertently slips back into a Nottingham accent. Boylie's terrace classic, "Might As Well Be United", goes platinum. Gary Neville congratulates the United board for standing against the immediacy of modern life. And off the back of the on-pitch success, United go from strength-to-strength off it too, with new commercial partners rolling in. In a single week in December, Ed Woodward announces a new tin opener partner in Malaysia, a Buckfast tie-up in Glasgow, and panty liner partners in Cuba, Bolivia and Uzbekistan.

This is all in stark contrast to the events over at the Etihad. Pep Guardiola is struggling to turn results around. Results are so bad, some fans start leaving before full-time. The pressure gets to Pep. The Sun report that he was spotted in El Rincon drinking sangria straight from the jug, weeping gently whilst cuddling a signed photo of Lionel Messi. The club issues vague denials, stating it was actually in Evuna. And the picture was not signed. On 6th January, shortly after a shock 3-0 defeat to Oldham Athletic in the FA Cup, Pep Guardiola resigns. Brian Kidd is put in temporary charge of first-team affairs, and in a bid to impress the City bosses, experiments with a bold 1-1-6-2-1 formation that sees John Stones as a rush goalie, and Ederson as the pivot. City lose 9 straight games and slip into the relegation zone,

where they will remain. They are docked a further three points after it is revealed Kidd's teams contains 12 players.
City turn to Sam Allardyce.

Allardyce immediately drops Ederson in favour of new signing Jussi Jääskeläinen (43), who he orders to kick long at every opportunity. City score a mere 4 goals over the subsequent two months, all from corners. After The S*n run an exposé on Raheem Sterling laughing just days after a City defeat, he is offloaded to Real Madrid in a cut-price deal.
As City's relegation is confirmed, the unthinkable happens and United win the league, with a month to spare. Jesse Lingaard scores the crucial goal against Watford, and the whole team choreographs a detailed flossing celebration by the corner flag. Jose Mourinho runs down the touchline and joins in.
Simplymartial69 points out that the meme of the goal celebration got more retweets than City's announcement of Sam Allardyce as manager.
With relegation for City, comes even worse news. News breaks from the Middle East that the oil has run out. All of it, everywhere.
Then Sheikh Mansour, in his end-of-season address to City fans, declares that he is bored, and is selling up. "I am bored, and I am selling up," he says in the video. The club is bought by Michael Knighton, who saunters onto the Etihad pitch before scoring a panenka past Claudio Bravo. Knighton announces a ground-share with Stockport County over at Sale rugby club. All season tickets will be a set price of £1600, which includes a free non-alcoholic drink in the Little Bee. Knighton declares that within 5 years he expects City to terrorise Europe. In a bid to reclaim past glories, Knighton doubles the height of the floodlights and builds a temporary stand without a roof. Unfortunately due to a mix up with the architects, the stand faces away from the pitch, but sells out in record-time.
Within two years, Knighton sells the club on to the Glazers. City's home kit is to be red in future and the club is renamed The Manchester Massive Mavericks.

Over a million people come out for United's trophy parade, at some points the crowd appearing to be almost two-deep along Deansgate. Jose Mourinho is made a knight of the realm, and a film about United's season, entitled "Jose's Giants", starring James Nesbitt, Terry Christian and Mick Hucknall, tops the film charts for a year.

Despite not keeping City up, Sam Allardyce is handed a new 7 year contract, thought to be worth north of £8m a year. He immediately hires Kevin Nolan and Sam Lee (not that one) as his assistants, and makes a £12m bid for Chris Smalling. Smalling eventually signs for City for £22m in early August, and the signings of Rob Green, Jonny Evans and Salomon Rondon soon follow. John Smith s Extra Smooth is installed behind the club bars, as main sponsors of the club, a deal thought to be worth £200,000 a year.

City eventually return to the Premier League in 2044, though by now a European Super League means there are only two leagues in England, and Rochdale are soon installed as title favourites.

And even if all that actually happened…….
Every single last detail……………..

It would still be preferable to Liverpool winning the league.

The Tottenham Hotspur Debacle

As you will all know by now, Tottenham Hotspur have got themselves into something of a pickle. The news emerged recently that their new ground will not be ready in time for its scheduled opening against Liverpool on September 15th and the club have provided no new date for when the opening will be. The ground still resembles a building site because, well, it is, so don't expect to see games there anytime soon. As a result, the game against Liverpool and the subsequent home game against Cardiff City will have to be played at Wembley.

In addition, if Spurs were drawn at home in the Carabao Cup, they were hoping to be named as the away side and it seems their Champions League group games will remain at Wembley too with health and safety issues delaying their move. With test events necessary before any switch, it looks like this is an issue that could drag on for some time. Spurs got Watford at home in the cup, and now want to play 50 miles away in Milton Keynes. Another fine mess.

Whilst this is unfortunate for Tottenham Hotspur and will no doubt hit them financially, it wouldn't normally be a massive problem as they continue to use Wembley until their new stadium is ready. And this is what they will do. Except, that is, when Manchester City are scheduled to play them on 28th October. On that day, Wembley is hosting an NFL American Football match, and that will not move for anyone. This leaves Spurs in something of a quandary – and the solution is that the City game will be moved back a day, to the Monday night.

Other options were no doubt considered. There was talk of switching venues to Twickenham, for example. However, the rugby authorities soon quelled such notions. Switching it to a City home game was never viable either as this it was seen to be interference with the integrity of the league. On top of this, Pep

Guardiola would never entertain the switch as it would cause a succession of away games towards the end of the season.

Now, apart from the concerns over the state of the pitch one day after an NFL match, and they are serious concerns, there are more pressing matters here.

You see, if the game had originally been scheduled for the Monday night, there would have been few complaints. But it wasn't. It was scheduled for Saturday at 3pm initially, then moved to the Sunday. And now it seems, it has been moved again. As always, then, it will be the fans who suffer. That is what grates in this situation. Of course, the stadium delays will inconvenience Spurs fans. But it is Manchester City fans who have been hung out to dry most by the October fixture.

Away fans, at least those of Premier League teams, tend to wait until fixture changes are announced for television coverage before making any travel plans. Once such changes have been announced, plans can be made safe in the knowledge the time of the game will not be altered. Except this time, the game was altered for a second time. This is not Manchester City's fault. However, any club has a duty of care to its fans and a club with annual revenues of over £400 million has an added responsibility to meet that duty of care.

But hey, match-going fans have been treated with disdain for a while now, so these developments should not come as much of a surprise. The modern game is packaged for the majority, the armchair viewer rather than the match-going fan. La Liga could soon play games in the USA, the Premier League could have a 39th game hosted abroad, a European super league is a constant possibility and it has taken endless campaigning to cap the cost of tickets for away fans.

There has to be a limit to how much fans can be exploited. Now it may well be that the only viable solution to the problem of when to play the Tottenham Hotspur/Manchester City match is to move it to the Monday night. I understand that City didn't have much choice here, and were probably backed into a corner. They don't want the game awarded to them, thus weakening their claims as true champions should they be top dogs come May. That was never going to happen anyway. They don't want to move the game to later, when there is barely time for players to breathe. It had to be played on the planned weekend/Monday. But once backed into a corner, you limit the damage caused.

You do that by taking the attending fans into consideration and ensure the move is as painless as possible. Firstly, there should be free travel laid on for all travelling fans on the day. City have done this. Good start. Tickets should be cheap. Yeah, like that's happening.

But most importantly - one of the clubs should reimburse all pre-existing bookings. And in that respect, the silence is deafening.

City's supporter services have already replied to a concerned fan on Twitter, stating that the club is not liable for refunds for travel costs for a fixture switch. This spectacularly misses the point. I'm not interested in terms and conditions, about City's responsibilities under the law if a fixture is changed. This is not a legal issue, it is a moral one. It is a duty of care to those that help fund your billion pound operation.

Now in a perfect world, this is where Tottenham would take ownership of the blame. They could have done the right thing and announced problems with the stadium build before Sky and BT announced their live football coverage for October. Instead, they waited until a couple of days later, probably only after the press got wind of the problems, by which time media coverage forced them to announce something. Either way, as those responsible for the wasted travel plans of thousands of City fans, there is a case to be made that they should reimburse everyone involved.

There is precedent for this. The Premier League forced Swansea to reimburse Sunderland fans in 2015 after the Swans moved a fixture due to the timing of an FA Cup tie. It was moved back 24 hours, as City's game probably will be, and Sunderland strongly opposed the move. On that occasion, there was compensation for affected fans. Will there be this time?

But if Spurs refuse, City should be the "bigger man" here and take the bullet. I doubt it will hit the club's financial results too badly. You see, City are in the process of electing various fan representatives to deal with a myriad of club issues, a great move. Yet at the same time, they continue to treat fans with disdain. When City were backed into a corner, they should have made their demands quite clear – yes, we will move the game to the Monday night, under duress, on one very clear condition – every single City fan that had already made plans for a Sunday game, a rearranged game, will be fully reimbursed all costs, either by Spurs or the Premier League. Agree to that and you have a deal. Without it, sod off.

That of course would involve thinking about fans. The whole affair will simply prove the growing disconnect between fans and clubs at the top level, where money is king. Further down the line there may be recompense for fans (there may not), but it shouldn't be up in the air. Where is City's ownership of this? Show you actually give a shit about the fan base. Because occasionally we need more than competitively priced Champions League tickets, confetti and scarves. The mooted move to Monday night was disclosed weeks ago, so everyone knew this was likely coming. City fans may get £10 or so back on cancelled train tickets, maybe a bit back on cancelled accommodation, but that is not good enough. It's not just City fans either. Tottenham fans are required to purchase fresh tickets for the rearranged games with the promise of future credit notes to reimburse them: the new tickets being more expensive than their existing ones. Astonishingly, Manchester United have now moved their game that weekend to the Sunday, inconveniencing two whole new sets of fans. You couldn't make this up.

On a website where I asked of Spurs fans should reimburse City fans for the fixture change, from 154 votes, 35% said no.

Imagine that – thinking that fellow fans should be screwed because hey, it's City. Fan campaigns for cheaper away tickets, like "Twenty's Plenty" worked because fans cast aside rivalries, rather than acting like pre-pubescent children on social media sites. And we must continue to do as long as fans are treated like an inconvenience. As soon as this fixture change was announced, City should have had concrete plans for all fans affected. The fact that those affected are instead greeted by a wall of silence really says it all.

Stick that thought in your next fan survey, City.

Tonight, I'd like to read you a charming little story from a book I picked up at the United Megastore™ sale. It's called **Little Garry Potter and The Theatre of Dreams**.

(FYI – Jose Mourinho had just made a deal after accepting a charge of tax evasion. You won't have seen it covered in the media)

Little Garry Potter was all comfy in bed, underneath his Phil Jones duvet, which his dad said would ward off the demons. "Glory glory Man United" was playing on his Deezer account, Manchester United's official music partner.

Dad had said he would read Garry a bedtime story as Garry was upset after hearing that United's glorious and successful manager Jose Mourinho could go to prison for something called tax evasion. He didn't know what this meant, but it sounded bad, and Mike Phelan would have to take over. Dad said not to worry as he had good lawyers.

His dad settled down next to him in a chair, only opening a story book once he had taken a sip of his Casillero Del Diablo cabernet sauvignon wine. The wine was a smooth, full-bodied Cabernet Sauvignon with cassis and black cherry flavours, complemented by hints of coffee and dark chocolate. More than 100 years ago, a man reserved for himself an exclusive batch of his best wines. To keep strangers away from his private reserve, he spread the rumour that the Devil lived in that place. Hence the name: Casillero Del Diablo, The Devil's Cellar. Casillero Del Diablo are proud to be Manchester United's official wine partner.

"Son, I want to tell you a story set in the near future, a story of a brave warrior brought to a land to restore a rightful heir, to bring back glory to where it belongs. It's a story about Jose Mourinho."

"The alleged tax evader?" asked Garry, fear in his innocent, young eyes.

"Son, I told you not to worry. Jose will be fine. The money was just resting in his account."

"Anyway, once upon a time, in a land far, far, far away..."

"Manchester?"

"Yes Garry, Manchester, a town in the north of England. In a land far, far away – Manchester – there once lived a man of great charisma, of great wisdom, a special one. He went by the name of Jose Mourinho. He was revered by all. He teamed up with a man named Ed Woodward, known also as the Equalizer, to bring back the glory days to Manchester United, in association with Adidas, Manchester United's official kit supplier.

Every day, Jose would arrive at the crack of dawn at United's training ground in his Chevrolet Corvette Grand Sport, to begin a hard day's work. The Grand Sport came with twin airbags, four wheel drive and the perfect combination of power and handling. Chevrolet are a principal partner of Manchester United.

"Dad, I don't understand what this has to do with Jose and the Theatre of Dreams?" asked Garry.

"Just setting the scene son, just setting the scene. Anyway, Jose was soon in trouble, for the evil owners who controlled his budget provided him with a mere £450m, which was barely enough to buy 3 full backs, 2 central defenders, an old youth player back for £90m, a striker and three more midfielders with barely enough money left over to pay off the legal fees for the physio he had slandered at his previous club."

"What was Jose to do? He knew his job and reputation, and relationship with his good friend Duncan Forts, depended on defeating his evil foe, Josep Guardiola. Jose had beasted Josep, who was bald and a fraud, many times in Spain, a hotter country where they both used to compete. Now it was time to do it all over again. And in the first year, that is what he did, with three glorious victories including the definitive measure of success, the community shield. Jose was king once more."

"It didn't last though. Evil forces were at work, determined to smite Jose at every turn. Apart from the aforementioned £450m, he was not being given the funds to compete with the mercenaries across the city. The only response was to try and buy every player City were linked with, ably assisted by Azam, official MUTV Partner in Botswana, Burundi, Congo, Ghana, Kenya, Namibia, Malawi, Rwanda, Sierra Leone, Tanzania, Uganda, Zambia & Zimbabwe."

"Once Alexis Sanchez became available, Jose and Ed sprang into action. Jose flew immediately to Chile to seal the deal, via Aeroflot, Manchester United's official carrier, as organised by regional partner Thomas Cook. Jose felt great, in no small parts thanks to Aland, the official wellness and nutrition partner of Manchester United in China. Next came Fred, who City definitely wanted, but who wanted to join the biggest team in the world instead. Manchester was red. As always."

"So what went wrong daddy?"

"Corrupt referees, players making mistakes, other teams fluking results. There was nothing Jose could do about it. Nothing."

"And the tax thing dad?"

"A simple misunderstanding. All sorted."

"Why did he plead guilty then?"

"Jose accepted the charge not because he was guilty, which he most certainly was not, but because he was not one to cause a fuss."

"Is that why Alexis Sanchez also pleaded guilty in February daddy?"

Garry's dad was getting exasperated by now. "Yes Garry, now focus on the real story. Alexis just didn't want to be away from his dogs."

"But daddy, I thought Jose demanded our respect? I know I am only three years old, but I fail to comprehend how a man who accepted a tax avoidance charge, poked a rival coach in the eye and harangued a female physio for simply doing her job to the extent she had to quit, can expect our respect?"

"Is there not a juxtaposition in those situations that hits at the strained relations not only between Jose and the media but also the disconnect between club and fans?" added the three-year-old.

A loud cheer went up from the living room downstairs.

"Son, son...", spluttered Garry's dad.

"Son. The media hate Jose. You must understand this. Fake news. Sad. One day, when you're old enough to play at City's academy, or go to Dab University, you'll understand."

"Ok. But dad, I thought this story was set in the near future? I know all this."

"Yes son, well I'm getting to that bit now. You see, social media domination and kit sales were not enough anymore. United were the most successful team when considering income minus net spend divided by points gained, as verified by the trustworthy International Centre for Sports Studies who Jose's friend Duncan had picked as their skewed results suited his agenda. But sadly there were no trophies for this. "

"Was Jose sad daddy?"

"Yes he was son. His left back kept eating burgers, his defenders kept making mistakes, his star midfielder spent most his time having haircuts and making videos, and players kept leaving to selfishly attend the birth of their children. He locked himself in his hotel suite, living off just pizza and You C1000, proud isotonic drink partner for United in Indonesia."

"Dad, is this mess of a story really just an excuse for sponsorship placements by United's official partners?"

"Of course not son. Not sure how you could come to that conclusion. That's the sort of rubbish you would never hear on Cell C, official broadcast partner of MUTV and Manchester United in South Africa. United are about playing for the shirt, the glory of playing for the red devils, as is this story. That's what's important. Then the kids and the wife, in that order. And retweets. It's a story about not having to win all the time, and life not being fair, and sometimes the oil-rich cheating mercenaries winning instead. Or god forbid, one day, the scousers."

"Is that what Citeh are, mercenaries?", asked Garry. He did his best impression of a Mancunian accent.

"Yes they are. Yes they are. They play for the money, we play for the shirt. They might as well be Celtic, son."

"You see, the moral of the story is that respect must be earnt through success alone, and only in England, subject to certain caveats that muddy the waters of what constitutes success. Jose has that respect, unlike any other manager in the Premier League, and that is why he is attacked so much."

"And so, in the near future Jose had to leave, because of unfair attacks. It's getting late now, but next time, I'll tell you how the "class of 92" led United back to the glory days, back to where they belonged. And with that thought, I will bid you goodnight son."

He rose, finishing off his Casillero Del Diablo wine and before turning off the light, weakly dabbed in the direction of Garry, who feigned a smile, before turning over and going to sleep with tears in his eyes.

Garry's dad milly-rocked his way to the kitchen and to a cold, refreshing Budweiser, a crate of which had arrived that very afternoon, from DHL, Manchester United's official logistics partner.

He turned on the history channel, and settled down to reminisce about better times.

Goodnight.

September

Premier League: Manchester City 2 Newcastle United 1

Be honest. You're reading this after the season ends, obviously, and you can't remember a single thing about this game. And why would you?

Well as we entered September, this was not the stroll in the park that many may have expected, but City got over the line. When Raheem Sterling opened the scoring in just the 8th minute, victory was almost assumed. But then a nice break from Newcastle and sloppy defending saw Yedlin snatch an equaliser. This started a trend that would see only defenders score against City in the league for quite a long period of time. City would prove adept at restricting opposition attackers, in the league at least.

In the end, victory was sealed from an unlikely place, Kyle Walker slamming in a long-range beauty that eventually ensured City took all three points. It was his first goal for the club. It may well be his last too, as a Kyle Walker shot is as rare as an Etihad full house.

Hashtag Banter.

Anyway, with Chelsea and Liverpool winning ahead of City, this was three much-needed points at this early stage of the season. City were largely dominant (78% possession, 24 shots), but were made to sweat for victory. Wasteful would be the key word, as chances were regularly spurned.

Fun fact: Manchester City have won each of their past 10 Premier League home games against Newcastle, their joint-longest run of home wins against a single opponent in the top-flight (also 10 v Wolves between 1900 and 1937).

Next up – another tedious international break. Yay!

Premier League: Manchester City 3 Fulham 0

As the storm clouds loomed, what was already being billed (not by me) as a must-win game was seen out comfortably in the end by the champions. A routine win, that slumped into a training match by the hour mark.

The rain held off, but with Liverpool winning at Wembley in the early kick off, City needed to avoid any signs of complacency, the thing Pep seems to fear more than anything.

It's impossible second-guessing a Pep team of course, but for once a hunch paid off, and Sane was back in the team. News of course broke last week that he was to become a father, which he now is, which rather pissed on the chips of those bemoaning his departure from the Germany camp, suggesting he grow up, which many a City fan did on Twitter without any facts to hand.

Of course this news does not mean he does not have an attitude problem. Maybe he wanders into the academy every morning, giving the V sign to the tea lady before smashing all her cups for a laugh, before spitting on the receptionist, but just maybe we should give him some time and let him grow into the season. He will have been pretty stressed in the past month awaiting the birth of his first child, and this would naturally have an effect on anyone, whatever their age or profession.

Elsewhere, Otamendi was randomly thrust back into the team, which is fine as he needs game time, having not actually had any yet. Mendy was nowhere to be seen, but it appears this is due to an injury. Let's hope it is nothing serious.

Delph came in to deputise, Aguero was up to by himself, and the two Silvas were paired together. Yay.

Nice to see two more "mature" mascots for this game. My, they must have seen some dross in their time, so I'd say they earnt this day. Of course in the old days there'd be a weak joke swirling around the internet about them making the starting XI, but times have changed in their lives and ours. Thirty-three managers have passed through during their time as supporters.

This had banana skin written all over it for a pessimist like me. A home game against a promoted side should not really pose too many problems, but Fulham are different to the norm, having invested heavily (and well) during the summer. Schurrle, Mitrovic, Seri, Sessegnon, Mawson and more are all great players.

Still, what do I know? In many ways Fulham did impress me. They pass out from the back, they pass well, they spread the ball, they are good to watch, with no shortage of skill. I suspected that Fulham would never sit back with ten men behind the ball, and that was the case. Perhaps they should have done, but it's not their way and all that. It made for an entertaining game until City shut down the match, but it also allowed the home side to flourish. They simply allowed the City players far too much space.

The key to Fulham getting something out of the match was probably to block the home side until frustration kicked in. So much for that plan. Within 90 seconds, the passing out from the back style was their undoing. Seri's pass was weak, Fernandinho nipped in, and crossed for Sane to tap in. Just who you wanted to score more than anyone, his inclusion in the side vindicated after 98 seconds.
We shouldn't take away from the finish either – yes it was in most respects a tap in, but the keeper's dive inches away from him was distracting, but he kept his eye on the ball. No baby-themed goal celebration though – disappointing.
A shame for the visitors, who had looked lively in the opening 80 seconds!
City were creating at will, even if the visitors were looking threatening from the flanks. Sterling will garner criticism for his miss one-on-one, but it was in fact one of his better shots, and

the keeper just did enough to deflect it onto the bar. Sterling did little wrong for me.

The pass was of course supplied by Bernardo Silva – more on him later no doubt.

Next was David Silva's 50th goal, a scrappy effort that he almost missed form close range, but still preceded by some neat build-up play. Fulham claimed in vain for handball, but it was off his chest, so even a real VAR operation rather than the trial in action that day would not have ruled it out.

There was time for a jinking Sterling run to be finished off with a low shot and good save, and for the traditional match official cock-up, a Sane goal wrongly ruled offside – Otamendi was offside but he wasn't remotely involved in the play. Same old, same old.

Never mind, because within a couple of minutes of the re-start, the game was effectively over. Aguero got the ball on the right, slowed things down, sprung back into life and crossed for Sterling to tap in from a yard out. All too easy for City, and after that the game resembled little more than a training match. City starved Fulham of possession, and they rarely threatened. The home side could have had more goals if needed you'd imagine, but with the Champions League on the horizon, game management sprang into action. Not the most entertaining final half an hour, but understandable.

Bernardo Silva had one shot deflected wide, and missed an absolute sitter. We'll let him off on this occasion. Jesus also had a golden chance saved.

Not quite the perfect day though – Aguero went off, hopefully as a precaution, but having felt discomfort in his ankle after landing awkwardly in the first half. We now hope Dr Cugat has him performing somersaults by Wednesday evening. Delph off too, with talk of that being a precaution, but with Mendy's situation unknown, we need at least one of the two fit over the coming week.

MOTM? Well it's time to talk more about Bernardo Silva. Most of it has already been said in recent months to be honest, but what a joy to watch. Just sublime, his control of a football unmatched in a squad of superstars. Just a shame he couldn't cap off the performance with a goal.

Other shout outs – Sane started with a goal, but did well throughout the game. Delph was a beast, with some superb covering, tackling and an all-round energetic display. And it was great to see Fernandinho back to his best. The key now is to manage him through a brutal eight months or so. Sterling too was his usual dangerous self, and it was great to see the Sterling/Sane/Aguero axis back again.

There was much criticism online for Foden not getting any minutes. This is not an issue that loses me much sleep, it's Pep's calls and he has his reasons for everything, but I tend to agree that he could easily have got half an hour with the game over after an hour. Aguero had to be one of the subs of course and Jesus is the natural replacement, Delph was protected so I get that, and the re-jig of the defence could not really accommodate bringing Foden on at that point. Now if Fernandinho had been subbed as I expected, that would have made sense for many reasons, and would have allowed Foden on, but by now Fernandinho was covering in defence with Delph off. The fact Sterling came off suggests he is a starter on Wednesday. Not an ideal situation, but there were extenuating circumstances on this occasion. Gundogan got on though, so why not Foden?

Job done anyway, and onto the Champions League once more. Lyon are in bang average form in the league, so let's hope for a great start to the competition.

The Champions League Campaign Begins

Manchester City 1 Lyon 2

Jeez. One of *those* nights. Poor crowd, poor performance, trams crap, man-flu approaching, so little sleep. I love waking up after a performance like that. #sarcasm

I doubt anyone is reading this, so I'll cut to the chase – little need therefore to dissect chances and the like. There weren't many after all. Just a shout out to Ederson for his great fingertip save from Depay in the 2nd half, to spare us even more embarrassment.

Now I am sick and tired of people criticising others for whether they go to a football match or not, those usually criticising obviously not there themselves, but even so, the attendance against Lyon surprised me. We as a fan base have an apathy for the Champions League of course, and we favour the league, the bread and butter, but still it surprised me. Maybe this country is on its arse more than I ever realised, but after the 100 point gain last season, I thought plenty of fans would be up for this. I was wrong. Their choice of course, but it must have an effect.

Apathy from the crowd, apathy on the pitch, seemingly. Time to stop booing the anthem, and create the right atmosphere for players to flourish. They should need no encouragement to perform in a Champions League tie though, so it works both ways. Play better and the crowd get up for it.
So how do you judge losing to a good team in average form? Which team turned up at the Etihad? Were we poor or were they great? As is usually the case, both is probably the correct answer.
City were sluggish, lethargic, sloppy and lacked intensity. Lyon were disciplined, skilful on the ball, and countered with precision and pace. Most importantly, their players did not make mistakes and ours did. That's the difference, and it is

something of a theme for City defeats. There's little place to hide in this competition, so when Delph misses a cross, the result has a certain inevitability about it.
But if that mistake had happened the other way round, would we have scored? Clinical we are not.

After games like this, you begin to doubt all players. After a single defeat. Well I do anyway, but that's what 10 minutes on Twitter can do to you. Laporte is crap after all when players get at him, Walker a flat-track bully, Delph just an adequate stand-in, Jesus a Championship player who runs around a lot, Fernandinho too old, Gundogan utterly useless, Silva too old to run two games a week, Sterling just a headless chicken. Sane was Ok though.
And Sane being the brightest player as a substitute makes the concerns of just a week ago seem rather distant now. Now we're questioning every other player instead.

I struggle to explain this performance though, I really do. Citing complacency seems too easy for me. They are playing Lyon, not Oxford United (gulp). If Pep had hair, he'd have torn it out. There is a problem with this competition, and this is proof as I suspected, that City still do not have a handle on the Champions League.

You see, I asked Sam Lee on Monday if City had progressed and evolved to the stage that games like these were now almost guaranteed wins. That we, like the European giants, can expect to coast through groups such as ours. I wanted verification from a neutral about where we were, evolution-wise. He thought we were close to that position, and I as natural pessimist, doubted it. Turns out I was being a realist. Fact is, Real Madrid win at home to Lyon. Pretty much always. So do Barcelona, so do Bayern Munich. We have a long way to go, and the sad thing is a lot of fans don't seem that bothered. Four defeats on the row in the competition, three home defeats on the bounce too, though all in different circumstances. Pep's record in the Champions League too will come under even more intense scrutiny after every performance like this. Don't get me wrong, we win the league and I'm happy. But that's far from a guarantee any more.

For me stability is key. There are too many games to play the same team for weeks on end, but change the team every single time, and you don't get that understanding. It took time for the players to take on Pep's complicated methods, but they got there in his second season. With news that he has been trying new things in training to try and improve our Champions League performances, you wonder if he has over-burdened the players again. After all, this competition is his weakness, and the main criticism linked to that has been his tendency to over-think.

The point will be made by hacks with their finger on the pulse that Arteta failed his managerial audition. Poppycock in my opinion – we can have little confidence that having Pep on the touchline would have seen a change in attitude, and Pep will have spent all week setting up this team. And he will have chosen it, more to the point (a reminder that Pep was serving a touchline ban for this game).

So Pep choses Sterling on the left, Bernardo out wide again despite us all knowing he flourishes in a central role, with Sane on the bench when he could have caused problems for 90 minutes. Lob-sided, but that's easy to say with hindsight.

Fernandinho tired? Sorry, I'm not having it. I'm not having it that this defeat somehow links back to the failure to capture Jorginho in the summer. It may well prove costly in the long run, but Fernandinho has played one game in the previous two weeks, and was at his worst early in the game, not the latter stages. It's a question of focus, and not being supported when pressed.

We need to talk about Jesus. He's not our saviour, just yet, and to be honest, I'm seeing no improvements over the past year. His goal threat is minimal, and he is not really suited as an out-and-out striker for me. I never thought he was the finished article, my hope being that by the time Aguero departs in two years' time he was ready to step up. That's not looking likely right now. He's young, had two bad injuries etc etc – he needs time, he will get it, but we're very reliant on Aguero, not that he did much when introduced in the 2nd half.

A penalty on Jesus? Probably, just, but we don't get them, and that's not some paranoia, just a Champions League fact. The number of penalties I've seen given for theatrical falls down the years. Just look at United's penalty on the same night to see how the world works for others. Having said that, Ronaldo of all people was the recipient of the worst decision of the night. No wonder he burst into tears, the delicate flower.

It's easy to get into pessimism mode now (I love it really) and bemoan the season ahead. The easiest way to get over it is to win our next game, naturally. Failure to beat an average Cardiff side will be truly worrying.
Anyway, this puts the pressure on the next match, at Hoffenheim. A draw in the other game was probably a plus for City, though only time will tell. Qualifying from the group is the key here, but this defeat has not only made that difficult, but lessened the chances of topping the group and thus perhaps getting an easier draw for the knockout stage. And to think we entered the game as favourites for the competition. Madness. Still, as there should not be any whipping boys in this group, and anyone could in theory beat anyone else, the points needed to qualify may well be lower than the average. City finished third in a group with 10 points because one team lost all six games, but 10 points should be enough this time around.

We're still terrible as a fan base at dealing with defeat, which in a way is good because it means it does not happen very often, but then it shouldn't with the squad we have. We can but hope that this is the kick up the arse the players needed. In the meantime we can all argue about what terrible fans we are for not going to every game, and the world spins on its axis as normal.....

Manchester City Fans & Human Rights

Just over ten years ago it began. A wonderful journey for Manchester City fans. A litany of caveats, an asterisk next to each achievement and a decade of wailing for rival fans.
Money doesn't buy you success. The sheikhs will get bored. The oil will run out. Always in our shadow. 'istory.
Wishful thinking.
New avenues were needed, so rival fans started counting empty seats, and they still are, decided that money does buy you success, and net spends proved it, whilst developing a keen interest in global human rights. But rather than dismiss that last point, I think it's worth looking at in more detail.
So, how do I feel about the fact that the owners of my beloved football club are strongly linked to the rulers of a state that has been highly criticised for its human rights record? It's a question that every City fans has had to consider at some point.
So let's cut to the chase – in response to the question as to whether I care about human rights abuses in the UAE, the answer is quite simple – no. I think I speak for most City fans by saying that? Got a problem with that view? Tough ****, couldn't care less.
There, that's that out of the way.

Ok, I need to drill down on that. You see, in 2007, I was not kept awake by the thought of the treatment of migrant workers in the Middle East, and I'm not now. I don't shed a tear every night at the situation in Yemen, which still sickens me when I read about it, nor about the situation in Burma or Indonesia, or Nigeria or.......
There's a lot of bad stuff going on in the world, as there always is with 7 billion people plonked on its surface. If I cared about all injustices, I would have broken a long time ago. Ten minutes on Twitter leaves me on the edge nowadays.
But surely say the critics, it is surely different when these people own your football club?
Nope.

And here's the thing. Rightly or wrongly, and that's for every individual to decide, and using a sample size from the internet that hardly counts as conclusive, it seems this is the majority view. We simply aren't overly concerned about our owners' ethics or practices and it would be a lie to pretend otherwise. We perhaps selfishly take our own priorities as more important, and following Manchester City over the past decade has brought untold pleasure, and has enriched us in ways we barely thought possible.

I am in no doubt that football fans will lower their moral bar in return for success. After all, would you erase a period of unparalleled success if you thought you could improve the lives of migrant workers in a country you know nothing about thousands of miles away? Most football fans would shrug their shoulders and say "nothing to do with me, nothing I can do about it". And if City were owned by a local fan instead, would anything have changed in Abu Dhabi in respect of migrant workers or human rights? A cop out perhaps (definitely?), but that's life, the reality of how most of us think.

Fans of other clubs would soon change their tune too should a similar situation happen to them. Would Aston Villa fans be protesting in the streets if a wealthy Dubai prince took over their club and took them to unprecedented success? I doubt it very much. Nor Newcastle fans or Derby fans or West Brom fans. They'd love every single minute, every single transfer link, every renovated stand, housing project, every day out at Wembley. Seeing that trophy lifted high by their captain, reminiscing about the goal that sealed the first title in 50 years, eagerly playing the season review DVD, crowing on social media, worshipping their star striker, drinking it all in.
And don't for one moment think it couldn't happen to any club in the country. Only last year a cousin of Sheikh Mansour attempted a £2 billion takeover of Liverpool, though talks eventually floundered. FSG are looking for investment however, and I doubt that it will come from the Co-Op. Liverpool are

making strides in returning to the summit of European football, and their owners will do whatever is necessary for that to happen. There will be few dissenters, because we're not talking about Manchester City here. It's just organic growth after all.

It's the hypocrisy of it all. People snorting cocaine every weekend whilst decrying the cruelty of riding elephants in Thailand. Do you think that cocaine was ethically sourced via a vegan collective in Chorlton, or does it suit you better not to give it much thought? Feel confident do you in criticising human rights in the middle-east whilst your amazon order is collected by an overworked person at breaking point on minimum wage, as you walk around in clothes made by children in sweatshops for pennies? We all tend to be rather selective with our morals.

The simple fact is this. Rival fans who couldn't care in the slightest about the welfare of a worker thousands of miles away are using City's owners to point-score. Their team is not as good as City's, they've exhausted every other area, the banter is feeling tired now, so let's pretend to be disgusted about City's owners. It's fine of course to have a genuine interest in such matters, to probe, to question, to demand reform, improvements, to state that the situation is abhorrent to you, if you have expressed such views consistently and campaigned on such matters previously. It's not fine if you're using the situation in the middle-east as part of a football rivalry, because you read an article on the internet that provided you with the ammunition you wanted.

One of the most important points for me however is that we as fans have never, or should never, look to football for moral guidance. A multi-billion pound industry will always attract all areas of our global society, and the sport has never been squeaky clean, and for all our outrage, never will be. Were you really looking for moral guidance and spiritual cleansing from your football club's owners? Now of course in a perfect world every club would be owned by a local fan, a passionate supporter with philanthropy in his or her heart, who doesn't take a single penny out of the club and helps the club through its glory years. Sadly, over a decade ago, there was no one that really fit the bill for City, and the club was not in a good state. Sadly, for most fans, that local hero does not exist for them either.

What's more, it's worth pointing out that English football is awash with "arab" money, as it is with Chinese and Russian money too, that money's origins impossible to ascertain much of the time – and it's best you don't ask too many questions either. So is it ok to have sponsorship deals with regimes we consider despotic and with poor human rights, or is it just ownership of clubs that we've suddenly decided is acceptable? There's Chelsea and the enduring suspicions that Roman's wealth isn't entirely legitimate. Over in Trafford, United get money from China, Saudi and the UAE. They have Aeroflot as a major commercial partner. In Liverpool the name on their shirt is Standard Chartered, who received a record fine for money laundering that involved drug and terrorist money. Their previous airline partner was Garuda, the Indonesian state airline and that country has a very questionable human rights record. And there's Tibet Water. Arsenal have Emirates of course. Arsenal have "Visit Rwanda" on their sleeves, West Ham's owners have their own niche history, and the list goes on and on.

In fact, here's CNBC with an update on Standard Chartered:
Standard Chartered remains under U.S. supervision six years after accusations it breached Iran sanctions, but Chief Financial Officer Andy Halford told CNBC that the bank is making "good progress."
In 2012, the New York State Department said the British lender hid $250 billion worth of transactions with the Iranian government. Following an agreement in the same year, where it reached a $340 million settlement, it has been under the care of an independent monitor to improve its money laundering prevention scheme.

MOVE ALONG, NOTHING TO SEE HERE. #ynwa

This is modern football, and it has its tentacles around many clubs, not just City. That's why Barcelona replaced the charity on their shirt with the Qatar Foundation, despite its questionable links. Atletico find themselves sponsored by the delightful Azerbaijan regime, and then there's PSG of course. The list goes on and on....

There is ignorance too involved when discussing owners whose culture differs from ours. "Arab" is often used with disdain, the religious beliefs dismissed when looking at practices in the UAE, the tense situation that pervades the region glibly reduced to a footnote. The UAE is a relatively new country, developing in a powder keg region and that must be taken into account. It took the UK a long, long time to reach what we call civilization, though it seems lacking at the moment when you turn the TV on. As an atheist I am not overly keen on many a religious practice in the middle-east, here in the UK, or around much of the globe, but there's little I can do about that, and I can express my own beliefs but that's where it ends.

The owners' religious and moral views have not spread to the clubs they own, the opposite being the case, as seen by the support for the women's team, Manchester Pride and more. PR guff perhaps, but still good to see. Values have not been imposed on the City Group, which would have resulted in a very different perspective from me and others.

The UK government is no better than most middle-eastern rulers, but they don't own my football club, or anyone else's. Nevertheless, many football fans across the nation voted for them, many of them (by which I mean most) will have shown little interest in our government selling arms to Saudi Arabia, repression of the poor, the brutal effects of austerity, the dismantling of the NHS for their own financial gain and much, much more. We can't be selective with our outrage to get one over a rival fan. The world shouldn't work like that. After all, you all sat there enjoying the World Cup in Russia, and despite moaning, you'll all do the same in Qatar in four years' time. No boycotts from fans, players or managers. A few angry words on Twitter will do, eh?

There must be a line though – a line that your owners cross that makes you decide that the situation is unacceptable, to rebel, to push for change. For me, the line was crossed by the end of the brief Shinawatra reign, from the stories coming out of Thailand. The current owners have not crossed that line. Stories of dodgy brothers, of the regime's human rights record and of children trafficked for camel races does not push me over the edge, because none of that links back to those I believe own and run this club. That may be convenient for me, it may mean I turn a blind eye and find the answers I want or have traded success for a lower moral code, but that's the situation, and I'll lose little sleep over it, because I don't run the club, I don't choose its owners, and nothing changes whether Sheikh Mansour owns my club or not – in fact the takeover has only served to focus attention on the UAE. The owners took on City as a PR exercise, and it is in their interests to project themselves as a forward-looking society, which they are in many respects even when judged by Western "standards", whatever they are. Of course some of the PR remit will be to cover up stuff as well, I'm not naïve in that respect.

But hey, I am selfish, like most fans – I could get run over by a bus tomorrow, and what the last decade of my life will have provided is memories that would last ten lifetimes, success I never thought I'd see, players I never expected to idolise. It's been a blast. That's what I care about – my own experiences, shared experiences, amazing highs and the occasional lows. And cat videos on Facebook.

So keep retweeting Nick Harris and his financial figures, rival fans. Keep quoting David Conn and Duncan Castles questioning the market worth of middle-eastern sponsors. None of us City fans could care less. And neither do you, really.

Premier League: Cardiff 0 Manchester City 5

Men against boys, and the easiest of victories for City, who had the game wrapped up by half-time. It wiped away dome of the memories of Wednesday's horror show against Lyon.

And boy, I will never tire of seeing Neil Warnock suffer on the side-line. The ****.

Two debut goals for Riyad Mahrez in the 2nd half sealed the deal, and it was great to see him get off the mark. He is settling in fine, though there are bigger tests to come.

Before that – three first half goals. Aguero slotted in from a Bernardo Silva pass in the box, before Silva himself looped a header into the far corner. I will assume he meant it.

Just before half-time, in atrocious conditions, Gundogan curled one into the corner, and it was already game over. A professional job was being done against a poor side.

Mahrez was only a sub on this occasion, replacing Aguero, but one simple goal and one nice finish from further out will help his confidence no end. This squad is packed with a ridiculous amount of talent now, especially in attacking areas, and he will have to earn that game time along with everyone else.

And with David Silva on the bench, Ilkay Gundogan showed his worth with a masterful performance.

Time for the Carabao Cup.

Carabao Cup: Oxford United 0 Manchester City 3

Another stroll to victory against spirited, but limited opposition, as you would expect.
More importantly, Phil Foden came of age with his debut goal late on, to cap a wonderful display in midfield. And whilst Guardiola made 10 changes from the side that won 5-0 at Cardiff City at the weekend, keeping a wealth of talent on the bench, this was still a strong side that showed that he is taking all competitions seriously.

Gabriel Jesus' close-range header gave them the lead at half-time and City gave the score-line a more realistic look as Oxford, second from bottom in League One, understandably tired late on. Foden, who had helped create Jesus' opener, produced a superb pass to put Riyad Mahrez clear for his third goal in two games, then got the reward his performance deserved with a perfect low drive with virtually the last kick of the game.
What a way to finish the game, and you could see what it meant to the Stockport Iniesta. Such a big future awaits. And another goal for Mahrez, which is nice. Plus some wayward finishing, which was not.

And credit to Oxford manager Karl Robinson too, who was full of praise post-match, especially for Foden, and did not instruct his team to be overly-physical as I originally feared.

Onwards and upwards, with Fulham awaiting City at the Etihad in the next round.

Premier League: Manchester City 2 Brighton 0

Routine win. Never got out of 2nd gear. No injuries. Excellent.
Bye.

Well, to be honest, what more is there to say? Pep commented after the match that he thinks the team are playing even better than last season, in the league at least, and it is shown in how the opposition's opportunities to counter-attack are so restricted in the majority of league games.

Many an opposition team are beaten before they begin, the hope being, forlorn most of the time, that they can frustrate and hope to nick something with a rare attack. In Pep's debut season it worked a few times as City failed to put games to bed, but recently opposition teams of Brighton's level are struggling to fashion a single chance. When City get a second goal, the game is effectively over.

Time to rewind – the line-ups are of course impossible to predict nowadays, the surprise this time being the inclusion of Zinchenko at left-back, though not an earth-shattering surprise, as his lively performance against Oxford United showed, and of course his performances in that position last season.

I was also surprised to see Fernandinho start – this was a game where Gundogan could easily have deputised, unless the idea is that this is the plan for Hoffenheim.

Anyway, it was an opening half hour of relative frustration, and I felt Brighton defended well, and kept their shape. Their recent league record is poor, with only 2 wins in their last 15 games (and I don't need to tell you who both victories were against), but they are still no mugs.

Opposition teams looking to defend for 90 minutes tend to get their best chance of scoring in the opening minutes though, and once the game settled down, there was still an inevitability about it all.

Still, nice to get that opening goal, on 29 minutes, to settle the nerves. Brighton ventured forward, foolishly, City broke, it was fed to Sane whose pinpoint cross found Sterling at the far post. 1-0.

Sterling forced a great save soon after, but the floodgates did not open. Was this another game man-managed by the players with the Champions League in mind? Maybe. Whatever, only one team was likely to score, and when the 2nd goal came on the hour, it was a thing of absolute beauty. I don't associate Sergio Aguero with dribbling runs, but that's what he did against Brighton, fed Sterling, who returned the pass for him to slam home the ball from 10 yards out. And that was game over.

On came Mahrez, Jesus and Foden, to little effect (not that Foden had much of a chance), and the game was comfortably seen out in the autumn sun. Job done, without changing gears, and City end the weekend top of the league. Where they belong.

Zinchenko once more impressed, having the most passes, touches and a pass accuracy of 95%. I'm so glad he stayed to fight for a place in the team, as there was little point us offloading him for £15m without finding out his true potential. He's worth more now anyway in the current market.

MOTM? Sterling for me. Sane was electric on the other flank, and we can stop worrying about his attitude and future at City for now, but Sterling continues to develop and is at his peak right now. Hopefully that development will see him trusted to start at Anfield. And hopefully that won't faze him if it happens.

Onwards then to Hoffenheim, an early kick off to mess with our brains and body clocks and a must-win game in all likelihood. Let's hope the response we have seen since the Lyon game continues with two important games on the horizon.

Ratings

Ederson – 6 – nowt to do. Sorry.

Walker – 7 – quiet, efficient performance, but not overworked either, so little to add.

Zinchenko – 8 – another great showing. At the heart of much of the action, as the possession stats showed.

Otamendi – 7.5 – getting a run in the side, and did what he had to do admirably. Brighton never threatened and he should take some of the credit for that.

Laporte – 7.5 – see above. Again, not overworked, so not easy to rate, but did what he had to do with his usual aplomb and seems to have developed a partnership with whoever starts beside him. Number 1 defender for Pep now? He always plays...

Fernandinho – 7. Not great, didn't have to be. Another player that was allowed a comfortable afternoon, and helped ensure Brighton never threatened to get back into the match. Could easily have been rested though.

David Silva – 7.5 – classy performance after subdued showing in Carabao Cup, he was his usual elegant self.

Bernardo Silva – 7.5 – by his standards, not his best game, but was still far too good for the visitors and helped the home team dominate the midfield and the ball.

Leroy Sane – 8.5 – those concerns of a few weeks ago seem a distant memory. Like last season, Sane is growing into the campaign, and was at his best against a defensive Brighton side. Constant threat down the left flank, and picked up a deserved assist for his efforts.

Raheem Sterling – 9 – Man Of The Match for me, he was electric, got a typical close-range goal through clever movement and terrorised Brighton defence from the off.

Sergio Aguero – 8 – not bad for a player yet again playing with an injury, his 2nd goal was a thing of beauty, the goal of the season so far for me. Vital to City that he stays fit.

Gabriel Jesus & Riyad Mahrez – 6 – both came on and did not have a major effect on the game. Was a good opportunity for Jesus to do so.

Phil Foden – N/A.

Into October.........

Champions League – Hoffenheim 1 Manchester City 2

Here are some things I learned and all that. Already, in a 6-game league, this had a must-win feel to it. Conceding after one minute didn't help therefore, but City quickly levelled before David Silva snatched a late winner.

There's No Easy Games In This Competition

That old cliché. Not strictly true of course, but we cannot expect our team to roll over every "lesser" team we meet. Hoffenheim are on mugs, they wouldn't have qualified via the Bundesliga if they were, and they play attacking, pressing football. I spent two decades watching Alex Ferguson's United teams grind out results like this in Europe (and before you ask, no - I've no idea why I watched the games), and the result was key. Games are not easy at the top level, and it would be boring if they were – might as well be Hearts.

This was not the perfect performance, far from it, but City were the better side, showed resilience after coming from behind, and the three points has lifted them straight into a qualification spot at this early stage. This was the most important game of the week for City, as another defeat left them with no wriggle room at all in the competition, so the result was everything. Job done.

City were too open in defence for my liking, but perhaps this was the result of Hoffenheim's attacking style. As disappointing was not taking advantage of the home side's own defensive holes in that first half where there seemed opportunities every time City attacked. But with spurned chances for Sterling, Aguero, Otamendi and more, this was the right result. After just one minute many of us were questioning what it was about this competition that brought out the worst in everyone, but thankfully that's a discussion that can be shelved, for now.

Defensive Midfield Remains A Problem

It's been discussed to death, but whilst Fernandinho was not poor against Hoffenheim, he has yet to reach the heights of previous seasons, and the fear is that age is catching up with him, as it does with us all. This is worrying with Liverpool on the horizon. His sloppiness was fatal against Lyon, and his sharpness was not overly evident against Hoffenheim either. Which begs the question of why he started against Brighton. Fernandinho, even if he was 23 years old, cannot play every game this season, it will break him at some point, and even if it doesn't the team's performances will suffer. But with Gundogan limping off in the second half with a hamstring injury, it seems we are as dependent on him as ever. Txiki and co. are surely already looking at a Jorginho alternative, and the sooner he arrives the better. John Stones came on in the second half and the new shape was a success, but he cannot seriously be considered as an option in midfield for any big games.

Referees Hate Manchester City

That's grabbed your attention. I'll be honest, I can't really believe in conspiracy theories, of UEFA's secret meetings whereby it's agreed that Manchester City and their oil money cannot be allowed to win the Champions League, so must be stopped, by any means possible. And hey, a "bent" referee (a description Duncan Castles would no doubt be comfortable with) would surely have sent off Kyle Walker given half the chance for a dangerous tackle. But it's undeniable, it's staring us in the face, it's **smacking** us in the face, that City have been the victims of a long, long procession of bad refereeing decisions in the Champions League (and beyond). You don't need me to list them, and I don't think we can use it as an excuse for our apathy for the competition, but you know, after last night's non-penalty, I did stop caring temporarily about the result. I'd simply had enough. I sat there laughing at the madness of it all. Which other team would have a player taken out by a goalkeeper and have play waved on? Where was the yellow card for Sane if it was not a foul? Why were City stopped from taking a quick throw-in when in an attacking part of the pitch? Why did Hoffenheim get every single decision in that first half? It's puzzling, if nothing else.

Liverpool deserved to get to the Champions League final last season, their football merited it. But they got breaks. Despite all of City's shortcomings, VAR or just competent match officiating would have led to a close outcome in the quarter-final. Until City start getting decisions their way, we'll struggle to make an impact in the competition, especially at a time when there is no outstanding team that can rise above the rest. Cup competitions often rest on very fine lines, and City could do with a few breaks at crucial times. Thankfully, not even Damir Skomina could find a reason to disallow David Silva's winner.

Sane Is Back

It seems a lifetime ago that we wondered what was up with Leroy Sane. Dropped from Germany's World Cup squad, he at least had the summer to relax, and we expected him to start the season on fire, raring to go, looking to prove a point. A disappointing 45 minutes in the Community Shield was what happened instead, and he spent the next month mainly on the bench. There was talk of attitude problems, and even his international team-mates waded in with their opinions. Well like last season, Sane has grown into the campaign, and against Hoffenheim I thought he was electric. Some of his runs were imply mesmeric, even if he did try too much at times. This is the Sane we love. Running at opposition defenders with poise and pace, the ball seemingly glued to his feet. He got one assist, but should have had at least two. Suddenly, he is one of City's most important players again. But hey, smile occasionally, it's good for the soul!

A Tight Group Means Every Point Counts

It's hard to know until this group has concluded what constitutes a helpful result for City in other games, but as in Round 1, the other game ended a draw in a desolate Lyon stadium (#emptyhad blah blah), which *may* be good news come December. City have exited this group stage in the past with 10 points, but on that occasion there was a whipping boy (Villareal) on zero points. This time around it seems the group will be tight – any team can take points off any other, so the points requirement to qualify should be lower than the average, possibly eight or thereabouts. Looking ahead, if City can gain 4 points from their Shakhtar Donetsk double-header then beat Hoffenheim at home, they will surely have qualified again with a game to spare, despite the opening day defeat. Then the last game becomes a winner takes all scenario perhaps. That's a lot of speculation I've collated, but I think it shows how the dynamic can change with a single victory when there are only two games to play. A mix of victories and defeats is better than a succession of draws.

About Those Referees Again....

It's a conspiracy, I tell you. A real one, not like the ones about jet fuel melting beams and flags on the moon. No, Manchester City, the best team in the land and all the world will never win Europe's premier club competition, because, wait for it, referees have got it in for us. The proof is there for all to see. The non-penalty for Sane v Hoffenheim, the spate of decisions against Liverpool in the champions league, and a spate of ridiculous calls over years of competition. Still, it's not as bad as some of the decisions made in Premier League matches. Those decisions would require a show of their own. There, leg breakers are the weapon of choice, even family guy harry kane getting in on the act last season.

But anyway the theme in the Champions League is quite simple, and tends to revolve around a total inability to give City blatant penalties. David Silva in Munich, and Micah Richards the same game. Then there's the Subasic foul on Aguero ignored in the 5-3 victory against Monaco. Naturally the visitors got a penalty of their own. Naturally Aguero got a yellow card. Sometimes the officiating is so bad that even Kevin De Bruyne has to be dragged away from match officials at half-time. At least City beat Napoli that night. Take note, Liverpool. Even Manuel Pellegrini, a man who would remain straight-laced if his lottery numbers came up, once called a Swedish referee unfit to officiate and suggested a bias towards Barcelona. There's the last-gasp shirt pull on Balotelli v Ajax that was not rewarded with a penalty. And who can forget that time that Samuel Umtiti stepped on Raheem Sterling's foot? The result? Well a yellow card for diving, naturally. Occasionally it works the other way, as seen by the red card and penalty when Messi was fouled outside the box at the Etihad, or the magnificently inept penalty to allow CSKA Moscow to draw level late on in their supposedly empty stadium. I'll have forgotten a dozen more no doubt, but you get the idea.

Of course any team over an 8 year period can catalogue decisions that have gone against their team in a cup competition, but it's a simple fact that penalty appeals are generally waved away when it involves City, as if we have less right to them, this in a competition where a player only has to fall to the ground to get a free kick. I don't think we can use it as an excuse for our apathy for the competition, but you know, after the latest non-penalty decision, I truly did stop caring temporarily about the result. I'd simply had enough. I sat there laughing at the madness of it all. Which other team would have a player taken out by a goalkeeper and have play waved on? Where was the yellow card for Sane if it was not a foul? Why were City stopped from taking a quick throw-in when in an attacking part of the pitch? Why did Hoffenheim get every single decision in that first half? I have no logical answers.

Liverpool deserved to get to the Champions League final last season, their football merited it. But they got breaks (sorry for repeating myself here. I'm not bitter, honest). Despite all of City's shortcomings, VAR or just competent match officiating would have led to a close outcome in the quarter-final. Hey, Robertson was even allowed to slide through Sterling at one point and even the commentators couldn't be arsed kicking up a fuss about it. In fact it was never mentioned again. Now imagine that happening the other way round. Imagine Sane's goal being disallowed for Liverpool, imagine us scoring an offside goal, then Liverpool wrongly having one ruled out in the 2nd half. Judging by the reaction to a correct red card for Mane last season, I can only assume there'd be a week's mourning on Merseyside and questions asked in the commons. But until City start getting decisions their way, we'll struggle to make an impact in the competition, especially at a time when there is no outstanding team that can rise above the rest. Saying that we're good enough to win it irrelevant of bad decisions just doesn't wash I am afraid. We're not that good that we can win despite refereeing incompetency, and no team can win without having a referee do their job – god knows Real Madrid have had enough decisions go their way in the past few years and beyond. Cup competitions often rest on very fine lines, and City could do with a few breaks at crucial times. Thankfully, not even referee Damir Skomina could find a reason to disallow David Silva's winner in Germany. After a run of City defeats, he finally got to officiate a City victory. I bet he was made up about that.

So why does this happen on a regular basis? I don't believe in conspiracy theories, and I cannot believe that there is a campaign to deny the likes of City and PSG, the cocky upstarts with no history and oil money. I do believe in corruption though, because it's stating the obvious that UEFA is riddled with it, and I believe in bias. Referees just seem to take a dislike to little old City. Maybe they just love that anthem so much they thought they'd teach us all a lesson. Insitutionalised bias I think you call it. Still, nothing we can do about it. Complain and Pep gets another ban, ask for clarification from the referees association or UEFA, and we'd no doubt get fobbed off. City are new money, and it seems that hasn't gone down well. Like Trevor across the road with his shiny new Jag. Hardly reason to key the car though, The truth is often the most boring though. Man did land on the moon, it would have taken more effort to fake it truth be told, and all theories against the landing can be debunked in minutes.
Likewise, the reason City don't get decisions might just be that referees are sometimes crap, and we're not getting the calls. I'm not convinced, but until I connect hidden symbols and find evidence of an illuminati linking Beswick and Michel Platini, it's all I've got I'm afraid. We might need a terribly written book by Dan brown to solve this particular mystery. Or we could just blame David Gill as per usual. If he had his way we'd just automatically hand over the Champions League trophy to United every season without having the inconvenience of actual games.

Of course soon the great saviour will arrive. VAR is inevitable, at home and abroad, and then everything will be sweetness and light. It will take a catastrophic power cut or suchlike for City to be denied their justice. Knowing our luck it will somehow work against us. Clear errors is what it is generally used for, so expect the definition of that to be reinterpreted before its widespread introduction. Or maybe the VAR and his team will consist of Kenny Dalglish, John "Nugget" Aldridge, Steve Mcmanaman and the cast of Bread. But surely, at last, we will see results based on merit. VAR is not perfect, it might reward the armchair fan, it might remove emotion from the game, but if I've learnt one thing from following Manchester City in the past 10 years, it's that it should benefit my club more than any other.

Premier League: Liverpool 0 Manchester City 0

Phew. It's over. The stress of an Anfield trip seems to have almost usurped that of derby day, and City didn't lose. I'll take that, whatever the circumstances.

Maybe I played down this game in order to make the weekend more bearable, or more precisely a potential defeat, but this did not seem like the all-important game that everyone like to claim it is. It is big of course, and City have many demons to banish, but it is October, there are three points at stake, nothing is decided by the result. Having said that, with an international break now with us, it would have been hugely disappointing to enter the break off a defeat to Liverpool.

But on the plus side, City at least went into the game top of the table, just. And ended it there, naturally. My fear weeks ago was always the possibility of entering the game with a points deficit against Liverpool, and it would have put huge pressure on getting a result. The prospect was there a fortnight ago of entering the international break five points behind Liverpool. The reality is instead we enter it not joint first, as Sky would have you believe, but ACTUAL first. You know, like we ended the 2011/12 season.

This was a team sheet to be met with trepidation, anticipation, perhaps dread. All the talk was of how that left-back spot would be filled. As it turned out, city's social media head had not been exiled to the naughty step, broken a metatarsal or turned up three hours to the match. Pep said that when Mendy was fit he would play, and so it turned out. And having not made the French squad due to possible injury concerns, he now gets a fortnight to work on fitness. Hopefully.

The rest of the team was not too surprising, except perhaps for the inclusion of Mahrez. Perhaps this was due to the feeling that he would contribute defensively more than Sane. And he did, to be fair. The two Silvas would play together centrally which excited but also worried me slightly, against a workmanlike, intense midfield.

And so to the match. The team bus didn't set on fire, which is always a bonus, and the team seemed relaxed enough, despite all the flags, the intimidating atmosphere that only Anfield can create (and nowhere else) and the predictable booing of Raheem Sterling, three years after fleeing the cult, I mean family. Still, Liverpool did dominate the early ball, and with Salah missing a half-chance early doors, there was some anxiety that this match was following a similar path to previous encounters. Thankfully that domination soon dissipated, and Liverpool would not craft another great chance all match.

Let's be honest, whatever I expected from this match, what actually transpired was way down the list of possibilities. And that's great news for us City fans. You see, it seems Pep, despite all his pre-match talk about only knowing one way to play, had introduced pragmatism to his thinking. The pre-match talk was a red-herring. He knew that a slow game is Liverpool's kryptonite. And so it proved. By taking the heat out of the game, the home side were blunted. So too were City to some extent, but the history of this fixture placed an emphasis on City to do something different, and a draw and an even game suited the visitors more than the home side, though it is no disaster for Liverpool either – both sides enter the break pretty happy with their league campaign so far.

Penalties apart, it could have been better for City, but the killer ball was sadly lacking. We should not denigrate our attacking players for this though – for the vast majority of the game the space was not there, for both sides – this was 90 minutes of imperious defending. Rarely will players of both teams have so little room to work with. We can criticise the performances of Firmino, Salah, Mane Sterling, Mahrez, Aguero and more, but it cannot be a coincidence they all failed to sparkle. This was a day where defences dominated, partly due to Pep refusing to allow the game become open and stretched at any point.

Liverpool's chief cheerleader David Maddock naturally led in the Mirror with the assertion that Van Dijk and Lovren were both world class, eventually praising Laporte and Stones too, but it was the City duo that were the best two players on the pitch – after all, they both didn't foul opposition players in the penalty area. Stones did not misplace a pass in the first half, and finished the game with a 98% pass completion rate. It's hard to separate the two defenders for City, they were that good. Good to have the partnership back.

Mendy was sloppy early in the game, but grew into it – again he won't get much harder games than this, off the back of an injury, so no sweeping conclusions from me. Just really glad he is back too.

Our attacking players struggled because of the tight nature of the game, so it's hard to draw conclusions again. Mahrez will come in for criticism for obvious reasons, but was probably our best attacking outlet. He was fine, with one exception. Bernardo was often excellent and continues to impress. Some will probably say Sterling was put off by the boos, but we can't know that, in a game where his performance was consistent with all other attacking players on the pitch. Aguero may well have been short of fitness, with his heal problem common knowledge, and for that reason I cannot really criticise his substitution. Hindsight is a wonderful thing, but I doubt any of us thought a late penalty at Anfield was a realistic possibility. Jesus could not turn the game after coming on, but was bright and showed more than in recent games. Sane of course showed plenty too, and should have turned the game, which brings us to...

Penalties. First off, there is talk of City possibly meriting four of them during the match. Not for me. Firstly, the Van Dijk hand ball is not close to a penalty. Close quarters, accidental handballs should never be punished, unless preventing a goal. The Lovren challenge on Aguero however was probably a penalty, but I cannot blame Atkinson for not giving it, as it took some studying of replays to ascertain that. As for Jesus getting clouted in the face, I am somewhat on the fence with that one. Another accident, but he was hit, ignoring the dramatic fall to the ground. Not obvious for me though. And nor was the actual penalty, at first glance. I thought it was soft, but then the replays showed it to be the correct decision, just – he did impact on Sane's lower leg. Such a needless foul, with Sane in no great position to create a goal-scoring opportunity.

And so late drama, and a chance for City to banish all their hoodoos and take charge of the title race. Ah well, maybe next time, eh? It has since emerged that the bench decided who took it, so Pep takes responsibility for this. To be honest, there was no outstanding candidate, so it's a tough call whichever way you look at it. I admire anyone who has the balls to take a penalty in such pressured conditions, and hope Mahrez brushes off the miss and moves on. He of course does not have a great penalty-taking record, notably missing one against City in a shoot-out last season in the Carabao Cup. But Jesus has missed his last two, the two Silva are not recognised penalty-takers, David Silva having missed his only penalty for City over six years (one of the worst penalties ever witnessed), and as Lionel Messi shows, the best penalty takers are not always the most skilful ball—players so Bernardo Silva may or may not have been a good option. He's got to want to take the penalty anyway – otherwise it's an irrelevant argument. Aguero was of course off the pitch, Yaya has gone. Kevin not quite fit enough to feature. That's life. Mahrez was scoring penalties all week in training, but you cannot simulate the match-day penalty experience. Penalties are missed, it happens. It just annoys me that he did not at least put it on target. That's basics for me.

After the miss, the fear was that it would energise the home side, and it did, so I was happy to take the draw as soon as the shot was blazed over the bar. Honours even, in a strange but intriguing match. City closed down Liverpool's threat, and dictated the rhythm of the match – in different circumstances they would have taken all three points, but it was not to be.

Nevertheless, this still has echoes of Chelsea away last season. The marker has not been placed down as emphatically as on that occasion, but the City team have made a point. They avoided defeat in possibly the hardest game of the season, and could have won. A point to each team is quite fair in the end, though points are not handed out on fairness. City shaded that game, no doubt about it, and that is something to cherish. Satisfaction, mixed with disappointment - quite an improvement on previous visits to the ground!

So that was City's first clean sheet at Anfield since 1986, and also means four clean sheets on the row in the league. Progress. We all know City have the firepower to win the league at a canter, it is why our goal difference speeds ahead of everyone else's within weeks of the season starting, but if City become Golden Glove contenders too, then they will be hard to stop. With three goals conceded in eight games, so far so good, especially as one of those three was punched in...
Onwards and upwards. City's next game is at home to Burnley at fortnight, and the hope is that Pep has a fully-fit squad to choose from. Kev is back, and his absence did not derail the season, nor should it have done. The team is in a good position.

JOY!!!! ANOTHER INTERNATIONAL BREAK!!!

Bluemoon Podcast Audio Script

Talking about anything football-related during an international break really is drawing the short straw, and I ran out of material ten years ago to be honest, but at least the new format of a nations league has given us a few matches worth watching, and of course a few that weren't.

Raheem Sterling ended his barren spell for England so people will have to find something else to talk about now regarding him, and they will. I hear that recently his car has been dirty again. The man really has no shame. A lack of shame that extended to him being allowed to be clattered by Lovren against Croatia, a foul that got the Liverpool supporters all giddy, the cult agreeing as one that bad fouls are acceptable when performed by a Liverpool player against an ex-Liverpool player. At least Sterling didn't walk off crying like Salah did in the Champions League final.

So with all that in mind, with little to fill my time beyond the British Bake Off, the Great British Menu, Masterchef Professionals, Saturday Morning Kitchen, Nigella Lawson's new series, Jamie In Italy and reruns of Floyd in France, I've been thinking about size, a delicate subject for men.

There's one thing that is always used against City away from seat-counting, a dig made with such a lack of self-awareness you begin to wonder if it's not just a series of bots set up by Ed Woodward. Yep, it's the big team jibe of course, and the size of your club.

People really seem to think it's a worthwhile debate, though thoughts turn to Talksport, where Danny Murphy recently dismissed Newcastle as a big club, and even Paul Dickov was in on the act saying City are now bigger than United. As what constitutes big is of course impossible to define – we may as well debate how long a piece of string is.

Nevertheless, fans who tend to have never been near their own team's ground seem to think it's a weapon to use against fans of a team who tend to be better and more successful than theirs. The lack of self-awareness angle is obvious – by belittling the size of another club, you are effectively admitting that club size is something attractive to you, and thus marks you out as a classic glory hunter. No true football fan, and I include long term local United fans in this, chose a club because of its size – be that its average attendance or revenue. No true fan chooses a club because load of people already support it, in America, Ireland, Scandinavia, Asia and beyond. And no true fan of a successful club feels the need to mention size because they've got nothing to be defensive about. Successful teams' fans brag about games won, trophies secured, magical moments, not retweets and social interaction numbers for their flop of a signing playing a sodding piano.

And this big club grading system seeps into every facet of club analysis – it allows questions to be raised about City sponsorship deals that fade into insignificance compared to United's. Or at least they did. It allows UEFA to consider reassessing the coefficient system to factor in previous success because some of the old big clubs don't get to bully everyone else anymore.

But hey, for a small club, City really do alright. Do you know one thing that sets apart little old City from the likes of Liverpool or Manchester United? Well it's the fact that none of our star players have left the club, demanded a transfer, engineered a move to sunnier Spanish climes? Tevez is the closest, but he stays nowhere for long, the littlest hobo of the footballing world, but Aguero, Kompany, Silva et al are still here and are going nowhere soon it seems, even after all these years. They must just love little clubs. Raheem Sterling may break that trend in a couple of years, but it's astonishing to see how many of our big signings have settled here, in a place with four seasons in a day, and that was just Monday, and never stirred up trouble and forced a way out. I would have been happy to get 3 years from the likes of David Silva and Sergio Aguero – to get over triple that blows my bitter blue mind.

What's more, it seems strange, considering City aren't a big club, that so many Liverpool fans seem so desperate to create a rivalry with City fans – maybe they just want to attach themselves to a club that has actually won something recently, which is fair enough. Of course they themselves must surely win something soon, so maybe they'll calm down then. And maybe I'll win the Booker prize and marry Margot Robbie.

Anyway, the size of my club is not giving me sleepless nights, I have to admit. They weren't the biggest club in terms of size of support when I started following them almost 40 years ago, so I'm hardly going to be stung by comments about their size now, when they are winning trophies.

Got more fans? I'll bear that in mind the next time I watch Vincent Kompany lift a trophy.

Think your club grew more organically? Something for me to ponder when I next watch my Centurions video.

Got that elusive history cos you think history means winning things 20 years ago? I'll keep that thought the next time Phil Jones vainly lollops after Sergio Aguero.

So mine might not be the biggest. My club that is. But it's what you do with it that matters. And my club is doing quite a lot right now, so that will do for me. The rest of you can keep counting seats and living in the past, I've got some champions to watch. Oh, and a piece of string is 90cm long by the way.

Premier League – Manchester City 5 Burnley 0

Some thoughts….

City Are Better Than Last Season

Quite the claim. Pep had previously hinted at this, and you wonder how you improve on a 100-point season. Well City are unlikely to reach that landmark again, but we should look past point totals. Pep has kept the squad together whilst adding the mercurial talents of Riyad Mahrez (more on him later). With Phil Foden developing nicely, the squad is certainly as strong as ever.
But it's not just about squad strength. Pep's ideals are never more apparent than now. Teams from lower down the division may well have been despatched with ease last season too, but there is now the sense of an even great dominance in such games, of an inevitability about the result that even an early red card for Kompany may not have dispelled. Burnley could not muster a single shot on target at the Etihad, and after being stubborn opposition on three occasions last season, there is a sense that City have found another gear to move up to. The limp defeat to Lyon is a large caveat, but in the league at least City are purring along nicely. The game at Spurs may tell us more about their current level.
And the reward for such superiority? The most pointless record of them all – the longest unbeaten run ever in 3pm kick offs.

Mahrez Is Settling In

There were a few raised eyebrows as Riyad Mahrez was announced as man of the match as the game drew to a conclusion at the Etihad, especially considering the stellar display put in by David Silva. Nevertheless, Mahrez had a great game, which is good news for him and for City. When you watch match highlights, you see why he won the award – Aguero spurned two glorious chances handed to him on a plate by

119

Mahrez in the first half, he could and perhaps should have had at least one other assist, and of course he scored the goal of the game with a sumptuous curled shot. He has had a slow and unspectacular start to his City career, and concerns from those of a nervous disposition have already begun to wonder if the move was wrong for City and the player. That's football for you, where we lurch from crisis to triumph in a matter of minutes. Bernardo Silva was proof that players do not have to make an instant impact to be a success at the club, and Mahrez is doing just fine. He's also City's 2nd top scorer, not bad for a so-called "bit-part" player.

Joe Hart has a future

Stating the obvious no doubt, but Joe Hart seems to have found a spiritual home after a nomadic two years. It's probably not the best time to mention this after he conceded five goals, but without him it could have been much more. He was not to blame for any of the goals, and was helpless against the onslaught. Two great saves from Aguero and David Silva in the first half showed he can still perform, and he was one of the few Burnley players to leave the pitch with credit on his first game against the club he left permanently in the summer. There was little joy to be had from seeing him concede a bucketful of goals, as he was one of City's great servants. Hopefully his rehabilitation can see him force his way back into the national squad, and fight off the claims of the plethora of English keepers at his club.
(another wonderful prediction, eh? – May 2019)

A Sean Dyche team never deserves to lose

Probably a bit harsh on a day when the visiting manager had valid claims to be a tad peeved. We must look at the incidents with impartiality, and there is no doubt that Vincent Kompany could have been sent off for dangerous play when swinging his leg to connect with a bouncing ball. Nevertheless, it was not a clear red for me, as he was, as I just said, kicking at a bouncing ball at waist height and seemed caught unawares by the sudden presence of Lennon. A red card would not have been an injustice though, so City can feel lucky to have gained a yellow – Kompany has a habit of occasionally starting a game sluggishly, as showed at Leicester last season, but the referee should not make the call on how long has gone in the game. A red card is a red card.

The other incidents had no bearing on the result – Dyche used the classic excuse for the 2nd goal about how that was the crucial moment in the game, but the visitors could have played for a week without scoring. I cannot tell conclusively if Sane was fouled, and after that Silva was probably offside and the ball was out by a few centimetres. Not that clear, as it has to be the whole ball crossing the line, but it was just out. Either way, City were winning this game, and even if you view Sane's petulant hack as a red card, the only consequence would have been City losing his services for three games, and not on the result of this game as City were way ahead by that point.

Dyche is of course old-school and views players like Sane falling to the ground as a disgrace, and I have some sympathy for him, as I'm not a big fan myself of players collapsing to the ground when they feel contact, but that's the game now and it has been like that for years. It's not still 1985. But Dyche is from the Mark Hughes school of "the world's against me", where his team are always cheated when points are dropped, whilst conveniently ignoring any discretions by his own, honest players. I've heard him whinge so many times now he's just another broken record with a microphone, last week bemoaning "where the game is going". Fuck off and suck on a Strepsil.

(obviously if I was a Burnley fan I'd love him, his character a major part in bringing success to the club)

City's Goal Difference Once More Worth An Extra Point

It might be tight at the top, but there's one metric that is beyond doubt, even at this early stage. Manchester City will once again finish the season with the best goal difference in the league, and that is effectively an extra point (kind of). Of course it may not matter, but it certainly has in the past. Some Liverpool fans may be still claiming that their team is joint top of the league, but in 2012 City of course won the league on goal difference, and for the 2014 title win, City's superior goal difference over Liverpool meant they only needed a draw on the final day at home to West Ham rather than a win, which rather alleviated the pressure (a bit). Nine games in, and City's goal difference is at least 10 superior to anyone else's. It's an astonishing chasm. They're not joint top. They're top.

Goals: Agüero (17' minutes), Bernardo Silva (54' minutes), Fernandinho (56' minutes), Mahrez (83' minutes), Sané (90' minutes)
Oh – and good to see Kevin De Bruyne back on the pitch as a substitute. Very good.

Champions League: Shakhtar Donetsk 0 Manchester City 3

Just what the doctor ordered. And after the horror of the opening game, City have recovered nicely to sit in a qualification spot at the half-way point of the group stage. In fact, they're top, which is some turnaround, helped by the other teams repeatedly drawing against each other.

Pep called this some of the best football under his management, so I will not disagree. It was a professional and ruthless display in a very tricky tie.

City dominated from start to finish, with captain David Silva and defender Aymeric Laporte scoring in the first half before substitute Bernardo Silva sealed the points in Ukraine.

Mahrez was in again, and after some nervy home attacks, he hit the ball wide when he should have scored after a scintillating counter-attack. The fact he was wearing gloves just irritated me further.

It wasn't to prove decisive, though there was still time for him to miss another glaring chance, the keeper saving his shot from in front of goal, from a great Mendy cross. David Silva back-heeled onto the post from a great cross from Riyad, before finally opening the scoring soon after with an excellent finish as the ball dropped to him on the left of the penalty area. Mendy had a pile-driver saved, and Laporte was left free to head in the resultant corner.

De Bruyne got seventy minutes under his belt, Bernardo Silva came on, surged forward and scored a peach of a goal almost instantly. Now that's how you make a substitution, and it was game over.

Onto the trickiest of games on a cabbage patch pitch on Monday night, a night on which football should never be played.

Premier League: Tottenham 0 Manchester City 1

As discussed below, an evaluation of the team seems utterly pointless considering the conditions. So the result was everything, and the result was great. Thanks to Lamela though for missing that late chance. Much appreciated.

The pitch played a huge part.

I've only ever seen Ederson hit a clearance long about 10 times, and 7 of those occasions were last night at Wembley. Have no doubt, the state of the pitch played a significant part in the outcome of this football match. It dictated the style of the game and probably cost the home side a point near the end. I take little from this game apart from the reassurance of knowing City won. Blaming the pitch can easily be construed as making excuses for a far from scintillating performance from the visitors, and we will never know if the players would have put in a similar display on a pristine surface, but personally I have little doubt that the playing surface dictated the style of play throughout. City players seemed restricted and cautious, and the ball spent far more time in the air than I expected. The result was everything in this game, and there's little more to take from a surreal night, though the apparent lack of any injuries on the cabbage patch pitch is another bonus. We could analyse Mendy's mistakes and Walker's loose passing, but I'd be more concerned if such displays happened on a regular basis, on a proper pitch.

Maybe we are spoilt watching the cash-rich Premier League "product" to expect perfect pitches week-in, week-out, but this was not some unfortunate consequence of a long winter or unforeseen circumstances. This was all the doing of broken promises and treating fans once more as 2nd class citizens (I include the Spurs fans in that). It was a shambles from start to finish, as shown by the NFL logo still being clearly visible in the centre circle throughout the pitch, and the empty seats in the stands.

Mauricio Pochettino did his homework.

No surprise there of course, but after his side were schooled twice City last season, Pochettino made some tough decisions, and despite the result they worked. It would have been much easier for him to play his strongest side, but by benching the likes of Eriksen and Alli, he plumped for what Pep later described as the most physical side he had played against. There was pace too in the side and it caused City plenty of problems. Maybe Pochettino too had one eye on the pitch, but he succeeded in limiting City's arsenal of attacking options, and a strong finish to the game having introduced his big guns off the bench almost paid dividends. It was not to be his night, but compared to last season, it was a step in the right direction.

A small consolation for Mahrez.

"The boss was very special to me. I spent four and a half years there, I have many memories of him. He was such a good person; a good human. When I scored, I put my hands up to the sky for him. He did a lot for me and for Leicester."

The tragic events of the weekend reinforced something I had long expected. Under the tutelage of their owner, Leicester City was a family, a close knit group of players, owner and fans alike, who lived the impossible dream just over 2 years ago. With that in mind, it would have been totally understandable if Riyad Mahrez's mind was elsewhere over the last 3 days. He may have left Leicester City, but a part of him will remain there. I did not expect him to feature against Leicester, but he started and he scored the crucial goal to take City back to the top of the table. His understated goal celebration was fitting and his strength of mind admirable. I am delighted that City won a tough game, but I'm even happier that Mahrez found a small piece of redemption on the churned Wembley pitch.

Fernandinho still holds everything together.

Whilst Bernardo Silva was, as always, impressive, there was only one Man Of The Match for me. Fernandinho has a huge weight to carry on his shoulders this season once the purchase of Jorginho fell through, but he says he feels like a 25 year old right now and he shows no sign of slowing down, no doubt helped by a break over the recent period of internationals. This was his type of game, and he was everywhere. So much for my concerns over him last month.

Racing back to make vital interceptions in the box when Spurs threatened, covering his defence, and roaming across the barren stretches of centre-pitch to keep the side ticking over. As always he was not afraid to deploy the dark arts when required, activating many a bulged forehead vein in Mourinho lickspittles, whoever they may be. Any successful side needs bite, slyness and the ability to compete physically, and Fernandinho ticks all the boxes. He is also extremely adept at walking the disciplinary line just well enough to avoid serious punishment, usually. As all City fans already know, replacing him will be one of Pep's biggest challenges, though that time shows no sign of approaching just yet.

Most tackles made (5)
Most fouls conceded (4)
=Most interceptions (4)

The juggernaut continues.

Six clean sheets. Three goals conceded in the league. Three defeats in the last sixty five league games. A plus twenty four goal difference after ten games. Four points dropped due to a handball goal and a missed penalty. No attacker or midfielder is yet to score against City in the league this season. Only one shot on target against Manchester City in their last 191 minutes of league football. Only four in the last four games. Seventeen shots on target against City in ten games (United have allowed fifty). Seven points away to three of the top five without conceding a goal.

There may well be debate over whether this City side has hit the heights yet this season, or is in fact even better than last season's, but the facts speak for themselves. City have recovered to top their Champions League table after three games. Raheem Sterling, he's top of two leagues, as after ten games City remain top of the Premier League, having ticked off four tough away games. They are unlikely to ever match the points total of last season, but as we move into November, they are well placed once more for an assault on multiple trophies, helped of course by the return of Kevin De Bruyne, who they could afford to send on from the substitutes bench. The vagaries of the league table meant that City could plausibly have ended this round of fixtures 5th in the league. Instead they are top, and as Lamela blazed his shot over the bar last night, Liverpool and Chelsea fans across the globe will have realised how tough it will be to dislodge City from top spot.

November

Carabao Cup: Manchester City 2 Fulham 0

Probably the most forgettable match of the season. Go on, name the scorers.

Well maybe you do remember, because this was the night Brahim Diaz scored two goals for City. And more importantly, Kevin De Bruyne picked up another injury, and we all slumped in our seats. It's looking like one of those seasons for him, which is even more of a shame after the stellar season that preceded this one. He is at his peak, and to miss out on playing is heart breaking for him and us.

Questions were naturally asked as to what he was doing on the pitch in the fourth most important competition, but I am not having that. He has to play some time, he can get injured getting out of the shower, and he needs match fitness. It's just bad luck, and the tackle itself was unnecessary.

Anyway, a great night for Diaz, though it would be his last. Soon he would swap Manchester's youth teams for Real Madrid's. That's his choice, but I would not expect him to be lighting up their first team any time soon. The lure is obvious though. You win some, you lose some. We snatch up some young players and we lose some. Jadon Sancho was snatched from Watford, then snatched from us. That's football for you.

So into the quarter-finals for City, with ten changes from the previous game not slowing down their march against a strong Fulham side who would soon change their manager once more. Then change their manager again. The less said about my pre-season predictions, the better.

(City have reached the League Cup quarter-finals in consecutive seasons for the first time since 1977-78 and 1978-79)

Premier League: Manchester City 6 Southampton 1

Some thoughts on the game. Probably five, that's the tradition it seems.

Pep Guardiola wary of complacency.

Manchester City may have taken some control back in their Champions League group, but there is still plenty of work to be done. Next up in the league is a certain Manchester United, so you could have understood if Pep Guardiola had looked at the upcoming games and made plenty of changes for the visit of a struggling Southampton side. But no, this was debatably City's strongest side, and showed that Pep is taking nothing for granted. Even after a 6-1 rout, he was still unhappy at City's defensive frailties during the match, and once more we are reminded of his quest for perfection. He will never rest, however well things are going, which is good for City fans, less so for their rivals.

Raheem Sterling is top of two leagues.

After news of Sterling verbally agreeing a new contract, this was great timing to show what we're getting for our money. And it seems we should pay him some more. Sterling had one of his best games in a City shirt, often utterly unplayable, frightening the Southampton defence into a deep level of passivity. Two goals, two assists, and much more besides, he was electric throughout the match, and however much wages he may or may not deserve, it was clearly vital that city tied him down to a new contract, rather than watch a £100m+ asset leave for free in 18 months' time. Next up, Leroy Sane and Phil Foden. Apropos of nothing, how is Jordon Ibe doing nowadays?

Benjamin Mendy is City's only current problem.

It's been a tough year or so for Benjamin Mendy, a serious injury seriously derailing involvement in City's record-breaking season and costing him the opportunity to nail down a place in France's World Cup winning team too. City fans should therefore show a degree of patience with a player who may take time to take on board Pep's complicated instructions, as many other players did in Guardiola's debut season. Nevertheless, the French left-back has hardly covered himself in glory over the past week. There were extenuating circumstances on Wembley's cabbage patch pitch, but against Southampton Mendy's turn of speed in defence seemed sluggish, his positional sense erratic to say the least. Pep will not be happy, and Mendy will no doubt become his latest pet project. With earlier stories swirling around about dissatisfaction from his manager about off the pitch travails, have no doubt that he will not find Pep patient for too long. Hopefully he can work on these aspects of his game in the coming weeks as we can all see just how destructive he can be further up the pitch. He is fundamentally a defender though, and that is what he will be judged on above all else.

Mark Hughes is football's Mr Beige.

Mark Hughes was a great footballer, but as a manager he has a self-worth greater than reality. There was little sadness when he was relieved of his duties as Manchester City manager, and his career has followed a steady path of mediocrity ever since. For the second successive visit to the Etihad, Hughes saw his side lose by five goals. For the second successive visit his team showed some spark (geddit?) in attack, but defensively had more holes than a Duncan Castles Ted talk on tactical fouling. He is a manager that is rarely to blame for his side's defeats, but also a manager without any obvious footballing philosophy. What is a Mark Hughes team? It's hard to say. Just eleven players on a pitch trying to kick a football to each other. His lack of defensive nouse has often been his undoing, and Southampton's decision to hand him a contract after he just kept them up last season may be one they will rue. They can do better.

The whiny, tiresome talk of domestic domination has resurfaced.

Manchester City won the title last season for the first time in a few years. They have never retained a domestic title. This season, they have not even been top on points until the end of this weekend. On Sunday they faced a Southampton side in poor form and low in confidence, whose manager conceded seven goals the last time his side visited The Etihad. A comfortable home win was hardly a surprise, a shellacking little more so. With Liverpool having to play one of the season's more difficult games the day before, a two point lead at the top should hardly surprise either. Next week the gap may be hauled back again. There's no overwhelming evidence that City will run away with the league as they did last season, with Chelsea winning yet again this weekend. They may end the season with over 90 points, but there's plenty of evidence they will drag a couple of teams with them.

So why the sudden tiresome talk from a minority of the media about the league being boring and the title race being a procession?

Let's be honest here. The talk exists because of City's wealth, where it originated, and where their owners reside. A sneering, morally superior mocking of "oil money" and "Arabs". A reaction to the football leak Financial Fair Play revelations that have been common knowledge for years but suddenly are being used to fulfil a particular narrative. Anyway, I hope these "impartial" journalists are right. Because the piss-boiling then would be enough to power a large City, and will be an utter joy to behold.

Needless, to say, United's "organic" domination of the league was fine, and did not distract form the attraction of the league at all. Money may well have skewed and corrupted this league, as well as restricting true competition, but that's not City's lookout. They're playing the game, one that has its roots way before City came to the fore.

SPOILER ALERT – City did not run away with the league.

Champions League: Manchester City 6 Shakhtar Donetsk 0.

12 goals in a few days at the Etihad. Us City fans were really being spoilt. Some thoughts….

UEFA are now great.

Yeah, that's probably stretching it a bit, but after a week of football leaks revelations in Der Spiegel, most of which we already knew(next up – revelations about a Dave Whelan FA Cup final broken leg), but revelations that certainly did not paint UEFA as the bad guys, in the eyes of City fans at least, the cherry on the icing on the cake came when the match referee kindly awarded Manchester City a penalty due to Raheem Sterling tripping himself up. City have had some appalling decisions go against them in this competition down the years, but this decision for them was as bad you could wish to see, and probably evens out all the other ones, such was the ineptness from the match officials.

Losing managers love to paint out that a controversial 2nd goal for the opposition was a turning point in the game, as Sean Dyche did the other week before his team got walloped 5-0, but there can be little doubt that this changed nothing. It's probably just as well, as I'm not sure the club would have survived a winner this controversial. Questions would have been asked in the Commons.

And they may still be. This was a tap-in for those wishing to have a go at Raheem Sterling, which let's face it is now our national sport, usurping football some three years ago. What a tiring week. It doesn't need me to point out the hypocrisy of it all, when we consider how Boly's handball goal against us earlier this season barely raised a murmur – in fact Paddy Barclay argued passionately that technically the laws of the game did not state it should be disallowed. Well the laws of the game do not state that City players should referee games, that's generally a job for whoever captains United, nor do they have a duty to point out mistakes. If players did point out all mistakes to referees about 30 offences a game would have to be changed. Players try to gain an advantage via cheating every single match – how ironic that now we have uproar over someone tripping themselves up.

Anyway, altogether now…. The Champions League, der der der der……. <standing ovation>.

(it should be pointed out that there are reports that Guardiola told the 4th official that it wasn't a penalty, and referees don't change their mind anyway)

City are proper Champions League contenders now

It's a fair point to observe that you should never make sweeping conclusions during the group stages of the Champions League – after all, Tottenham topped Real Madrid in their group last season, and cup competitions can never be called, never accurately predicted with true certainty. What's more, city qualified from their group last season with ease, so perhaps you could argue that they have been contenders for a while now. Probably true, but there is still the feeling deep down that somehow the last couple of games have been different. This win was not only City's biggest in the competition, but it was the ease with which a skilful opponent (who defeated Dynamo Kiev at the weekend) have been swatted aside twice, with 9 goals scored with 0 in reply. This Shakhtar side might not be as good as last season, I don't know, but they top their domestic league once more, I doubt losing Fred has completely destabilised them, and the difference in the games between this season and last, even if one was a dead rubber, has been stark.

But, but…it's a cup competition, and one bad error, one bad tackle in the knockout stages could mean this progress counts for nothing. Nevertheless, for the first time since City qualified for this tournament, I believe that they have as good a chance as any. This is especially so considering that the traditional giants are hardly setting the world alight. This could be the best opportunity to strike.

The defeat to Lyon increasingly looks like an aberration, an outlier, especially as Lyon conceded a two-goal lead against a 10-man Hoffenheim as City hit Shakhtar for six. So after an opening day defeat, City have virtually qualified with two games to spare, an impressive turnaround. They have been helped by every single non-City game being a draw, and whilst a Lyon victory against Hoffenheim would have guaranteed qualification, the comeback from the Germans may be advantageous for City should they wish to win the group, which they surely they do. The only way City can't qualify now is if they lose to Lyon, Hoffenheim defeat Shakhtar, then defeat City at the Etihad, probably by at least 2 goals. I'm saying nothing.

The stats continue to impress

I may well be repeating previous points here, but this Manchester City team just keep producing ridiculous statistics. Twelve goals in four days at the Etihad is impressive in itself, but then extend the analysis to the past eleven games and you realise that City, since that defeat at home to Lyon, have scored 35 goals and conceded 2 in 11 games. There's a 0-0 in there too. Next up though is the derby, and anything can happen in that, as last season proved. United will be buoyed, but City's firepower, from multiple sources is frightening for any opposition team as is the depth, as showed by bringing in Jesus and Zinchenko and then recording their best ever Champions League result.

Jesus the timely saviour

There has been plenty of discussion over a certain Gabriel Jesus this season, thoughts turning to whether he was fulfilling his undoubted potential. In recent weeks, his sporadic time on the pitch has certainly shown more promise, and so there is no better way to answer critics than by scoring a Champions League hat-trick. Now of course two goals were penalties, one of which should not have been given, but as shown at Anfield earlier this season, scoring them is hardly a given, and both were expertly dispatched. The third goal however is the one that will live long in the memory, and perhaps a sign of what can be achieved by him when he has the confidence to believe in his own talents. Sergio Aguero is still the main man, of course, but Jesus did his cause no harm at all and this bodes well for the future.

City fans need a new hobby

From media coverage this week, you'd think Jamie Pollock had just scored a spectacular goal and City were slipping towards the third tier of English football. But no, look at the stats, look at the results, look at the players that wear that blue shirt, look at their skill, look at those goals, remind yourself of their passing, their mastery of the art of football. And then wonder why you're in such a bad mood all week if you're one of those to frequent Twitter. By the time you read this the last part of Der Spiegel's revelations will be out – and if there's no smoking gun in there we can shrug our shoulders and move on, and not get annoyed because of the rantings of a series of articles that seem to have been scribed by the lovechild of Mark Goldbridge and Duncan Castles.

Don't get angry anymore because Mark Ogden has got a hot-take on Raheem Sterling falling over or because John Cross has suddenly become an expert in European law, free trade and financial markets. Don't bother because some pre-pubescent Salah fanboy shrieks that we should be thrown out of competitions. Be careful what you wish for, there may be more revelations to come. This will be chip shop paper by next week – hey, who's talking any more about rape claims against Ronaldo? Or the state aid Real Madrid, Barcelona and others had to repay in 2016, or Liverpool's losses of a few years ago that would have seen them fail FFP if they had been good enough at the time to be in Europe.

So tonight I will have a nice meal and watch Gary Delaney tell some rude jokes and have a nice break from the dull, soul-sapping Twittersphere. And the bonus is that for a brief while at least, I'll forget that the Manchester derby is looming on the horizon. Oh dear god...

Raheem Sterling Signs A New Contract

The news we all wanted to hear. Raheem Sterling signs a new contract, and ties himself to City for the foreseeable future. Quite the turnaround considering Pep DEFINITELY wanted to sell him to Arsenal last summer. Yeah, right.

I will have mentioned it before, but I am massively protective of Raheem, after the journey he has been on. I have rarely felt as much pride as when watching him improve in a City shirt. To have him sign a new deal warms the heart.

Premier League: Manchester City 3 Manchester United 1

So it's over my least favourite biannual event, derby day, though of course it always has the potential to end as one of the best days of a season. And so it proved – I don't know what I was worried about!

United have never been such long odds to win a derby match, and somehow that worried me more. I'll never change. We all know City are better – we went into the game 9 points ahead, with a goal difference 28 better than United's, and we will surely finish ahead of United for the sixth season on a row come May. But this is derby day – City haven't won at home since 2014, away teams strangely dominant in recent years, and we saw how last season's match, in unique circumstances that day admittedly, suddenly turned with little forewarning. City have picked up a few famous victories as the underdog, but this City team is something else, so the odds were pretty accurate as it turned out.

No surprises with the City team, Mahrez in ahead of Sane the only talking point, the consensus in the pub pre-match that Sane would come on against tiring legs, which is how it panned out, though slightly earlier than I had anticipated. The United side was as underwhelming as it comes, with Pogba out and Fred and Sanchez benched. Good news, because Sanchez seems to prosper against City whatever his form has been recently, and Pogba relishes a game like this, whatever his form has been recently. Their midfield was physical, workmanlike and uninspiring, their defence a damning indictment of wasted transfer fees. But with some pace up front, it could work in the same way Liverpool use their midfield to supply the ammo for a dangerous front three.

Seven of Pep's signings started the game. Two of Mourinho's did.

But first we remembered those who had fought for our country. The on-pitch display was beautiful, but I felt rather baffled at the lack of a one minute silence – a misunderstanding by the referee? Either way, I'm sure it would have been impeccably observed by both sets of fans, so it was disappointing.

Having attended the 11am remembrance in St Peters Square, we absconded before they started singing the National Anthem.

Anyway, form certainly seemed to dictate the opening quarter of an hour. City were superb, as dominant as the opening stages of last season's fixture. United could barely get near the ball, and a goal was fitting reward for a game between men and boys. Sterling's dangerous cross was brilliantly anticipated by Bernardo Silva, who could have shot himself he was so close to the goal, but he laid it back. David wriggled and jinked his way into space and slammed the ball in off De Gea's outstretched arm. 1-0.

At the time of the goal, City had completed 96 passes in the match. United had completed 6.

The hope was that City would rip United to shreds thereafter, but this did not materialise, as Mourinho retreated into park-bussed mode. He brought two of his attacking trio further back to protect the defence and stop the midfield being overrun, and the game suffered as a result. The move might have bene understandable, as taking the heat out of the game was progress for United, but it showed up this United side for what it is – a limited bunch of expensive footballers.

Do not dismiss the fact though that this United side still contains a wealth of excellent footballers, and they were well drilled in defence, can pass the ball excellently in patches, and limit space. But they are so utterly lacking in players to unlock defences, and it's one or the other with them – defend well and offer little in attack or be more open and concede chances. They are light years behind City, but a decent, progressive manager would still halve that gap in my opinion.

Anyway, City were still dominant, but the chances were not flowing. It reminded me of the derby at Old Trafford last season for a while – City were clearly the better side, but the clear cut chances did not reflect that, and on that occasion it took two pieces of errant defending to aid City that day. On this day too, Mourinho commented afterwards that the game was won on three mistakes, but that was drivel – it was won because one team was far superior to another team. The only mistake was by a City player, allowing United their only shot on target, their only real chance. Damning for all United supporters. Aguero was the closest in the remainder of the half, shooting into the side netting, when a squared cross probably would have brought a goal.

Onto the second half. The 2nd goal by Aguero, again flicking the hand of De Gea, was a huge relief, the domination bringing daylight between the teams. It was a classic Aguero finish after United had once more conceded possession after being pressed in midfield. Within 5 seconds, the ball was in the net.

And at that point, the game was virtually over, but then United were handed a lifeline, and you wondered if history was cruelly repeating itself. For the second league game in succession, Ederson rushed out from goal and conceded a penalty. And it was a clear penalty. He is of course a proactive keeper whose style is essential to the team's successful style of play, but he will have to learn to temper this rashness in such situations. For both incidents, there was no imminent threat of a goal – if Ederson had simply waved the player past, they would have had work still to do. Lessons to be learnt.

Credit to City though, for they did not wilt. United could not fashion another chance for the rest of the match, in the same way they couldn't fashion one before the penalty, and the nerves were lifted with five minutes to go. And how - 44 passes, the opposition ground into submission, and a lovely deft finish from Gundogan at the end, on as a sub and making his mark when it mattered. If this move told us anything, it simply rammed home the chasm between these two teams.

Earlier, Sane was on too for Mahrez, as anticipated. This was understandable, as whilst Mahrez had played fine, he was not at the heart of City's attacking play, the ball channelled through Sterling more often (though credit for his delicate Aguero assist). Sane simply gave United's defenders a new problem to deal with, and a reluctance therefore to pour forward, not that there seemed too much desire to do so anyway.

After that, City probably could have had a couple of more goals if need be, as United's heads dropped. But the game was seen out comfortably, and City went 12 points and 32 goals clear of United. Drink it in.

At the end we saw some showboating from Sterling and a rebuke from Pep as he left the pitch. I can see both sides of this. Pep wants his team to remain humble, to never "take the piss" or goad opposition teams, and I support that. It also only takes one incident like this and Sterling is left with a broken leg after the opposition defender takes offence, as Mata did on this occasion after the ball went out of play.
However. This is a Manchester derby, so fuck 'em. The City players are not there to please Juan Mata, this game needs

needle, demands it, and needle is fine, that is what derbies are about, and showboating hardly crosses a line.

Duncan Castles can sit in his South African bunker, tin hat on, quoting Amnesty International reports and Fernandinho's tactical fouling all he wants, but a proper journalist, a real one, would have pointed out after the match just how utterly imperious the Brazilian was. With over 100 touches of the ball, more than any other player, he ran the midfield, and was a potent threat with his passing too into dangerous areas, chances for Bernardo Silva and Raheem Sterling springing instantly to mind. Yes he is 33, but he does not appear to be letting up. His age seems irrelevant, and you can see why Pep seems unwilling to rest him even for "smaller" games. His control allows City the freedom to attack, safe in the knowledge that he is behind them to mop up, or cynically tackle without punishment, depending on your point of view, or paymaster.

So Fernandinho was Man Of The Match for me, but there were so many contenders. The Silvas dazzled as they usually do, Sterling was once more electric, Stone and Laporte as classy as ever, the full backs comfortable and dependable.

As for United, they are equidistant now between City and the relegation zone, and as one scribe commented on Twitter, Mourinho's greatest trick has been to persuade some United fans that he couldn't have done a better job with the resources at his disposal. Staggering. The day he is relieved of his duties will be a sad day for all City fans.
Sadly that day may not be far off. Though as we know, United stand against the immediacy of modern football and are renowned for not sacking their managers, apart from all those managers they have actually sacked.

And a great experience all round. Full ground, electric atmosphere, silky football, and the morning rain long gone. This is what it's all about.

So another international break, so we can all worship Wayne Rooney. Great. Normally I'd welcome it, as it gives (some) players rest and allows Kevin to move closer to a return, but in current form I'd probably welcome a game every day. Anyway, City stay clear at the top of the table, having chalked off another potentially difficult game, and Manchester is blue, apparently.

Suck on that Nick Harris.

NEXT UP – AN INTERNATIONAL BREAK! YAY!!!!!!!!!!!!!!!!!!!!!!!!!

Bluemoon Podcast Audio Script

Well what an interesting 10 days that has been. On the pitch, it could not have been much more perfect, swiping aside Shakhtar Donetsk and then of course a mid-table Manchester United with little difficulty. Manchester is blue and all that, as we look forward to the prospect of finishing ahead of United in the league for the 6th season in succession. We truly are the noisiest of neighbours.

Normally the lead up to derby day the media coverage is dominated by wheeling out the likes of Paul Scholes, the notoriously shy family man, to explain how city will never be as big as united. This time, things were rather different.

I am not going to go over old ground with the football leaks and the hatchet jobs on our club's reputation. You're probably, like me, sick of it all. The reaction from much of the English press has been hysterical, in every sense of the word. In the same way that Brexit has given casual racists the confidence to be more open with their prejudices, so the leaks from Der Spiegel allowed those journalists that have always had a distaste for City, their financial strength and owners, to show their true colours and have a field day at the club's expense. I wrote last month that all football fans are essentially hypocrites, who have very selective moral compasses, happy to decry ownership models of rival clubs that they'd love to have at their own club, professing faux outrage at human rights issues in the middle east for which they couldn't really care less, whilst sparing not a moment's thought on how their clothes were made, their phone constructed, their food killed, or closer to home, showing no distaste at their own club's sponsorships deals with questionable regimes. It seems sponsorship deals are fine, it's just ownership that's a problem. Funny that.

As for Financial Fair Play, sod it, I don't care if we didn't meet thresholds, as long as we get away with it. All clubs will be up to questionable practices in a global money-rich sport where power is everything, so rival fans should be careful what they wish for. And yeah, I'll enjoy the amazing football being served to me on a weekly basis, and rival fans can whinge all they want, it makes no difference to us blues. Who's the bitters now, eh? You see, it's easy for rival fans, or more commonly, journalists who support less successful teams, to take a moral high ground and claim they'd walk away from their club should they ever be taken over by some gulf state-linked billionaire, but I assure you that almost all of you would not – you'd enjoy and appreciate the greatest period of success you'd ever seen and realise that nothing changed whether you are there or not. Take a selective moral high ground if you wish, or enjoy your short time on earth.

Anyway, that's all a bit too serious, so instead, I mused on twitter on what the next revelations could be. I commented on a Nick Harris exclusive, and how it focuses on City fans' claim that they signed Sergio Aguero whilst United signed Phil Jones, and the deception in the song that ignores amortisation costs, market values and re-sell fees that suggest, per se, that United actually got the best deal.

So with the help of some cracking replies and the twitter City family, I thought it may be a good time to look at some more of the revelations that will follow the Nick Harris expose, as Der Spiegel go after the shocking, brazen inaccuracies in much of City fans' chants. It may shake you to the core.

On Friday, news will break on the latest revelation that will only further damage City's already tarnished reputation. The leak will document how City fans not only failed to condemn but actually regularly encouraged Etihad and other Abu Dhabi sponsors to further inflate already overvalued sponsorships in order to pay Yaya Toure more money. It is alleged that the constant demands by City fans to increase their Ivorian midfielder's financial package led to overspending and the inflating of commercial deals to cover their tracks.

And there's more. City fans blatantly lied, despite all the evidence to the contrary, about their lack of success, trying to claim they had fewer points than they actually had. Der Spiegel have documents that prove beyond doubt that they did in fact win both at home AND away, and not only that, but that this was achieved on a regular basis. The article will claim that there is clear evidence City fans do give a fuck about results, are not entirely always intoxicated, and that at times in their history, this modest club were definitely not O.K.

Further allegations have emerged that Shaun Goater's scoring prowess was not reliant on an intake of food prior to him shooting, and that a regular low-fat diet, training and practice were bigger factors in his performances. What's more, it is claimed that Shaun Goater is not the greatest of all time, nor a goat, adding further fuel to the fire.

Next Wednesday , the German newspaper will run with accusations that by claiming to be fans of the Invisible Man, and claiming they are not really there, City fans are trying to both inflate the official crowds in their half empty stadium whilst also playing down crowd numbers, possibly as some form of tax dodge. Their ditty, you saw me standing alone, seems a further attempt to avoid paying what they owe on gate receipts. In a song about a particular derby result, City fans have enraged many within UEFA and FIFA by claiming it should have been ten, a clear dig at poor refereeing that they seem to think has cost them further goals and perhaps actual silverware. UEFA are not thought to have taken such an accusation well, and have asked for the club to comment on such claims.

With the club's reputation now in tatters, it will not help with to hear rumours that Uwe Rosler's grandfather will be posthumously tried for war crimes committed in an airplane just outside Manchester in 1941. The final nail in the coffin, one that may force City's owners to walk away, surprisingly concerns the attire of one of City's ex-players, the beanpole striker Niall Quinn. Ewan Mckenna, whose stomach has literally churned all week at City fans' complicity in genocide in Yemen, has released a stinging rebuke to the claims made in a song about Quinn's trousers in which he argues that said pants did not reach Quinn's chest, starting around the hips, before travelling down to his ankles, that claims that the pants are better than Adam and the Ants are subjective and could not be proven in any court of law, as is the claim that they are simply the best, as this would require comparison with every other pair of pants globally, an undertaking even the oil-soaked wealth of Abu Dhabi could not fund. Such claims could not have come at a worst time for the club.

With news that the song Raheem Sterling – he's top of the league has incurred an additional UEFA fine after the song was sang despite the fact that Liverpool had played earlier that day to go temporarily top of the league, City's PR department will certainly be busy in the coming months. When Nick Harris finds out that all City fans are not without a love of their own, that in a game once, the boys in blue did effectively give in, that the club does not guarantee to make fans happy when skies are grey, the blues have rarely marched on, and the craven inaccuracy about being the only club to come from Manchester, well, heads will surely roll.

All in all, worrying stuff, as our club's name gets dragged further through the mud. And yeah, I'm joking about seemingly serious claims. And I'll continue to, cos the moral arbiters can quite frankly sod off. I'll always support my club, and have little control over it. I'm going to enjoy this team whilst I can, and if that makes me, every other fan, the players manager and staff bad people then so be it. We're no different to anyone else. Except we're not as bitter as other fans. Until next time….

As City prepared for a visit to West Ham United in the premier league, Jacob Steinberg, Guardian journalist and West Ham fan, asked me some questions to help with an article he was writing.

1. Do you think that Manuel Pellegrini was a success at Manchester City?

It's a tough question to answer, as his reign was one that peaked early before gradually petering out to an uninspiring end. I would class him as a moderate success, and am thankful for his contribution to City's recent history. He essentially filled his brief, which was as a glorified caretaker manager, there to fill the "holistic" brief that City's owners demanded, the calm after Roberto Mancini's fiery reign. His debut season was one of City's best ever, an avalanche of attacking play, a season where goal-scoring records were broken with aplomb and the League Cup was added to the Premier League title. Winning two trophies in a season was uncharted territory for us all. It was just a shame that he could not maintain that style of play, and by the 3rd season, he was treading water, essentially a dead man walking.

2. Some say he only won the title because Chelsea and Liverpool blew it - unfair?

Totally unfair. I speak as a football fan and not a City fan in saying that I hate the idea bandied about that a team can only be a worthy winner if they lead the league throughout the run-out, which is the implication when many suggest City got lucky, as if overtaking a team late-on in a season is somehow fortuitous. Leagues are decided at the end, not near the end, the middle or in November. City's mental strength, a recent addition to their armoury, was key in overtaking two competitors in title run-ins. The team at the top at the end of the season tends to be the one that deserves the title, and I doubt one of Manchester United's titles has been downgraded because Kevin Keegan's team imploded late-season. (some classic whaboutery there). The suggestion that Liverpool "blew it" is based on one single defeat anyway, at home to a fellow title contender. It was never a game they could expect to win easily, so the argument is weak. Even if they had beaten Crystal Palace by an 8 goal margin, they'd still have entered the final week of the season in 2nd place.

3. Why do you think City struggled to challenge in his second and third seasons?

The 2nd season is harder to evaluate, but the starting point has to be by repeating the errors that followed Mancini's title-winning season, namely poor player recruitment, failing once more to strengthen from a position of power. The purchases of Mangala and Bony were disastrous, Fernando little better, and undermined Pellegrini's efforts to retain a Premier League title for the first time in the club's history, never an easy task. Alvaro Negredo's form had disappeared ever since a picking up a shoulder injury at Upton Park the previous January. Yaya Toure's goals dried up, and even David Silva was not at his best. Suddenly the squad that had delighted so many the previous season seemed old and stale, and Pellegrini must take some blame for not being able to get the performances out of his players. There was no shame in exiting the Champions League to Barcelona, but the two domestic cup competitions were feebly surrendered. City did finish 2nd in the league though, but this was now considered failure. As for Pellegrini's final season, he was the archetypal dead-man walking. City's board had at least learnt from the mistakes of the previous summer, by bringing in the likes of Kevin De Bruyne, Raheem Sterling and Nicolas Otamendi, but Pep Guardiola would reap the rewards of those signings more than Pellegrini once they had settled. There was simply a lack of dynamism at the club by now, from the manager or in the play, and the manager got much of the blame, his public persona considered a factor in some lethargic displays. The team was regressing, and only just qualified for the following season's Champions League after a dour draw on the final day at Swansea, yet amongst all this he took City to the semi-final of the Champions League, but still got huge criticism for the team's total lack of ambition as they lost the second leg at the Bernabeu. But despite being handed a season-long contract extension in the summer, everyone knew the score. This was his final season, everyone knew Pep was on the way, and the season reflected the situation at the club - one of just getting by, and the anticipation of an exciting new era at the club.

4. Do you think the squad struggled for motivation with Pep already on his way? Was he let down by signings?

Yes and yes. It is natural I guess, because it is the manager that transmits energy to the players, and the feeling was there was a lack of energy in his final season, the players' talents getting them through most matches as they slept-walked towards the ends of the season. Few of us fans know what Pellegrini is really like, but his public persona certainly did not inspire, though there is a value to the calmness he seemed to exude too. His signings definitely did let him down, especially the disastrous recruitment after he won the league. Many like to argue that Jose Mourinho had a much harder task rebuilding the squad when he took over compared to Pep, but if you look at Pellegrini's squad for his final game at Swansea, it is filled with weaknesses. Despite the funds he had been provided with, there was huge under investment in full-backs, and the squad was ageing and lob-sided. He must take part of a collective blame for that.

5. Do you think he achieved as much as Mancini?

An impossible question to answer! Most City fans, if not all, will definitely answer no to that question, and I am inclined to agree. Pellegrini's debut season was as good as any, but whilst money has played a huge part in all of this, Mancini helped change the mentality, ethos and history of the club forever. He was the one that delivered a first trophy in 44 years then a title too, in circumstances imprinted on our brains forever. He took on Alex Ferguson and beat him, and he had charisma and fire in his belly. He was the right man at the right time, but history is dependent on fine lines sometimes and he was seconds away from being a failure. There's nothing Pellegrini can do about any of that though, so he is blameless in many respects. He arrived in different circumstances and probably with the expectations higher than ever, and did a good job in unusual circumstances. But Mancini will always be considered the more successful of the two.

6. If he had been replaced by anyone other than Guardiola, do you think he would have deserved to be sacked?

Yes, because I think the on-pitch performances were simply not good enough - 4th in the league certainly wasn't, and a 2nd league cup triumph was hardly enough to save him. Of course without the axe hanging over his head perhaps results would have been better, but the previous season suggests otherwise. I don't feel sympathy for Pellegrini though. He knew the score. City's Spanish duo had been after Pep since the turn of the decade and it was always assumed that Pellegrini was there as a stop-gap. He will have known this, got paid well, moved on, got another job. He understood the industry and handled it all with the upmost grace throughout and I have huge respect for him because of that. The nice pay-off will have helped, obviously.

7. Do you think he might be better suited to building up a club like West Ham?

Yes, probably. As long as he is given time of course, a precious commodity in the modern game. It's hard to define Pellegrini, to truly understand his philosophy when he is a man of such few words. But just look at his time at Malaga to see what he can do without constant media scrutiny or a massive budget. He will have to temper his attacking philosophy with some defensive steel, and my concern is that his hiatus since City from European football will mean he will take time to impose himself on the team, but it's good to see him back, and I think he fits West Ham perfectly. I don't think he will have been damaged by his time at City or Real Madrid, but this feels like the right sort of challenge for him at this stage of his career.

And then I asked some questions of my own. I caught up with West Ham fan Jim Kearns to talk all things West Ham, with a bit of City thrown in too. Jim is author of The H List (https://thehlist.blogspot.com/) and can be found on Twitter too (@TheHList).

1. Before we look at the current situation at West Ham, it's probably best to ask about what has gone before. You've commented in the past that West Ham have become a lost love as long as the current owners remain in charge. Has anything changed in that respect? Or is there a huge groundswell from fans for a change of ownership?

I would be keen on new ownership, because I think the club has no future with David Sullivan in a position of importance, but I think most fans are wary of the potential for disaster with new owners. At this point Sullivan and David Gold are the devil we know, and most supporters would rather put faith in Manuel Pellegrini to transform the club than risk a Massimo Cellini type owner coming in and somehow being worse than the incumbents. That said, they are not remotely popular, despite their pathological need to be. Fan unrest is generally always linked to performances on the pitch, so as long as Pellegrini keeps us above the relegation struggle I suspect they will avoid the public calls for their heads that dogged them last year.

2. As for the ground itself - has the situation improved at all, or is there still the wish that you had remained at Upton Park? (sorry, Boleyn!). Is it the fact that it is not designed for football that is the problem, or also the reluctance to leave the Boleyn? Was this the only way West Ham could hope to compete at the top?

There's a lot to cover here, but dealing with them in order the answer is that no, the ground hasn't improved and is very unlikely to unless we buy it and commit to an incredibly expensive remodelling that brings the stands into the same postcode as the pitch, and provides some (any) modern amenities for supporters. All of the failings of the London Stadium are only going to be highlighted further when Spurs eventually open their ground up the road, and in the end one has to concede that you are right – it wasn't designed for football and it shows. It's a desolate place to watch football and quite possibly built on an Indian burial ground.

But part of that is because the team is so mediocre. I think it's fair to say that there was a vocal minority who never wanted to move, but also that a majority of supporters were happy to go to the new stadium because we believed in the dream we were sold about greater revenue, better players and a change in fortunes for the club, and could see no other way to punch above our weight. Whether people loved Upton Park or not, there is no doubt in my mind that they would have embraced this crappy stadium if the club had delivered a decent team. As we will come on to discuss, football fans will forgive a lot if they have a team worth cheering.

And this is the crux of the problem. It's not just that Sullivan hasn't delivered that, it's also that we know he doesn't have the ability to do so. Thus we continue to have the worst transfer policy in the league, and a decidedly average team who could have been just as easily assembled at Upton Park as in this stadium.

If it was going to be done, it had to be done well. And it wasn't.

3. Sum up briefly anything else that would explain how the club's been mis-managed/run in recent years. Have bad managerial appointments been key or have managers been on a hiding to nothing?

The owners. Everything comes back to them. The lack of vision, the lack of a culture, the lack of planning, the lack of standing for anything. West Ham is the worst run club in the league and I'll happily arm wrestle any Newcastle fan for the title. Leaving aside the stadium debacle, we have seen money repeatedly wasted on old ageing players, a failure to invest in young players or the Academy and a series of off field mishaps that almost defy belief. Karren Brady is a part time CEO but a full time drain on the payroll, Sullivan sits in his mock Tudor mansion in Essex and plays Fantasy Football using agents as scouts and buying players without the managers' knowledge, while Gold is everybody's favourite, confused uncle.

It is too much for them, and while I don't think their managerial appointments have been great, the reality is that even Pep would struggle to manage in this structure. Nothing about West Ham is normal. Consider this; the owners teenage son has been made Chairman of the newly formed West Ham women's team and is making a reality TV show about it; the club are refusing to meet with the FSF-affiliated West Ham Independent Supporters Association and instead want to constitute and appoint their own fan forum to represent supporters; we have been linked with paying Samir Nasri for £80,000 a week even though he's not actually fit enough to play football anymore; one of our youth team coaches kept his job after going on a Far Right march; and the club have leaked details of Declan Rice's contract requests to a preferred fan website, seemingly in a bid to undermine his standing with supporters.

Does that all seem a bit weird? Well, that has all happened in the last month at West Ham. I have ten years of this shit I could tell you about.

4. Were you happy with the appointment of Manuel Pellegrini?

Absolutely. People of his calibre just don't end up at West Ham. There were concerns about his motivation given the huge wages and the fact he'd disappeared to China previously, but trying to be optimistic, he is a cut above anyone we've appointed for decades. The ghost of Avram Grant looms large, after all.

5. Sum up the season so far - how has he done?

Poorly, to be honest, but I think you have to see that in the context of a very difficult start. Our opening fixtures were brutal and he's picking up the pieces of a club that has been in a downward spiral for quite some time. He had a lot of money to spend but, again, you have to place that in the context that it's been spent with Sullivan's involvement meaning that he won't have had full control over all the signings. I was hoping for better, but once we get this match out of the way, things will hopefully perk up.

6. What would you say his playing style & philosophy has been?

I think we've seen a commitment to attacking, and I have definitely seen the green shoots of some better, more incisive football being played. He seems slavishly wedded to variants of the 4-4-2 formation, which Moyes abandoned last year due to our defenders being so crap. They aren't much better this year, which generally leads to us going behind and Pellegrini then just chucking endless forwards on in pursuit of goals. I'm not saying this game will be a blood bath, but anyone not captaining a Man City player in their Fantasy League team this week just isn't trying.

7. Of the summer signings who has impressed most and least?

Weirdly I would say the best signings have been Fabianski, Diop and Balbuena, despite the fact that we have been defensively pretty poor. I don't really know what that says about us, but I'll be willing to bet that Sergio is excited about tomorrow.

Our worst has been Jack Wilshere, who was unsurprisingly injured within ten minutes of signing and now presumably earns his money trying to keep Andy Carroll out of prison.

8. Manchester City - you may have noticed they've been in the news a bit recently. What are your views on the club, in respect of how success has been achieved, the owners, and fans' ability to turn a blind eye for success on the pitch? And historically too - is there a bond between the fans of the two clubs, as many suggest regularly on Twitter?

In an ocean as fetid as that of professional football, why bother getting upset about a single tidal wave like that of Manchester City? I'm not a fan of brutal regimes or humanitarian abuses (who is, after all) but modern football abandoned morality a long time ago. Football fans are not responsible for the actions of their owners, and I don't blame City fans for turning a blind eye to all that stuff because we don't get to choose our football teams. I'm sure I should do more than shrug my shoulders, but I haven't got the energy when there is so much else wrong with the game.

I found the FFP abuses to be predictable but disappointing, and all part of a wider pattern where UEFA acquiesce to richer clubs in order to prevent them disappearing to their vaunted Super League. If I have a particular criticism of City it is that. It didn't take them long after joining the Big Six to start pulling up the drawbridge and demanding a greater slice of revenues and resources and doing their bit to start making it harder for smaller clubs to compete. Witness the new overseas TV deal being carved up to give a greater proportion to bigger clubs, as an example. Truthfully, I don't understand how it can be satisfying to be a fan of teams who are doing everything they can to rig things in their own favour, but perhaps City are different and I've been unfair to them. That said, my main feeling about the big clubs is that I can't wait for them to fuck off so the rest of us can actually pay our season ticket and Sky money and have something to aim for above finishing seventh. For what it's worth, I wrote more widely on this topic in the summer (https://thehlist.blogspot.com/2018/07/lets-fix-modern-football-pipe-dreams.html) I'd be interested to know what City fans thought of those proposals.

As for the link between the clubs, I do remember that from when I was kid and perhaps it's been exacerbated by having some shared popular players like Bishop, Sinclair, Lomas and Bellamy in recent times. I think there is also probably something to be said for there being a sense of commonality once, as a result of us both being criminal underachievers and "proper" fans because we kept turning up in big numbers despite being shit. I think those days might just be gone though....

9.   Thoughts on Pablo Zabaleta.

It depends. If it's a Friday then he's a wonderful footballer, a warhorse and a much needed professional presence in a club that was chronically short of them.

If it's a Monday, he's a prime example of our ludicrous transfer policy of signing players five years after their best and an example of the chronic short termism that has held us back for years.

10. Just how good is Declan Rice?

I am always wary of answering questions like this too effusively because one man's wonderful young youth prospect can grow up to become another man's Phil Jones. That said, Rice is the best player to have come through our system in a long time and is already crucial to our team. He can play either in midfield or centre half, and looks very comfortable playing off either foot.

He offers little in an attacking sense, but is a genuine holding midfielder and if he chooses England I could see him in the squad for Euro 2020, because it's a position of weakness for Southgate. He is already better than Eric Dier, as an example.

11. How do you think Pellegrini will approach this match? Reluctantly.

12. Which players should Guardiola be most wary of?

Marko Arnautovic is our best goal threat and Felipe Anderson has looked lively recently, but in truth I doubt Guardiola will spend much time worrying about them. West Ham are several rungs below City and won't have the ball enough to cause much damage.

13. If you could have one City player at West Ham, who would it be?

For a one off game, I'd take the wonderful David Silva but to build a team around I'd take Kevin de Bruyne. To be clear, if you're offering, I'd take any of them. Any. Of. Them.

14. Prediction on how game will pan out, and score prediction too.

Same as usual. You'll spank us. I'd guess we might keep it to 3-0 with Fabianski but it's hard to say. My overriding feeling approaching fixtures like this is one of apathy. I just want it out of the way so I can get back to watching real football where we play teams we can actually compete against. That doesn't feel like a good thing for English football.

Premier League: West Ham 0 Manchester City 4

And so City stay 2 points clear of Liverpool at the top of the table, as they scored four at West Ham for the third time on the trot. West Ham put in their best performance of those three games, and could have had a goal or two themselves, but even after the international break, and with a couple of players not quite at their peak, it was business as usual, as the machine powered on.

Just the 36 goals better than United in the goals difference chart, as they staggered to a goalless draw at the Theatre of Nightmares (they own the trademark now), and the table suggests a two-horse race, for now, as Chelsea were beaten comprehensively by Spurs.
Maybe we should invite Spurs to the race instead? They just keep on going, after all.

For City, it was done and dusted before half-time, and the second half was an exercise in player management. Sane and Sterling were electric, both scoring, both assisting, both making football look easy. Credit to Manuel Pellegrini for giving it a go, for West Ham troubled City's defence more than most other teams this season, and should have scored at least once.
They did not though, so another clean sheet for Ederson and City are still to concede in the final half hour of a match this season.

This was a team without Kevin De Bruyne and Bernardo Silva and Benjamin Mendy and with John Stones rested. It makes little difference any more it seems, though a midweek trip to Lyon will pose a much sterner test. And it surprised few to learn that Benjamin Mendy was injured once more, with knee surgery to follow. Worrying news indeed, and the decision not to bolster the left-back spot in the summer was coming back to bite City on the behind.

Goals: Silva (11' minutes), Sterling (19' minutes), Sané (34' minutes, 90'+3 minutes)

And so back to the Champions League. A big game in Lyon, where avoiding defeat would probably be good enough.

Champions League: Lyon 2 Manchester City 2: Five Things I Learned

In yet another entertaining match in Group F, Manchester City came from behind twice to book a place in the knock out stage of the Champions League. It was yet again a tough night for the City players against their French opponents, the visitors thankful for some bad misses in the first half before they struck with two headers after the interval to share the spoils. Here's five things I took from the match.

Foden still not ready to shine.

It was the big talking point leading up to the match, one that overshadowed the group standings, permutations, form and all else – would Phil Foden get to start in Lyon with City leaving behind a trio of injured midfielders?
No, he wouldn't – he got 90 seconds instead, so at least an appearance bonus is his to cherish. Pep spoke about how he was ready to star in this team, but this was still a big game against a top class side and clearly he felt he was not quite ready on this occasion. Don't be surprised if he gets a start in the near-dead-rubber against Hoffenheim, but the question many City fans want an answer to is when does he reach the point in his development to start any game?
Bournemouth at home this weekend is another opportunity to select the Stockport Iniesta, but don't really expect that to happen, even if the mini-injury crisis does not ease by then. Many fans are frustrated at his lack of chances, but he already has more minutes on the pitch than the whole of last season, and there is no rush.
The only certainty is that, at some point, his time will come.

Lyon are good!

Bet that came as a surprise, eh? This is a team brimming with exciting young talent, power and pace, which makes it all the more surprising that, whilst recent league results have been OK, they are 15 points behind PSG in the league and there are rumblings of discontent off the pitch. Admittedly, PSG haven't dropped a point all season, so it's hard to keep up with such a pace, but games like last night's are often good for perspective. Lyon's victory on Match Day 1 at The Etihad always seemed like an outlier, not because Lyon were good, but because City were so, so average. Well, in the return leg at times, Lyon made City look average again, though the Citizens had more fight in them on this occasion.

The crazy thing is that we may not even see this exciting side in the knockout stages of the Champions League. After Shakhtar Donetsk's late victory against a 10-man Hoffenheim, Lyon must travel to Donetsk for their final group game, where defeat would see them knocked out of the tournament. That would be a shame, as this is one of those teams you want to see more of. In this group their games have ended 2-1, 2-2, 3-3, 2-2, 2-2. Many have compared them to the Monaco team of two years ago, and the hope is that this Lyon squad does not suffer the same fate – an asset-strip followed by the appointment of a Sky Sports pundit. They deserve better than that.

City's squad might have depth, but there's no substitute for world-class talent.

We all know that this Manchester City is packed with talent, with a depth to the squad never seen before at the club. However, take out Kevin De Bruyne, Bernardo Silva, Benjamin Mendy and Ilkay Gundogan (yes, really) from any squad and you'll be worse off for it. And City suffered without these four players against Lyon. It resulted in Pep shuffling the pack, and it left gaps across the pitch as a result, and much of the performance felt disjointed. City have no right to roll over every team they meet, and this game should be a timely reminder that this team, no team, is perfect. And despite all this, City have qualified with a game to spare having lost the opening game, and only need to avoid defeat at home to Hoffenheim to definitely top the group. Job almost done.

<u>Winning away in Europe is not easy, whoever you are.</u>

There's a dichotomy here, it seems. Lyon underwhelm domestically but look world-class on the European stage against City. City are so dominant domestically that there is talk of the league becoming boring, yet they struggle twice against Lyon, and seem like a different side at times.

Lyon definitely seem to raise their game on the European front, though as already mentioned, chasing a PSG side that never drops points must sap the spirits on a weekly basis.

Fact is, no team, however good, has consistently travelled across Europe and swatted aside all they met, certainly not in recent years. Look at Liverpool, last season's finalists, just a few weeks ago. Last season they lost their away leg in Rome and should have lost to City too, truth be told. Barcelona's winning squad of 2010/11 drew in Copenhagen and at Rubin Kazan before losing at Arsenal in the Round of 16. Real Madrid have already lost away this season to CSKA Moscow. Alex Ferguson's United side spent many a year churning out hard-fought single-goal victories around Europe. It's not easy, it's a different mind-set to domestic games, and it's something we have to accept as fans.

Against Lyon, City showed fighting spirit to come back twice but struggled to impose themselves on the game, or create chances in open play. The new formation lacked shape and allowed spaces for Lyon's attackers to exploit.

That's life. City have pulled out some great away performances in recent years in Europe, but that does not mean we should expect them every time we travel. Football does not work like that, and if it did, it would be pretty boring. Might as well be Celtic.

<u>Pep's Champions League hoodoo must be overcome.</u>

Pep Guardiola last managed a Champions League finalist in 2011, a long time ago for a man generally considered the best in the world at his job. As City qualify for the knockout stage of the Champions League for the 6th season in succession, the only English team to do so, this may seem like a strange time to mention this fact. But some nagging suspicion about the draw in Lyon remains in my head that Pep succumbed to his previous weakness in this competition – tinkering, and over-thinking the situation. Whenever City seem to have an off-day the opposition can usually be found to have a settled side, they have stability, where every player knows their role. Now Pep had no choice but t tinker with so many midfielders injured, but two midfielders in Delph and Foden remained on the bench whilst Sterling's central role, one he has performed before, was not a particular success. Forming conclusions with hindsight is easy, but I still feel replacing like-for-like might have benefited City more in Lyon.

What's more, if Pep wants to break his hoodoo in the competition, he may have to abandon some of his attacking philosophies too as he did to neuter Liverpool in the league recently.

Oh, and to state the obvious, Laporte is pure class. But we all knew that anyway.

December

Premier League: Manchester City 3 Bournemouth 1

Not the walk in the park that some may have expected, but City got over the line, and opened up a five point lead at the top – though Liverpool have a game in hand. And with David Silva on the bench and Sergio absent with a muscle problem, it took until the 2nd half for City to seal the points.

And we need to talk about Leroy. And no doubt we will continue to do so, the man becoming something of an enigma. When we was left out of Germany's world cup squad, I not only wondered why that happened but what effect it would have on him. His early season form suggested a pretty bad effect, but now we are seeing him back to his best, and against Bournemouth he was electric.
And let's deal with facts – despite questioning him we are talking about the Young Player Of The Year, who has more assists since the start of last season than any other Premier League player. It's 20 by the way, Raheem Sterling 2nd with 17.

And talking of Sterling, in a game like this, without much of the old guard, like Aguero, De Bruyne or David Silva, he is taking on responsibility now, and delivering. He is getting older before my eyes, maturing and becoming the world-class player I knew he could be.

City, for once, had some luck too. At 2-1, a stupid nudge from Fernandinho should have resulted in a penalty for the visitors, but the referee thankfully waved play on. A fortunate escape. But in the end, 2nd half goals from Sterling and Gundogan were enough. None of the goals will win awards, but the slick passing was there for all to see in bursts.
And a shout out too to Zinchenko, who continues to develop in a role he perhaps thought he would never play.

What that equaliser did show late in the first half, was a season-long tendency for City to "ease off" after establishing a lead. I guess it is understandable, as game management is key when fighting on four fronts.

Meanwhile, over at Anfield, Liverpool's run of ridiculous luck, I mean superb victories began as Jordan Pickford decided for reasons only he knows to palm a Van Dijk miskick back into play allowing Origi to head home for a 96th minute winner in a game they deserved to lose.

As City prepared for a trip to Vicarage Road, I sent a few questions across to my old boss and Watford-supporting friend, Rob Smith. This is what he had to say.

1. First up, how happy are you with Watford's performances so far this season?

Very happy. We've only really had a couple of bad performances – most notably losing 4-0 at home to Bournemouth, but this can happen with any team. I think the bigger thing with results like this is how you bounce back. In seasons gone by, perhaps heads would go down, and there would be a spell of bad results. This season is different – we came back to get a dominant win away at Wolves – their first defeat on home territory in many months. We have more fight, more organisation, and more 'never beaten' attitude than ever before.

2. Which of the summer signings have impressed most - and least?

I think the best acquisition this summer was Ben Foster. With Gomes getting on, and beginning to show the odd sign of important mistakes, it was a logical time to bring Foster in. Albeit he is no spring chicken, he has made some important saves for us, and probably earned us a fair few points already.
 I also have to give an impressed nod to the move towards youth. Ben Wilmot came in from Stevenage, and looks extremely assured on the ball, even when used in midfield, rather than his preferred centre back position.
Also Domingos Quina – a last minute snaffle from West Ham looks very exciting – with a wonder goal in the Carabao Cup against Reading already under his first team belt.

3. Javi Gracia - impressed with the job he's done so far?

Maybe the jokes regarding our head coach turnover will stop, for a while now?! Gracia has just signed a 4.5 year extension on his contract. The first since Malky Mackay in 2011. Whilst occasionally, I think his tactics can be slightly suspect, overall, he is spot on, and sets us up well against teams. I think much more importantly, he has done an astounding job in bringing a real team spirit, where everyone works for each other, with a smile on their face. He inherited a bit of a mess after Silva threw us under the bus when Everton came calling. The players had already stopped playing for Silva, and our habitual second half of the season decline looked to have started. Gracia came in and instantly picked up great results, and has built on that in to this season, to his great credit.

4. How well have Watford's owners, the Pozzo family, run the club?

Following on from the previous question, I would say that the reason why this has been allowed to happen so quickly, is the way we are structured by the Pozzos. This is overlooked by the majority of the press, and pundits, but we are set up to cope if a head coach doesn't work out.
The operative words here are 'head coach'. I think to the untrained eye, fans think that a manager and a head coach are one and the same. Perhaps in some clubs, but certainly not Watford.
Transfer targets are planned long in advance of any move, with a system whereby the targets in each position are categorised as to their preference. Of course, the head coach is liaised with, as to positions the team feels is most important, but ultimate responsibility of what player comes in isn't the head coach's. This allows the head coach to fully focus on quickly getting his philosophy across to the players, which I feel aids individual improvements, and ergo, morale. On a business level, the Pozzos are known to be ruthless negotiators, and the model of developing little known, or out of form players, and selling on for a large profit continues to work well (thank you Richarlison!).

5. Troy Deeney - how big a legend is he at Watford, and why?

Come off it – he's been working hard in the gym, he's in great shape now! Troy might not bag you endless goals, but his hold up play and backtracking has been vital to us in recent seasons. He shoots from the hip, which in the main, is refreshing in a footballer.

I guess sometimes he can take that a bit far – as with cojonesgate, but even then, it was simply a fair reflection of how he viewed Arsenal in that particular game. He's had his doubters in the past season or so, but has used them to come back from injury stronger, and is looking hungry again. I do feel that he needs to be up there with an out-and-out goal-scoring striker, which currently we don't possess, but he still offers plenty to the team. He kept everyone galvanised, and I think helped the <few> loans we had in the couple of seasons before we got promoted, which I felt at that time was crucial.

6. Views on City, and how they have gained success. Is it unfair? Are fans responsible for owners?

They're OK I suppose – have their moments! In all seriousness, they are a joy to watch even when they're not at 100%. The fluidity or movement and one-touch passing Pep has drilled in to them now is mighty impressive. In terms of how City have gained their success, I find it quite ludicrous that people try and slate them. Jealousy is an ugly trait.

I saw a stat the other day showing Liverpool and Chelsea having spent more on transfers in the past few years than City. The argument of "buying the league" is ridiculous – every team buys players, and FFP exists for a reason. I guess it's all part of the process of being a fan though. Any other club would do the same, and I can't have a go considering my own club know how to use the system to their advantage.

You also look at the investment in to the area surrounding the Etihad, and what the owners have done for the community, and it's difficult to find fault in their approach. I can't possibly comment on the sponsorship deals City have 'created' though...!

7. If you could have one City player at Watford, which one would it be?

On the basis of what we need to improve our squad right now, I'd say the silver fox Sergio. We're missing a consistent goal scorer, and Aguero certainly fits that bill. I could see Deeney holding the ball up and laying it in to his path pretty successfully. Have a word!

8. How will Gracia approach the City match? Will it be different to how they normally set up?

I think it'll be much like the Liverpool approach. Not sitting too deep, and trying to play our game on the counter, rather than sitting back waiting for an attack. Organisation will be key, and for an hour against Liverpool, it worked well. Sadly though, matches are 90 minutes, so it'll need to be 100% concentration all the way.

9. Which Watford players should City fans be wary of?

Deulofeu, whilst fairly inconsistent, has the ability to unlock defences. His tricky feet, and rapid finishing can cause anyone problems, but it all depends on what kind of day he's having. Doucoure too is a marauding midfielder who can be tough to stop.

10. Score prediction.

I think even with the home advantage, City will be way too strong for us. We are susceptible to lapses of concentration when it matters, and an early goal I think will kill us against City, despite our revitalised approach to going down in matches this season. 0-4.

Premier League: Watford 1 Manchester City 2

A rarity this game as I missed it, due to attending a Ride acoustic set to celebrate 30 years in existence (them, not me). I tried to get rid of my ticket, as I am loathe to miss a match, but to no avail. Instead I had the excruciating experience of following via the internet intermittently whilst watching the gig. Well the 2nd half at least.

With that in mind, you're probably already aware that some searing insight and tactical analysis, the sort you've been used to in this book, will not be forthcoming. To be honest, from watching the highlights and from what I have read, I did not miss a classic.
Sergio Aguero remained side-lined with injury, top scorer Raheem Sterling was rested and an entirely different back four was brought in, including Kompany, Walker and Stones. Mahrez and David Silva were two of those rested at the weekend and both returned and were influential throughout.

So file this one under "job done". City made the last few minutes nervy, but once more got the points. It was a game that City were no doubt expected to win, and City's record against Watford is excellent, but it is not the easiest place to go. With Watford, you also are stepping into the unknown for me – you still don't know which Watford you're going to get.

In the end a goal in each half, from Sane and Mahrez was enough. Sane's goal came from a Mahrez cross, a clever improvised chest into the net, and Mahrez swept home six minutes into the second half. City remained five points clear, but it's really two once Liverpool inevitably win their game in hand.

Bluemoon Podcast Audio Script

Hello...?.....Hello.......?

I send you this short message from the year 2030. I'm somewhere south of Bishop's Stortford, close to where National Tyres used to be, near the A1060. I'm underground naturally, it's not safe to go out there, not since the Great Purge. FYI, time travel for audio clips was invented by Professor Brian Cox in the year 2027 A.D. hence why you can hear this message. There are four of us here, in this bunker, surviving on a diet of baked beans, spam and our wits. I dream of chicken Balti pies and a half-time Bovril. We hear screams from up above sometimes but we can do nothing about that. Gunfire too. A gang tried to lure us out by playing Mumford & Sons on a constant loop, but we stayed strong. We open the security door, and all our lives will be at risk. We must look after ourselves now, what few of us are left.

Anyway, there's a reason for this message. I wanted to tell you about what happens in the future, and warn you to get out whilst you can. Switzerland would be my tip, or the Dordogne, though only if you can get hold of a bottle of Chateau le Grandfont, 2012.

I'm waffling, and I don't have much time. You'll know some of this already, naturally, the signs were there. How a set of football fans set off a catalyst of events that ended with a post-apocalyptic wasteland, like Middlesbrough on a vast scale. Blues blamed Brexit and that Trump guy, but we knew they had only a small part to play. He's still President by the way.

God, it's crazy to think how it all started. The smallest spark created the biggest fire. Why didn't we take the accusations seriously? Why did we abandon our moral boundaries in pursuit of cheap, oil-soaked success? I wish I could go back in time like this recording and change it all, I really do.

It all kicked off in 2018 of course. Some leaked emails were published by a German newspaper, and the world lost its shit.

Barry Glendenning called City fans cowards and suddenly everyone was interested in human rights thousands of miles away, just as Manchester City got really, really good. This was just one of those coincidences you read about now and again. A British man who was definitely innocent, I mean he was British so he must be, was sentenced to life in the United Arab Emirates for spying. Things really got pretty hairy from then on. He was soon pardoned, but the damage was done.

Then City fans started taking credit for his release. After all, it had been our moral duty to raise the issue of his incarceration, Sam Wallace at The Telegraph, a paper that was heavily funded by Chinese state money, told me so. When this same fan base was later nominated for a Nobel Peace Prize, there was uproar. This was when the shit really hit the fans.

The battle lines had been drawn. On one side, carrying out their own morally acceptable version of the Crusades, was the British press, now fully briefed on Middle East geopolitics and legal systems. Sports washing they called it. Liquid football we called it. On our side, a merry bunch of moustachioed gentlemen from south Manchester and human rights abuse deniers who saw only joy in what their club's owners did. As Tim Booth commented, we were living in extraordinary times.

Everything snowballed very quickly. There were small demonstrations on the streets, organised via Red Issue's twitter account. Scuffles at matches. Social media spats. Barney Ronay had to enter a witness protection scheme, his safety no longer guaranteed.

If only City fans had risen as one and demanded action. There was talk of a delegation being sent over to Abu Dhabi to have a word with the sheikhs. Some names were mentioned, though I never found out if the rumours were true. Martin Lewis, Benjamin Mendy, Noel & Liam, Kevin Kennedy, David Mooney. But no, they – we - did nothing. We just wanted to watch David Silva, tactical fouling and drink dark fruits at half time. What's wrong with that? Others disagreed though. We had a moral duty to intervene, to say NO MORE, to demand the UAE model itself on UK democracy, a leading light for the rest of the world for centuries. Just ask the Northern Irish. I did write a strongly-worded email to Sheikh Mansour, but I never sent it. Didn't know his email address to be honest.

The world was disgusted. Questions were asked of us in the House. Soon City fans were being held accountable for all the world's ills. They were even blamed for fishing quotas in the North Sea, X Factor results and smaller Wagon Wheels.

City fans had inadvertently triggered a Western Spring, which was like the Arab Spring but with added sarcasm. Everything spiralled out of control.

You see, you might not know this yet, but it turns out Sheikh Mansour was testing City fans. By us lying down meekly, he felt he had carte blanche to do whatever he wanted. Obviously they didn't call it carte blanche in Abu Dhabi as English is not their first language.

We should have spoken out. Mansour would have listened to Dave from Marple and Alan from Hazel Grove. He'd have seen the error of his ways if we had just spoken up. He'd have remodelled the region in the style of a Western democracy. Slashed benefits for the needy, eradicated legal aid for suspected spies, wiped out half the police force, set up food banks across the emirates, sold off Etihad so it could be run better privately, and thus finally be accepted at last as a fit and proper owner by those whose acceptance he craved, such as Stan Collymore and Duncan Castles.

But by remaining silent, the City fans were implicit in what followed.

So the sheikhs turned up the heat. The UAE rulers put up the price of oil. They jailed 100 women for inadequate reverse parking. They bought every other Premier League club and ran them into the ground, except United which they left untouched. Sheikh Mansour also spread a rumour City wanted to sign Peter Crouch. United nipped in and signed him for £40m.

So how did we get to where I am today? Well my battery is running low, so I'll be brief. Once City had killed football for everyone, forever, society itself soon unravelled. Petrol was too dear now for most, so stranded in their home cities, social unrest was the inevitable conclusion. In the hot summer of 2020, the hottest since records began, as City fans celebrated their team's third successive Premier League, and a League Cup too, though by then it was known as the Haribo Fangtastic Cup, the country burned as riots hit all major cities. City fans were held responsible for the breakdown of society, not helped by Sheikh Mansour purchasing Tesco and renaming it Umtilat, which is Arabic for bitter bertie. Men with moustaches were hunted down and beaten, and anyone who defended the UAE was ostracised. A thousand City fans were left barricaded in at a Blossoms gig due to rioters outside baying for blood. Eventually lead singer Tom Ogden started a rumour on Twitter that the United Megastore had a half-price sale on, and the crowd dispersed.

But by now, law and order was gone. Gangs roamed the street, fans openly smoked on the spirals at City matches and I feared for my safety. On my CB radio I heard that there was a safe haven south of Cambridge, so under the cover of darkness and the haze caused by a burning City academy, I headed south, faking an Irish accent and hitching my way to here, Bishop's Stortford. I cancelled my subscription to Private Eye and set my guinea pigs free. My information was wrong though – anarchy ruled here too, but by selling my collection of Oasis CDs, I gained entrance to this bunker. There was once 20 of us here, but now there are four. The future is bleak, if there is one. The Bluemoon Podcast still transmits as a pirate radio enterprise from off the coast of Anglesey, and provides me with a link back to my old life. There's been no football for five years now though, since the new Communist government seized power in 2024. The purge of intellectuals, doctors and City fans happened soon after.

I thus send you this message, as the last hope for humanity. I know I shouldn't mess with history, but how can I make things any worse? So to any City fans that this message reaches.......

175

Please, I beg you, act now. Stop going to matches. Once rival fans see empty seats we can expect to gain their support. Send a strongly worded email to the club. Downgrade your season ticket from platinum. Bring your own food to matches, don't enter Cityzen competitions, leave the cup schemes. Unfollow City on Twitter. If possible, get yourself a Guardian column so you can bemoan the state of your football club. Leave matches before the 90 minutes are up. Do what you can. It's not too late. Act now, and the world might turn out to be a better place. If you don't, well, you've got blood on your hands. And you'll never make it to Switzerland in time. Most of Europe has fallen now too.

To those that do act in future, thank you blues, though I guess it makes no difference or else I wouldn't be here recording this message….or would I? I don't understand time travel. Anyway, thank you again, and good luck. Oh, and one last thing - put all your money on City to beat Bournemouth this weekend by the score of….. <transmission ends>

Chelsea 2 Manchester City 0. Thoughts on City, Raheem Sterling and being a football fan.

Here we go again. I missed watching the Chelsea v City game live as I had other plans that clashed, so will stay away from commenting on the tactics of the match, having watched it later from behind a couch. If you're reading this in a book, you're probably happy for me to skip this match anyway, right?

It was Dara O' Briain I had to see this time, and he was surprisingly good.

I always felt that not playing a striker was the wrong decision, whatever we think of Jesus's form, and the lull I have mentioned (on podcasts) in the past week or so seems real now. There is definitely fatigue setting in I reckon and injuries are following as a result, as they have for many teams. It was a hugely disappointing result, but it happens, this team cannot always be the best, however certain parts of the media have portrayed it.

The repeated claims that the league was now boring because of City look even more laughable, if that's possible.
City not being top of the table at any point now in a season feels like abject failure. I have forgotten how to deal with it. I'm in a foul mood as I write this and will be for the rest of the day. Not even salt and pepper ribs can rid me of this fug, though they may help a bit. We will see.

Quite a few in the media are keen to point out imperfections in this City squad and how you can get at them when a defeat occasionally trundles along, as is their right as football journalists. But was that not obvious anyway? Like those laughing at the thought of City going undefeated all season when no one but journalists had even entertained the possibility, claiming that City can be vulnerable is stating the bleeding obvious. Pep Guardiola is managing brilliantly what is the best side in the Premier League, and one of the best in Europe, but they are not football's version of the Harlem Globetrotters. What's more, their rivals have collected some of their best squads in many a year too. City will simply not get everything their own way every time they step onto a football field, and the sport would be pretty boring if they did. Some are saying it already is, but that was a kneejerk reaction to provide content when City have not even retained a Premier League title yet, when no one has for a decade.

As for this game, City dominated but did not make it pay. Once they went behind, their response was lacking. That is a shame, and hopefully just a temporary blip.

Regrettably, the day after the match and the main talking point is not even the match itself. Us City fans should be grateful for that, until you realise the reason for it. Yes, yet again we find ourselves talking about Raheem Sterling.
And by that I mean, racist *****in the crowd.

First off, and even despite what wrote earlier about my current mood, it still staggers me to this day the state people get in at football matches. It's always apparent to me that a lot of middle aged men go to a football match to escape from their real lives. Fair enough. Real life is tough, and we all need an escape, in one form or another. The problem for those that use football as an escape is that they have no control over what happens. We are mere voyeurs in the scheme of things, hoping that a set of men we have attached ourselves to make our day a good one.
I don't know at what point the incident occurred that has hit the headlines today, but as Chelsea were not behind at any point in the match, their mood could not have been that bad. Yes, City out-passed the home side for a while, but whilst the scores remained level, there is little cause for panic or football-induced depression. But some men, always men, simply have anger management issues at football matches. That hardly excuses the path to outright racism, as we have all heard at some point.

The sight of fans straining to shout abuse as an opposition footballer takes a throw in or corner is as old as time itself, and I'm baffled as to why it has always been met with a shrug of the shoulders. You can get thrown out for standing up nowadays, but outright abuse, racist or otherwise is often palmed off as passion or atmosphere. You really have to wonder where your life is at when you find yourself screaming abuse, spittle flying out of your mouth, as a young man you know very little about comes to pick up a football near you. I can only assume your life has been a failure, intellectually at least.

So how did we get to the point of Raheem Sterling being abused on Saturday evening, and laughing it off because the regularity of it has probably left him feeling helpless?
Well, at this point we must distinguish between sports and news reporters. The campaign of harassment and stalking accompanied with an undercurrent of racism fuelled by the disgust that young black men can have lot of money and thus spend lots of this money, has come almost exclusively from the news reporters. It is front page news, not back. It is these people that have questions to answer, but I doubt they care that much. The ones writing the pieces are no doubt following a pushed agenda, on shit wages to satisfy the needs of those higher up the hierarchy. I don't have the answers as to how this can be stopped. At least in recent months it dawned on many a sports reporter that Sterling needed some kind words in print. They took their time though – it's been going on for years, whilst they just stared vacantly into middle distance twiddling their thumbs, wondering if he was worth his transfer fee or exorbitant wages.

Journalists that expect City fans to denounce their football club's owners are highly reluctant to apply their own moral guidelines to denouncing fellow journalists. They look after their own, on the whole. But perhaps that should change now. Let's see how far your moral code stretches. Brave enough to

denounce your own employers?
Thought not.

But above all, these ramblings should end with a shout out to Raheem himself. Such dignity and such restraint in the face of such vile, cancerous vitriol. I couldn't have been this restrained. Most of you reading this couldn't either. What a role model he has turned out to be. His mum must be so proud. And credit too that he has not made this all about him, but about the problems faced by all players who suffer prejudice, abuse and a different type of media portrayal solely due to the colour of their skin.

Yes, Sterling himself has finally felt the need to comment on what has gone before. Even this comes with its own dangers, as can be seen by the knuckle-dragging Neanderthals on social media who still can't see what the problem is. Only one of this group oversaw phone hacking on an industrial scale, for the record. People are talking about stamping out racism, but you never will, especially in the current political climate. You'll never stamp out any of society's ills, but that is not an excuse to turn a blind eye. This should be a clarion call on many issues, including what is acceptable behaviour inside a football stadium. We bemoan the lack of atmosphere in modern stadia, but such instances are not how you rectify the problem.

Maybe this is a turning point in media coverage of Sterling. I won't hold my breath. Within a week the Daily Mail will be reporting on how he has eaten a £10 bagel just days after being dropped for the game against Hoffenheim. If Sterling is excused in future, certain newspapers will simply move onto someone else. Hits are more important than a moral code.
And the FA? They'll do sweet....

And where are all the Liverpool cabal that made his life hell for daring to want to leave the Liverpool family, for daring to want to better himself? They're all applauding his current stance, those few that have found a voice, without naturally recognising that they enabled all this. Their stance was never racial, it was due to a player wanting to leave their club, a concept they simply cannot grasp, but they unwittingly set in motion a sequence of events that leads us to the current day. They should be fucking ashamed.

Bluemoon Podcast Audio Script – Part 2

Hello..hello....the light's on good. I guess we should begin.
#ynwa

It's me again. I'm talking to you from the future once more.
2027 this time, one day after Professor Brian Cox has invented
time travel for audio clips, as there is no time to waste – things
are most definitely not getting better. You lied to us Brian.
#ynwa

I'm here to apologise. Last time I told all City fans to take a
stand against their owners, for the good of the world. Because
by failing to do so would lead to a post-apocalyptic world where
those that survived the purge of 2025 rummaged through bins
for food and fought off rats and cockroaches in a daily bid for
survival. Yeah, well you'll laugh at this, but turns out THAT was
the better option. #ynwa

You see, once my original message reached you all and went
viral on Lad Bible, not forgetting of course the 6450 page thread
on Bluemoon, you bitter blues all listened to me. You shaved off
your moustaches, broke free from your chains and stood up to
"the man". For the first time, empty seats started appearing at
matches. Cityzens went bust. Sales of pies plummeted, and a
boycott of City Square devastated the local community. All good
you say, but the problem is that I had not for one moment
contemplated the dire consequences of all this. I thought we'd
be making the world a better place. I was wrong. #ynwa
For some reason, rival fans did not applaud our moral stance,
but simply laughed at empty seats. The boycotts affected the
team's performances. Pep left, the Sheikh got bored, City
plummeted down the table, confidence draining away from the
mercenaries in blue day by day. And then IT happened.
Liverpool won the league. #ynwa

I repeat – Liverpool won the league. It gives me a chill just thinking about it, 8 years later. Feels like 80.

From that moment, it was all downhill for us all. Naturally the celebrations on Merseyside were as intense as they were long. A red haze hung over the north of England, Ireland and much of Scandinavia for many months. Jurgen Klopp was knighted, and became the face of Colgate. Similar honours were bestowed on James Milner and Jordan Henderson. Books were written, plays acted out, and then there was the poetry. The endless poetry.

If you can dream—and not make dreams your master;
If you can think—and not make thoughts your aim;
If you can meet with Benteke and Aquilani
And treat those two impostors just the same;
If you can fill the unforgiving minute
With sixty seconds' worth of distance run,
Yours is the Earth and everything that's in it,
And—which is more—you'll be a Sir James Milner, my son!

It was hell. A never-ending hell. A hell, that got worse, got hotter, somehow. Liverpool strengthened further in the summer, and soon, with City no longer rivals and Jose Mourinho signed up for another six years at Old Trafford, the coast was clear for Liverpool to dominate Europe once more, especially once rebellions started against Barcelona's Qatar state sponsorships, and Real Madrid's controversial appointment of David Moyes as manager. By now, Sarri lived permanently in an oxygen tent. #ynwa

Soon Liverpool football team and its fan base ruled the world as they had always wanted to. They could finally walk the walk as well as talk the talk. There were a lot of memes in the summer of 2019.

The power they had energised them further and seeped into society. They were everywhere – I guess it was inevitable that soon they would hold positions of power, and assert themselves on society as a whole. Now they control every facet of daily life, and they cannot be defeated. A cult can only destroy itself.

183

I try and keep the window shut most of the time not just because of the music, but also cos the constant pyro stings my eyes. The rulers are big on flags, and symbolism. Everyone worships he that is known simply as King Kenny, a mysterious other-worldly figure thought to look over "the family". That's what we all are now. The family. #ynwa

Every night we all have to eat a lamb or beef stew. It was nice the first time, kind of, less so the 300th time. I work six days a week, making flags and scarves. It pays for the stew, kindling and re-education lessons for the kids. The biggest flag I've made was over 20 feet tall, with something on it about chicken kievs. It made little sense to me. #ynwa

Boss Nights are now compulsory for our own sake, where we all congregate in a nightclub and sing Liverpool songs. Allez allez allez. The party ensure attendance, via their gangs of Redmen. Their tickling sticks are not what you think they are. Failure to do so means a month-long shift making Liver bird pin badges in a dusty basement. No one wants that.

A copy of Gideon's The Theory And Practice of Oligarchial Gegenpressing is by everyone's bed. Jurgen is infallible and all-powerful, though he still acquiesces to Kenny when necessary. It's not all bad though. I get an extra day off on Sunday, as it is Virgil Van Dijk day. It is recognition not just of him being the greatest defender in the history of association football, but also of his 7 consecutive PFA Player Of The Year awards. #ynwa

Life is a struggle though. You'll Never Walk Alone plays over loudspeakers in the street 24/7. It's driving me insane. Every day is a different style. It was being played on a harp yesterday. A fucking harp. To make matters worse, whether writing or speaking, we have to end at least one sentence a minute or each paragraph with the hashtag ynwa. #ynwa.

I mean, just listen. <opens window>. Occasionally it is broken up with Ferry Across the Mersey or the Theme Tune from Bread. Apparently that's linked to why I live on Boswell Street, next to Avaline Place.

I digress. I must cut to the chase. It is not too late, if I understand time travel correctly, which I still don't to be honest. We must try though. Try and change history. Yet again that duty falls on you blues. The world watches and the world waits. This is what you must now do, and I am sure this time. Nothing can be worse than this.

So ignore what I said on the last recording. Be blue, be proud. Stand up for you club. Support your team, go to matches, Drink in the success. Buy a £3 kit kat at the bar. Buy every kit. Rubbish FFP on Twitter. And when you see Raheem Sterling, give him a hug from me. He wins the Ballon D'or eventually, you know? Well almost, he was pipped to it by Trent Alexander Arnold. Anyway, don't get downhearted when Wigan knock us out of the FA Cup again in March 2019. And February 2020. And January 2021.

Keep the faith. Walk on through the wind, Walk on through the rain, Though your dreams be tossed and blown, Walk on walk on with hope in your heart. Oh shit, the indoctrination has worked. It's too late to save me, but it's not too late for you. #ynwa

And I'm being honest here, a post-apocalyptic landscape is not *that* bad, now I come to think about it. It has its perks. Like when you find some fresh road kill, or the acid rain eases off for an hour or two. I for one welcomed our new communist overlords. The weather hasn't changed much so you'll see the sun occasionally too. Just think of the alternative, and decide what future you want. For you, for your children, for their children. For your guinea pigs.

Oh, and put all your money on Harry Redknapp winning I'm A Celebrity, Get Me Out Of Here in 2018. No, seriously. I hope this reaches you in time to make a few quid.

Good luck blues. We're all counting on you. #ynwa

Champions League: Manchester City 2 Hoffenheim 1

A game of little value with City safely through already, and top spot 99% certain, as it turned out. Leroy Sane scored twice as City reached the knockout round for the sixth successive season. Nevertheless, City had to come from behind, after the visitors scored a 16th minute penalty. The intensity was clearly down for this game, and the sloppiness that followed would surprise few. Hoffenheim themselves had slight hopes of qualifying for the Europa League, but you wonder if they truly believed that was something to aim for on the night.

Laporte's foul to hand the visitors the initiative, a rare blot in his copybook, spurred City into life, and eventually the home side prevailed.
And how. The equaliser will be forgotten in the annals of history, in a season of astonishing moments and a glut of goals, but it was a stunning free kick, on the stroke of half-time. The 2nd half winner could never match that, but was still a nice finish after a good counter-attack that he began before exchanging passes with Sterling.

So after that opening day disaster, City rallied to somehow top the group with 5 points to spare. As alluded to previously, this was helped not only by them winning lots of games, but the astonishing number of draws in non-City games. The other three teams struggled to string together victories, which eased City's passage considerably. Though naturally, 13 points was always going to be enough whatever the other results. This gave Pep the confidence to allow Foden game time, who was denied a wonder goal by the keeper tipping over an angled volley late on. And thus, as group leaders, City have a better chance of a reasonable draw for the Round of 16. Fingers crossed.

BUT MOST IMPORTANT OF ALL - this was the week that Phil Foden signed a new contract, and committed his future to City. I was never worried he would not – he has no desire to leave the club, ever, but it's still great to see it confirmed. He's one of our own, and I can't wait to see him flourish in the coming years. There will be much debate about the amount of game time he is getting, but he is still just 18 years old. He has time on his side, everyone needs to be patient. Pep does not want to loan him out, preferring to see him learn from the world class talent surrounding him on the training pitch, and I am fine with that. With time, he should get more and more minutes on the pitch, and only next season will we see him fly, I imagine. What a talent.

Premier League: Manchester City 3 Everton 1

It's the time of the year for hard-earned wins.

Manchester City may well be in a lull right now. It's hard to tell when the bar is set so high, but have no doubt they are not at peak levels right now, like most other teams I imagine. It's mid-December, freezing rain is lashing down, players are dropping like flies and the opposition are on the up (in my opinion). All in all it was job done for the home side, needing to perform having been knocked off the top of the table the previous weekend, a feeling they have not experienced very often. With Liverpool playing the next day, against mid-table fodder*(ahem), there was a certain amount of pressure on the Citizens therefore, and they responded well. This was no classic performance, but it was enough, and whilst the visitors could easily have scored more, the home side could have scored a lot, lot more. What's more, having played on the Wednesday night and then asked to do so Saturday lunchtime against a side that had the midweek off, it was most definitely about the result and little else. The added bonuses were much needed goals for a maligned striker, a run out for a returning star player and a loaded bench suggesting City have much of their squad depth back for subsequent games.

Gabriel Jesus is back.

It's easy to forget that Jesus has a Champions League hat-trick under his belt this season, but it was still clear that he needed a goal or two. Sometimes we forget that players are just human beings like the rest of us, doing their jobs, with worries, stress and heartache off the field, because they're no different apart from their ability to kick a pig's bladder hard and accurate. Gabriel Jesus has travelled across the world to a new culture and a very new climate as a young man and is expected to perform week in and week out. After the game he spoke of how his family are now in Manchester and how that has helped him, and the results are clear to see. Gabriel has always been a team player and there has been no lack of effort from him in that respect, but there have been signs that his game was improving in other areas recently, and with Sergio still not fully match-fit, this was a perfect time to add goals to his game. Let's hope he now kicks on, confidence enriched, the support of his family removing the stresses of everyday life, allowing him to flourish on the pitch.

As are some big names….

No Premier League team has ever recorded a 100% win rate over the Christmas period, which shows how brutal this period is. The Centurions of course fell short at Crystal Palace last season, and very nearly lost their unbeaten run too. Teams like City can hardly complain, their squad depth allowing them to rotate, a luxury teams such as Palace can ill-afford to do. Nevertheless, the human body is not designed to play high-level sport so incessantly, so it is reassuring to see some of City's absent stars back, or close to being back.

Kevin De Bruyne may have shown rustiness when he stepped onto the Etihad pitch, but boy was it good to see him on there. Sergio Aguero's abductor injury was thankfully not too serious as he made the bench, and City could even rest Raheem Sterling and John Stones. The long-term injury to Benjamin Mendy and the medium term one for David Silva are the only notable absentees, which is not bad at this time of year, though an injury to Ederson will ram home the consequences of Bravo's long-term injury too, whatever you may think of him.

The absence of Silva and also Danilo for an unspecified period of time are inconvenient, as against Everton Kyle Walker and Bernardo Silva were two players who looked like they need a break – they are needed right now though, as putting John Stones at right back was hardly a roaring success against Hoffenheim, and Phil Foden is not yet fully trusted for tough games.

Changing the defence has its pitfalls.

Rotation is of course inevitable at this time of year, if not throughout the season. No player can play over 50 games a season even if super-fit, and even Aymeric Laporte got a game off recently. However, I've always felt that a stable defence relies on a central defensive partnership, and that it's one of the most important areas of the pitch. Laporte and Stones certainly seemed to have built such a partnership, but recently they have often not played together, and the opposition has been afforded much more chances per game. There may be other extenuating circumstances of course, in fact there almost certainly are, but the rotation has certainly taken away some of the defensive steel, temporarily at least. Nicolas Otamendi did not have a good game against Everton, reverting to his old self, leaving Fabian Delph as the last line of outfield defence a few times in the centre of the penalty area. Everton's goal deflected off Delph, whilst Walcott nipped ahead of him to fire over when he should have scored.

Wobbles aplenty, but this squad should be able to cope. Should City win at Leicester this week in the Carabao Cup, then January will be just as hectic, so the rotation of players will not stop anytime soon.

Everton's future is bright.

City's 2nd and 3rd goals against Everton seemed to suggest a woeful absence of competent defending, City's goal scorers finding themselves in acres of space yards from the goal. In fact, the first goal too showed the visitors' inability to pass out from defence and a habit of panicking when pressed. Nevertheless, there is a lot to admire in this current Everton squad, though after the Sam Allardyce reign, I guess it's easy to be positive. This team is talented though, with a better balance to it before, the likes of Digne, Mina and Bernard added to an injection of promising youth players and the old guard next to revitalised players such as Keane, Sigurðsson, and England's Number 1 keeper, meaning they can be confident about the future. For me Walcott is still a weakness in the side, and that area needs boosting, along with a top class striker, but Silva has got the team ticking over nicely, even if results don't quite prove that just yet. The problem is that they remain stuck in the second tier mini-league that exists in the Premier League. If you had told an Everton fan a couple of years ago that they would be jostling for league positions with Manchester United, they probably would have been overjoyed, but it turns out that this simply means they still have a lot of work to do. Breaking into the top 4 or 5 will not be easy.

Goals: Gabriel Jesus (22' minutes, 50' minutes), Sterling (69' minutes)

*United, obv

CHAMPIONS LEAGUE DRAW

And it is Schalke that come out of the hat – and we can't complain about that.

Jose Mourinho departs – Bluemoon Podcast Audio Script

It was the news all City fans had been dreading – the news you knew would come one day, but you woke up each morning hoping, praying, that this was not the day. A serious injury to Kevin De Bruyne? A transfer request from Leroy Sane? Season ticket prices going up again? Being moved from your normal seat for one game? No, much worse than that – Manchester United had finally parted company with the special one, Jose Mourinho.

So off he trundled, just the £20m or so richer, freed from his prison cell at the Linton Travel Tavern, for a short break before he poisons another club. And despite all that poisoning, astonishingly he still retained the support of a hard core section of the United support, who in a cult-like frenzy repeated the mantra that the problems lay elsewhere. There were of course many problems elsewhere, but if you couldn't see that the sulking, spiteful, miserable egotist at the helm was not the main one, then I pity you.

And I have a theory as to why United fans did not accept, at least publically, what was staring them, and the rest of us, in the face. That Jose Mourinho was a lousy, lousy manager for United. There was desperation for him to succeed because of the two failures that had preceded him, and because they had to pretend to like and support a man they had previously despised. For so many reasons, it had to work, and some never gave up hope that it would even when United resembled a pub side week-in, week-out.

And accepting defeat would mean admitting what they've known for a while, the elephant in the room, that Jose Mourinho was hired specifically to win the title for United, and to put it in even plainer terms, he was appointed as a direct response to City hiring Pep, and to get one over him. Now remind me, how did that go?

Yes that's right, little old City, the team whose name nobody knows, the irrelevance of a joke club, now call the shots in Manchester to the extent of making our cross-city rivals, if you can call them rivals, make desperate last-chance appointments to try and stay on an even keel. And not only managerial appointments either. Can there be little doubt that the likes of Alexis Sanchez and Fred were signed not to address problem areas in the squad, but to try and make a statement to City and the rest of the footballing world. Now remind me, how did those two signings go?

But with Mourinho, the PR war waged by the likes of Comical Ali himself, Duncan Castles, made sense in the battle to persuade United fans that not only was Mourinho the right man for United, the man to bring back the glory years, a born winner, but that he would beast Pep Guardiola, the manager they secretly wanted, the manager many journalists were saying preferred to go to United even after he had privately agreed to join City. Gary Neville has said this week that when Mourinho arrived, he was a banker, almost guaranteed to win the title. They made a pact with the devil because they truly believed he was their saviour, bless 'em. Funny old world isn't it?
Of course it's a different world now. United are no longer the playground bullies, and they have made disastrous decision after disastrous decision trying to rectify the situation. What more proof could you have of a power shift than City pulling out Rotherham, Schalke and Burton Albion in three recent cup draws? We've truly arrived now.

But back to United for a cheap laugh. This desperation to beat Pep and win a title permeated throughout the club and led to all long-term plans for progression being thrown out of the window. It permeated into the transfer deals they carried out, the final nail in the coffin, the need to throw huge amounts of money at ready-made players with little or no re-sell value because they wanted success now. By the end of Jose's reign this week, they're further away than ever from achieving their goals.

Ed Woodward knew this when he hired Mourinho. Plenty of board members foresaw how it would turn out too, but Woodward rolled the dice, and gambled on getting Jekyll rather than Hyde. It was a terrible call. The reaction this dismissal is telling. Sadness amongst the laughs from rival fans. Spanish newspaper Sport wonder why Madrid would be interested in Jose, saying his football clock has stopped and the game moved on. They also call him 'the most toxic and poisonous character who has passed through Spanish football'. That's quite an achievement.

The current situation is farcical, but the likes of Woodward and the Glazers just keep on digging. Now they have a caretaker manager for six months, and I can only assume this is because they have identified someone in the summer that they cannot get now. But if Ole Gunnar Solskjaer had never played for Manchester United, would anyone be calling his appointment a good one, with his track record? If we assume not, then why is it a good appointment because he did play for them?! Ah yes, that old chestnut about him "understanding" the club. I wonder just how many extra points United will gain because their manager understands the club, whatever that may mean? What is it he understands precisely? Their legendary DNA? The need to attack and play youth? Which set of fans does not want those two things anyway? United fans are no different. It was this flawed idea that an insider would work best that has had me pleading for it to be given to Giggsy til the end of the season, or others from the Class of 92, for over 5 years now. One day, though this will have to do for now.
And when Paul Ince is arguing about the need for a United man, then you know the idea is flawed.
He said this week that "the caretaker manager should have an understanding of Man United, and if you look at who has links to the club but is external, that doesn't leave many realistic options. You'd look at someone who has managed at a decent level, and knows it inside out." He then suggested Steve Bruce or Mark Hughes. This stuff really writes itself sometimes.

Whilst the likes of City and Liverpool move on and progress, United's treading of water whilst dressed in a gold sequined bathing suit has left them years behind. They don't have the players for someone like Pochettino to turn things around in a matter of months. They need another transition period, to follow on from the previous four they've had since Alex Ferguson left, a man who sowed the seeds of destruction himself by ostracising previous owners over the small matter of some horse semen then suggesting David Moyes as his successor. They truly are the owners of cups for cock ups now, as City prepare for their 10th cup semi-final in a decade. One day United will get things right, they're too powerful and too rich not to, but in the meantime we may as well enjoy the ride, for however long it lasts. Because for United fans, the worst thing that could happen was to hit a period of gross underachievement just as their two main rivals got their act together and sped off over the horizon. Just wait until Leeds get promoted.

Carabao Cup Quarter Final: Leicester City 1 Manchester City 1 – Manchester City win 3-1 on penalties.

Groundhog Day at the King Power Stadium as City once more draw 1-1 before progressing on penalties to reach the semi-final of the League Cup. Once more it was not a game that captured the imagination, but it featured Kevin, so I'm happy.

Yet again, City are doing just enough to progress in a tournament that is way down in the list of their priorities. As it is for most of their opponents too. Pep's line-ups may not be stellar, but they are strong enough to prove that he wants to win everything. Time will tell where such an approach takes us.

Thankfully City are becoming quite adept at penalty shoot outs. And they needed to be, though this was not the perfect set of kicks. Leicester's were worse though. A low-quality shootout saw Leicester miss three penalties while a dinked attempt went wrong for Raheem Sterling before Zinchenko emphatically thumped the decisive kick into the top corner to send his side through.

De Bruyne calmly put City ahead after 14 minutes. Other chances were not taken before sloppy defending allowed Albrighton to equalise after 73 minutes. No extra time anymore, so straight to penalties it was, and I make that 5 in a row for City. Long may it continue.

In such a competition, at this time of year, this is the definition of the result being king. Analysing anything else seems pointless. This tournament has been terribly kind to City in previous years and given us fans loads of great memories, but if City fail, then so be it. Little sleep would be lost.

But what was even more helpful was the subsequent semi-final draw. The strain of a long, brutal season and a packed Christmas schedule meant games were unrelenting. There were two big teams left in the competition, and one unexpected one in Burton Albion who shocked Middlesbrough in the quarter finals. City drew Burton, taking the pressure off by avoiding two games against Chelsea or Tottenham.

The Week of Hell: Manchester City 2 Crystal Palace 3, and Leicester City 2 Manchester City 1.

It's best I group these two together – I'm sure you'd rather I moved on. I commented previously that no team has ever won every game over the Christmas schedule, and right on cue. City blew their chances to break that particular record. It's hard to know what went wrong over these two games, but they have undoubtedly put a dent in City's attempts to retain their title. No invincible tag, no lead at the top of the Premier League. A disastrous week.

City do not lose many games in which they score first, however difficult the opposition maybe. To do it once is careless. To do it twice in a week, against "mid-table" opposition is almost inconceivable. In the first game Ilkay Gundogan opened the scoring after 27 minutes, yet by half-time City were behind. It got worse after half-time, before Kevin De Bruyne fluked in a consolation goal. Against Leicester, an early goal from Bernardo Silva seemed to calm the nerves, but slack marking soon saw Albrighton (him again) equalise before they scored an 81st minute winner. That was a cracker of a shot, as was Andros Townsend's earlier goal of the season contender, and it was one of those weeks.

The performance levels were hard to explain, perhaps the season simply catching up on the players. There was a lethargy in the play missing from the opposition, and the end result was a seven point deficit at the top of the table, with Southampton away and Liverpool up next.

Not good. Not good at all.

Kyle Walker was disastrous against Palace, and his form is creating murmurs of discontent. In his defence, we are talking about one of a number of players who have been playing football almost continuously now for 18 months. The strain was bound to affect some, if that is indeed the reason for his slump. No surprise therefore to see him on the bench for the Leicester match.

And to top it all off, a red card, a weird one for Fabian Delph too. It wasn't a clear red, though his reaction after kicking the ball away was unconventional, but either way, you get the feeling the caution will place him on Pep's naughty step for a while to come.

Crystal Palace were actually prove to be an excellent side away from home during the season, but still....and Leicester were in poor form, with their manager under pressure and soon to depart. By the end of the season, his successor would have gone too. These were damaging, unexpected results. And with 2019 yet to arrive, City's league campaign was in danger of collapsing. A defeat to Liverpool would mean the end of that campaign, by the early in the New Year. Defending a title was once more proving tougher than anyone could imagine. With the knives out, discussion once more turned to a quiet summer of transfer business, with Mahrez the only arrival. Had the league champions once more failed to drive home an advantage from a position of strength? It seemed to be the story of the past decade.

Happy New Year all. And bah humbug.

Premier League: Southampton 1 Manchester City 3

The vultures can be called off, for now. City fashioned a competent and mostly professional performance to get partly back on track, and see out 2018 with three points. They had to.

Ralph Hassenhutl was now in charge of the home side, which worried me further. I wanted the old useless manager in charge, the one and only Mark Hughes, not some new, vibrant whippersnapper with fresh ideas and a reputation to enhance. Damn you footballing gods.

So with the season in danger, there was probably little surprise to see Vincent Kompany back in defence, and also Zinchenko too, now bizarrely our clear first-choice available left-back. Like the guy he replaced, he too would have an interesting 90 minutes.

Anyway, nothing to worry about. City won. It helps to have David and Fernandinho back, and Riyad Mahrez got another start.

It was nervy though, no doubt about it. Twice in the first half Charlie Austin found himself in space but messed up his big chances. City were creating too, as the home side showed little intention in shutting up shop. In the end that probably suited City. And with just 10 minutes on the board, City got ahead. Mahrez to Bernardo who crossed for David Silva to thump home the ball. It was the 9th goal City had scored in the opening 15 minutes of a match this season.

Aguero then had a point-blank chance saved, from just three yards out. Mahrez burst forward and curled the ball just wide, but he had options to either side.
And for a short while, it seemed that City would pay for their profligacy. Southampton were edging their way into the game. And when Zinchenko dawdled on the ball, Holjberg

dispossessed him, burst forward and lashed the ball in from just outside the hour.

Worrying times, but with a bit of luck and better finishing, City turned it round. Before that though there was a strongish claim for a penalty after Zinchenko collided with Ward Prowse. It was on the edge, and the young Ukranian was having his shakiest 15 minutes of the season. You've seen them given and all that. To be honest though, it was more of a dive than a foul, and not some miscarriage of justice for Liverpool fans to spend the summer poring over.

Though obviously they will anyway if City prevail.

And then some real luck — it seems a rarity nowadays, not that City require it most of the time. A Sterling cross deflected twice before finding the back of the net, and City were thankfully back in front. Soon after and Zinchenko made amends with a nice cross that Aguero rose to head home off the keeper's soft hands, and somehow City were two clear at half-time.

Phew. And that is how it ended. A game of two halves. Southampton rarely threatened as City held on to what they got. There was still time for Aguero to clip the bar though and for Sterling to have a glorious chance saved. And even for Mahrez to have a one-on-one saved too. Oh and a red card for Holjberg. By the end, City were utterly dominant.

The deficit remained seven points. And next up was the big one.

2019: January

Premier League: Manchester City 2 Liverpool 1

Wow. That was intense. I aged last night, but at a rather quicker rate than normal. That was pure football, on the edge, 90(+5) minutes of distance run. Blood, toil and sweat. This is descending into shit poetry hour, my apologies.

But what a game. Two sets of players that gave it their all, a game decided on very fine lines. 11mm from a goal, lunging challenges, vital blocks, 13km distance run by Bernardo, saves, misses, penalty appeals, Vincent calling Salah a pussy, and ultimately one team re-igniting a title race.

This was City playing a different game at times, and having to against a team that are undoubtedly the real deal. It will be rare that City won't dominate possession, but they didn't need to in the end. On another day the result could have been different, but that is football. Liverpool have had so many breaks in this fixture in recent times, that I guess we were owed one, though still they reminisce about the injustice of a fully deserved Mane red card over a year ago. Perhaps it's time to wipe clean the slate about who has had luck and move on – 4 points is the difference and there is all to play for. Well, move on after I mention it again later in this piece.

And whilst I suggested pre-match that this was not an absolutely must-win game (just a not-lose one), looking at Liverpool's kind fixture list in the coming weeks has rather altered my previous view – don't expect the lead to dwindle any further in the coming weeks.

Still, as the pessimist I often I am, I declared in the lead-up to the match that I hate football and sometimes wish I was not so passionate about it. Instead of three days of nerves and erratic bowel movements, I could have had the heating whacked up to full whilst relaxing watching Luther. But then football, And City's 14 players and one manager reminded me **why** I, we, are so passionate about football. It gives you experiences like no other.

So, a game of fine lines. I personally felt that, whatever your views on the Kompany tackle, it was foolish defending, putting a referee in a position where he could make a decision that could wreck our season. Since then my position has softened, as many have pointed out that the poor Stones pass left him few options, and that such moments are a part of football that are depressingly rare in the modern game. Either way, I don't think it was a clear red, so it's hardly a major controversy, unless you are clutching at straws of course.

And perhaps this match answered some questions raised in recent times about City's mental strength in adversity, as adversity is something they rarely have to encounter in the past year. Well there was mental strength in abundance last night, no more so than after Liverpool's equaliser, when many a City team would have buckled. City on this occasion did not, and rose to the occasion.

I read a few mentions to that this was not a high quality match. I couldn't disagree more – it was the epitome of quality. Quality does not have to mean scissor kicks, 30 yard free kicks or last-ditch tackles. Miguel Delaney called it one of the best games he has been to in recent years. Every player gave their all, and quality play was in abundance, especially from the likes of Fernandinho, and Bernardo Silva, beating his own "distance-covered" record, a record previously achieved at Wembley v Spurs. Bernardo clearly puts the yards in for the big matches. Or, in the words of Barney Ronay: *Bernardo Silva, a man born to glide and twirl and address the ball with his own feather-quilled left foot, careered about the place like a city-centre nightclub bouncer on New Year's Eve.*

And like at Anfield earlier in the season, despite the fact that Sane and Aguero and Firmino scored, was not about the wealth of attacking talent on the pitch. For me it was more about midfield, and that was where the game was won and lost. This is why Fernandinho's and Bernardo Silva's performances were even more important. And credit too to Laporte, in difficult circumstances putting in a good performance, limiting Salah to 32 touches on the night. But this was not just about how good players played, but attitude, effort and mental strength. City's players passed the test when many, me included, doubted them.

And as these instances never, ever get reported (can't think why), for the third time Robertson got away Scot-free for a penalty area foul on Raheem Sterling. I mean, if we want to talk about injustices during the match, we must surely mention this, yes?

Of course it would not be Liverpool if defeat was accepted and we all moved on to the next game. Hey, it's not surprising from such a deluded minority that they truly believe the vast majority of football fans are behind them winning the league. When City's merry bunch of bitter-ex-Chelsea-fans-plastic-oil-funded-human-rights-abuses-deniers are getting more support than you, you need to take a serious look at yourself. Petitions over goal-line technology, cries over no red card for Kompany, and even complaints about grass length and pitch watering. Let it go. The complaints about Kompany would be raised by any set of fans, but the other talk is quite frankly embarrassing. After all, their team is great, the pressing is mechanical and effective, their team have an innate understanding of each other's position, their passing is precise and crisp, their attack electric. You still won't win them all though, and whilst every team has had luck this season – Lamela missed a great chance late on at Wembley, Fernandinho could have conceded a penalty at a key time at home to Bournemouth, Everton's early miss from Richarlison the other week etc etc – Liverpool have more than had their share, so there's little to be gained by bemoaning luck now. It does not all "even out" of course, the world does not work like that, but they have escaped injuries to key players (though a good training regime has surely helped), got an amazing break against Everton, and have won games aplenty whilst underwhelming. We won't dwell on Mahrez's penalty.

So we're back to a three-horse race, talk of the league becoming uncompetitive shown to be a tad premature. Spurs will be as happy as anyone that City won, whilst bemoaning the possible consequences of losing at home to Wolves – let's hope City don't make the same mistake.
And so onto the domestic cup competitions, and a raft of changes no doubt. Perhaps we will see De Bruyne as he seeks to regain full match fitness, Pep's decision not to introduce him to the intensity of last night's match proving to be a wise call with hindsight. With Foden no doubt returning and the out-of-favour Walker surely featuring, it could still be quite a strong side, as should the side against Burton, the desire to get the job done in the 1st leg surely key. The quadruple is not necessarily back on track, but the result against Liverpool will hopefully be a springboard for the a successful 2nd half of the season.

Manchester City 7 Rotherham 0 & Manchester City 9 Burton Albion 0

Well this was a weird week. It's not often (by which I mean, never), that you see your team score sixteen goals in front of you within a few days. But that's what happened.
This was of course City's return to domestic cup competitions, and proof that sometimes Pep Guardiola cannot win. If he had played really weak sides, he would have been criticised. As he was, he was accused of disrespect by playing a strong side. Mark Ogden even commented as such at City scoring more than six goals. You really couldn't make this shit up.

Now I wasn't entirely sure City needed to play teams this strong against much weaker opposition when there is a long season and four fronts to fight on. But Pep knows rather more about this football lark than me, and I understand his logic that the first team needs regular football, needs rhythm by doing so, and he needs to treat all opposition seriously.

Anyway, for me, limping to both games with ankle ligament damage that may or may not have been caused by celebrating Sane's goal v Liverpool a tad too enthusiastically, I was able to enjoy a constant stream, no torrent of goals. And to be honest, when David Silva missed a sitter at what may have been 6-0 or 7-0 in one of the games (they merge into one), I was almost relieved. I was getting embarrassed at the ease of it all. City were clearly on course to break yet more goal-scoring records this season. And another trip to Wembley was now assured. I'm kinda glad they didn't score ten too. I was there in 1987 v Huddersfield, that will do me.

It should also be pointed out that nowadays Pep can make 10 changes and the team still looks super-strong.

For the record, the 16 goals were scored by Sterling, Foden (2 – the first a bit of a fluke), Jesus (5), Mahrez (2), Otamendi, Sane,

De Bruyne, Zinchenko, Walker and an own goal. Some nice stat peddling, and Jesus got 4 in the Burton game. De Bruyne even scored a header. Crazy days.

And so City become the first side in the top four tiers of English football to score at least seven goals in back-to-back matches in all competitions since Leeds United did so back in October 1967 (9-0 v Spora Luxembourg in the Fairs Cup and 7-0 v Chelsea in the top flight).

As for Pep: *"I am off for a glass of wine with Nigel Clough. I know how important his father was for English football, he was a genius. Incredible. It will be a pleasure to share some minutes with him."*

Class.

Manchester City & Respect

Ah respect. A cherished thing, sadly lacking in modern society it seems, especially in the football arena. Give me just a little r.e.s.p.e.c.t. and I'd be happy, as would City's fan base, no doubt. So let's find out what it means to me.
Sorry.
Respect is earned of course, organically, like United's success in the 1990's. The football authorities tried giving some to referees too, but that initiative soon died a death. After all, it seems it is a footballer's right to shout at referees for 90 minutes. And if you are Arsene Wenger, Neil Warnock or Sean Dyche, amongst others, the manager's right too.
But let's run through how City could have been more respectful over the past fortnight, as a few journalists with their own hot-takes have suggested respect has been lacking.
They could of course have cut the grass, not watered the pitch, not sang an edited version of one of Liverpool's songs that they themselves had pinched from another team, not allowed their keeper out of his area late on in a game already won, played a string of youth players in a cup semi-final to make it more competitive, but having not done so, at least had the decency to have scored a precise number of goals, namely six, so as not to disrespect the professional players they were up against. And all this to avoid becoming the first team in the history of football to be criticised for **trying too hard**. They should have played Phil Foden in every match irrelevant of the squad needs, especially more senior members who needed to build up match fitness. Sterling could have avoided doing one step over in the presence of Juan Mata. We could have avoided singing about going to Wembley when the 1st leg of the Carabao Cup semi-final had not even finished, the team ahead by a mere 9 goals. Arrogance and disrespect there in one handy package.

Of course, the morons that shape social media discourse could have engaged just 5 brain cells (excluding most Talksport presenters, admittedly) and realised that City youngsters played in the Checkatrade Trophy at Spotland 24 hours before the Burton match, and with each victory the tournament becomes more and more important. Should we throw that competition just so some two-bit journalist is happy? Answers on a postcard. Anyway, we've got it all to come again, as the Checkatrade tie against Sunderland is the day before the 2nd leg, and the football authorities won't move it. Pep might have to play a strong side again. Or dig deep into our academy.

But back to respect. And what of the instances you may not know about? The past fortnight, after all, is just scratching the surface. What of the many times, the nouveau-rich oil-soaked blue berts have disrespected rival clubs and fans in the past few years? You may need to sit down if not doing so already, as some of this may shock you. I'm surprised Duncan Castles hasn't mentioned it all previously. After all, there was little more disrespectful than flaunting the club's wealth than getting 100 points in the league. Why didn't we ease off when we hit 90?

But respect comes in many forms. Which sadly, brings me on to empty seats. Nah, you really don't want to hear any more on that tedious topic. But there are a couple of side issues that do baffle me, though more fool me for trying to explain the rants of the cretins that inhabit twitter and make it a no-go area even after my side has scored nine goals or eased past a tricky Wolves side, or even beaten Liverpool. We all know the real reason that the jibes come. Because our team is better than their team, so they need a new angle. The human rights faux outrage soon died down as Liverpool surged ahead in the league.

Anyway, those side issues – the first one is the idea that a magic money tree appears for fans of successful clubs, like the one Teresa May has when she's in trouble. You see, when fans and media criticise seats not being sold, who precisely are they criticising? Are they criticising the lifelong fans who have had to make sacrifices for a blindingly obvious reason. That reason is this - I can go to a fewer percentage of City games now compared to ten years ago not because I am less of a fan, but because successful sides play a lot more games than unsuccessful ones, and all the time my wage stays as low as ever. Please buy my books. Now I get round this by having debt, but plenty of people are actually sensible with their finances. As our football team has got better in the past decade, money has not suddenly appeared in my account to pay for 10 Wembley visits, 17 semi-final ties, Champions league ties galore, season DVDs and a lot more besides. So if you're not having a go at fans for not automatically aligning their wages to match City's rise, and you're not attacking people for not having enough money, then who else are you blaming for the empty seats? Families who refuse to put their kids to bed after midnight when there is a midweek game? The only other possible answer is that you are criticising unknown people for not becoming glory hunters and supporting City once they started winning stuff, thus filling in the gaps. What a truly bizarre and tedious argument.

The second is a peculiar British trait or disease if you will, the bizarre reluctance to accept the thought that just maybe it is not scandalous for bigger grounds allowed to have empty seats. Or any ground for that matter. The bizarre notion that having 45,000 fans in a 50,000 stadium is embarrassing compared to a full 40,000 stadium. Do you think the Spanish banter boys are out on force on a weekly basis on twitter mocking Barcelona, and their average of 30,000 empty seats? Somehow I doubt it, as they have better things to do, like grouting or clearing out ear wax.

As I mentioned on Twitter this week, I once debated empty seats with a United fan more sussed than most. He's Mancunian and goes to matches, though has strangely lost his passion in the past few years. I mentioned to him that United have empty seats at some matches too, as they have many times since that conversation. He said that was different as they had a bigger ground. I pointed out City had a bigger ground than Rochdale, so what was his point? He changed the subject, because as always with these moronic arguments, there's no thought or logic between the claims, it's just part of the need to attack,

attack, attack, and if you can't do it about the football, then other ways must be found. His argument was essentially thus; that there is a magic stadium capacity, agreed as correct by United, Liverpool, Arsenal fans etc above which it is ok to have empty seats but below which it is not acceptable, at least not if you're called Manchester City or are quite good at football. Conveniently this magic figure that is shrouded in secrecy is greater than City's capacity and lower than United's. And that just about sums up how stupid most of these arguments are.

This is why fans of the team that have scored 18 more goals than any other team in Europe are faced with endless crap online even after a great result. Because the morons have taken over the internet, and destroyed any chance of reasoned debate. Micky Flanagan joked in a live show that idiots used to hide away in society, but now they loud and proud about their own stupidity. And they spend most of their time typing on a keyboard that Manchester City have 11 fans, before getting their mum to make their tea. Imagine being so utterly dense to type that and think you've been funny and burnt a few City fans. So in the end it all comes back to respect. Whatever City do, whatever they achieve, they will never get any, and I think most of us City fans are aware of this and accept it now. Because if we're not winning enough games we're winning too many games too easily, or our fans are not appreciating the football by staying at home.
So what does respect mean to me? Well, it has to be earnt. City's football has earnt some, and for those that can't appreciate that, it is their loss. They know it deep down of course, but respect works both ways. It about time sections of our media started earning some themselves.

Premier League: Manchester City 3 Wolverhampton Wanderers 0

Another professional performance against a side that would become a thorn in the side of many a big boy this season. As they already had done previously for City.

This was one of those rare occasions however where the match officials may well have given City a helping hand. And it was Boly at the centre of the controversy once more. With Sergio and Kevin on the bench, any help was gratefully received. But in the end victory was pretty stress-free, with Gabriel Jesus adding another brace to his recent tally. Despite sporadic time on the pitch, he has quickly headed up the goal scoring charts.

Also good to see Danilo in the team – not that I don't want to see Zinchenko. Danilo though has been really under-used for me, and rarely seems to let the team down. He's a perfect squad player, but he needs more football. We'll struggle to keep him otherwise.

It should be pointed out that the red card in the 19th minute came when City were already ahead. With 10 minutes gone, Sane burst down the left and a square pass easily found Jesus for him to slot home.

But once Wolves lost a man, it was probably match over. Boly slid in on Bernardo Silva as a loose ball was contested by both, and a red card followed. I can see justification for it, dangerous intent and all that, but it was harsh for me. One foot, on the floor, and if it's relevant, he got the ball too. It was a yellow at most I reckon. I wasn't complaining in my seat though.

Wolves had one half-chance, but once Sterling won a rather soft penalty (no dive, but contact was fleeting), then it was game over, as Jesus slotted home, before a Coady own goal with 12 minutes to go in the second half. Another three points, and that's all City can do for now – keep winning and hope Liverpool slip up.

Speaking of which – many City fans think Liverpool will implode at some point, when inevitable injuries hit, or the pressure of a title race. We'll see, but I'm not convinced.

Two days previously Liverpool had won 1-0 at Brighton, via a Salah penalty, after he was fouled. Fancy that, eh?

Premier League: Huddersfield Town 0 Manchester City 3: Five Things I Learned

With Liverpool scraping past Crystal Palace the previous day, it was another must-win game for the reigning champions as they travelled to a seemingly doomed Huddersfield Town, who disposed of their manager during the week (mutual consent my arse) and thus provided something of the unknown with caretaker manager Mark Hudson in charge. Despite being turned down for one of the most blatant penalties of the season, City ultimately cruised to victory despite a lacklustre first half. With a late winner for Spurs in the other game on Sunday, the title race remains very much alive.

After You, No After You

And so it continues. Liverpool win, and open up a 7 point gap, City then win to return the gap to 4. But not next time around. Without scanning the rest of the season, it's still probably safe to assume that Liverpool and City will have a large proportion of their remaining league games televised, so don't expect them to play at the same time any time soon. And next time around City play first, midweek, giving them the opportunity to close the gap to a single point, at least for 24 hours. A chance to put pressure on the league leaders, but they have to win. Fail to do so, and playing first will be a poisoned chalice and take the pressure off Liverpool. City have a great record at St James Park, and Newcastle's home record this season is woeful, but that was before Cardiff came to town. It will not be a walk in the park.

The Top Teams Are Not On Fire Right Now

Liverpool and Spurs crawled over the finishing line at the weekend with three points, and whilst City's score line suggests a much more comfortable afternoon, this was not a classic, it's fair to say. City did a job, and by the end it was fairly comfortable, but this was not the high intensity approach I had expected in another must-win game, especially in the first half. It is perhaps churlish to discuss negatives after a routine victory, but the lethargic nature of the first half was baffling. The home side may have had a bounce by changing their manager, kind of, but they are a poor side this season who have only mustered 13 goals in 21 games. Caretaker manager Mark Hudson made 6 changes, but whoever they picked, they were there for the taking. Pep Guardiola's posture in the dugout on the first half told its own story, and he no doubt had plenty of things to say at half-time. It worked, and a new and improved City side put the game to bed pretty quickly in the second half, then settled for what they had as they often do. Having said that, despite the appearance of easing off when a job is done (though not against Burton, obv), City passed the 100 goal mark during this game, easily the best tally in Europe.

Clean Sheets Should Always Be Cherished

It shouldn't have been a clean sheet of course, Mounie missing a sitter right at the death, but City will take it. After a long run without a clean sheet, City have now not conceded for 386 minutes. The opposition may have been varied in quality, but the clean sheets should give the defence confidence as we head towards the business end of the season. It should be noted that during that period City have also scored 23 goals. Liverpool's title charge has been built on the bedrock of a solid defence, but with injuries starting to hit at the back and three goals conceded against Crystal Palace, it will be interesting to see if that solidity has gone and costs them in the long run.

Sane is different class

If you apply the high standards that someone like Pep Guardiola would, you could easily claim that Leroy Sane is still a player who is developing, with further improvements to come. That is true, which makes what he is already so frightening for opposition defenders. Another goal for Sane, another assist. He is the stats king. Sane has provided 24 assists in the Premier League since the start of last season, at least six more than any other player in that timeframe. He has now been directly involved in 17 league goals for Man City this season. And he can, and should, get better.

Utter consistency is not his yet, and his decision making is not always perfect, but this is a player with the highest of ceilings. He must be near-impossible to play against when in full flow, his agility and tight ball control at speed a constant menace. It just baffles you even more to think he did not make the Germany world Cup squad in the summer. Whilst the early games of the season suggested a hangover for Sane from that snub, he has progressed nicely back to the top player we know he is. He can easily become one of the best players in the world within a couple of years.

Preparation Is Not Always Easy

Marcelo Bielsa has hogged the headlines this week as he laid bare to the world his methods and obsessive levels of opposition analysis. One comment he made this week that won't have received much attention was his point that he could not analyse Stoke's manager and his methods at the club as he was of course a new manager, so there was nothing to analyse. Instead he looked at his last batch of games at his previous club Luton instead. It did not do him much good, as they lost 2-1. A new manager is dangerous, and for obsessives like Bielsa, present a headache. You simply don't know how they will approach their first match until the team sheet lands and the match starts. Pep Guardiola is of course an obsessive too, and faced a similar dilemma this week once David Wagner had departed Huddersfield last Monday. And Mark Hudson stuck to the script by making six changes and injecting a bit of vitality and pace to the line-up. With the chasm in quality in the squads it should not matter of course, and in the end it did not, but the lack of penetration in that first half perhaps suggested that preparation can be undone by factors out of any manager's control.

Meanwhile, over at Anfield, a calamitous error by Julian Speroni - making his first appearance since December 2017 - handed Liverpool an advantage with the match poised at 2-2, the visitors' keeper scooping the ball towards his own net for Salah to poke in from on the line. You seriously have to wonder....

Carabao Cup: Burton Albion 0 Manchester City 1

In a way, the most pointless game of the season, but a new ground ticked off, and time to plan a trip to Wembley. To be fair, that planning was done the second the draw was made. My ankle ligaments had really given up functioning by now, so I hopped into the ground and out. The performance was irrelevant, but the team was still a bit stronger than I expected. Respect from Pep once more.

The main memory was how bloody cold it was, and how our fan base can annoy me so much sometimes. Mahrez was getting slagged off from minute one, whilst some clearly drugged up arses in the 2nd half were a disgrace, before a woman who had had enough of being criticised tried to start a fight with them at the end, and I did not blame her.

Some young lads let off a flare right in front of my face, but that was fine as they were a good laugh and harmless. It's the middle-aged, aggressive coked up angry men that are the problem, as any visitor to Wembley can probably confirm. Away games can be hard work.

At half-time, just to top it all off, someone let off a flare in the bar so it had to be evacuated. How we all laughed. Top bantz! Hey ho. We move on.

FA Cup: Manchester City 5 Burnley 0

A potential banana skin match, in a competition we have not
excelled at, which is a shame as I hold it in great esteem, and it
was the tournament that started off this great journey we're
currently on. Anyway, as it turned out, it was navigated with
ease.
City have now scored 30 goals in seven games in 2019 and won
all eight matches since losing 2-1 at Leicester in the Premier
League on 26 December.

Another strong side from Pep, as we have now come to expect.
Perhaps he sees this competition as one he needs in the
cabinet, after last season's limp exit. After all, he accumulates
trophies like I accumulate Just Eat receipts.
Danilo at left-back again, Jesus still up front, Kevin back and the
likes of Fernandinho, Bernardo and Gundogan further cemented
a strong line up.

City had gone close to scoring twice before Jesus obliged after
23 minutes, after a scintillating run. He keeps scoring, and this is
the type of skill we want more from him. If we must criticise
him, and we are allowed to, even at his tender age, it is the fact
that he has never felt like a natural goal scorer to me. In fact,
I've never quite decided what his position is, and that's
troublesome. Whilst some will say his recent spree has the feel
of flat-track bullying about it, goals give strikers confidence, and
something to build on. This opening goal was surely evidence of
that, as he closes on in Aguero's season goal tally.

After that, it was the definition of plain sailing, bar one good
chance for a Burnley equaliser early in the second half. City
went up a gear after that, and added four more, including an
own goal and a penalty from substitute Aguero.

And their chance? Yeah, Otamendi having one of his moments.
It's easy to forget that he was in the PFA Team Of The Year last

season, and was a rock that helped the team make history, having eradicated his sliding tackles and errors of judgment. All defenders have them, but I doubt he will be happy with the game time he has had this season. Life moves fast, and already you wonder if City are planning for a defence without him and the likes of Kompany in the coming years – or as soon as next season. We should be thankful that the likes of him and Danilo are at the club – the depth in this squad is sometimes taken for granted, but it is ridiculous.

The thing with this team is that if you miss a chance like Vydra's then they will make you pay, and that is what Bernardo Silva did soon after. The game felt over at this point. The fifth round beckoned, especially after Kevin De Bruyne's screamer from 25 yards in the 62 minute.
Oh, and 50,000 for an FA Cup match is damn good. But you knew that anyway.

Onwards and upwards....

Premier League: Newcastle 2 Manchester City 1

And back down to earth with a bump. I'm not sure what has just happened, but I'm pretty sure City's title challenge is over for this season. And yet again, they let a lead slip to lose a match they shouldn't. It's beyond frustrating, and Liverpool fans probably can't believe their luck this morning. Because win their game at home to Leicester City tonight, and they will be 7 points ahead, and the league title is within sight.

And all in a game where City scored after 24 seconds. I mean, how do you mess up from there?! Because of defensive sloppiness I guess, and the inability to kill off a game you have in your grasp. City once more seemed content to take what they had, before suddenly having nothing. They only have themselves to blame.

City tweeted yesterday about City's amazing record against Newcastle, being unbeaten in 22 games, 19 of which were victories. Some saw this as tempting fate, because that's how football fans work. Maybe they were right all along.

But first the good stuff, and the downright bizarre. City were ahead within 30 seconds, with the strangest of assists from Silva as he slipped, and all seemed well. Then they scored again.

Except that they did not. Kevin De Bruyne took a free-kick that Aguero expertly swept home. De Bruyne's reward for such quick-thinking was a yellow card for taking it before the referee had given permission. And thus, the goal was wiped out.
Now I understand that the referee might have given out instructions, though if you re-watch the clip there seems very little if any dialogue between the referee and De Bruyne. But to book him? I mean, seriously, when have you ever seen shit like this happen to ANY other team? It's laughable.
A free-kick is supposed to be an advantage to the fouled team. Why remove that advantage? Over the season I would see many

other moments of quick-thinking from such situations, but only one where the goal was disallowed and the taker of the kick booked. Go figure.

Nevertheless, City were not putting in a vintage performance. Newcastle were happy to sit deep and look to occasionally counter. But sadly for City they did not play as dead as the previous season's fixture that City won 1-0. And hey, we can't expect to just rock up at St James Park and stroll to victory. Rafa Benitez would prove once again this season that he can get big results and get more out of a side than the sum of its parts.

But still, after an early goal, this was a poor performance, and rather self-inflicted. Half-chances came and went, with David Silva having a header blocked on the line when perhaps he should have scored. But City could not double their lead, and Newcastle were occasionally dangerous. In the second half Sterling missed completely what could have been a simple tap in whilst David Silva had a shot straight at the keeper. In a away though, their two goals still came out of the blue. A bouncing ball prodded home by Rondon centrally, somehow, then a stupid concession of a penalty by Fernandinho. The damage was done.

Premier League: Liverpool 1 Leicester City 1
Oh hang on. Scrap everything I said the previous night. It's back on!
Against expectations, Liverpool could not take full advantage of City's slip up, and we still had a title challenge with a good few months of the season left.
So Liverpool increase their lead at the top of the table this week, yet it almost feels like a moral victory for City. Bullet dodged, for now.

Bluemoon Podcast Audio Script

It's embarrassing, but I'm going to tell you anyway. Different times and that. As a child, I used to go to my cousin's house a street or two away adorned in full City kit, socks included, to watch two teams none of which were ever Manchester City, play in the FA Cup Final. Not sure why, but there you go. In those days the day of the final was an occasion, after all. The tribalism was largely absent, the game itself was simply a big, big deal, in a world of three TV channels and games of conkers without protective eyewear. Still, normal attire would have sufficed, but I guess it was an event for all fans.

The TV was turned on in the morning, and stayed on. The build-up to the match was a major part of the event, from the recap of the road to Wembley, the discussion on teams, to the excitement as said teams disembarked from the coach, with cheery waves and occasional moustaches bristling in the London breeze. The mythical Twin Towers, Wembley Way, the pomp and ceremony, Abide with Me. Over-tight shorts, jumpers for goalposts. Different times and that. FA Cup moments have become enshrined in clubs' folklore. It matters.

And to me, Wembley was mythical. As the years progressed, it became even more mythical, as I harboured little hope of City ever playing there, carried scant hope of watching my team walk out the tunnel led by Mel Machin or Alan Ball. Or Steve Coppell, who couldn't even stay at the club long enough to manage just one FA Cup game. Eventually City broke the duck in typical fashion, a 3rd tier play-off final. Not how I had envisaged it, scrapping for survival on a miserable, rainy day, but thankfully the occasion had its own charms, as it turned out. You can stick your treble up your arse, sideways. I had experienced the thrill of Wembley, in the best possible manner. FYI, Full Members Cup Finals don't count.

Anyway, last week my Manchester City booked their sixth final date at Wembley in the past decade. Let's be honest, they had essentially booked it earlier than last week. Those 6 visits are before you chuck in a few semi-finals, a few Community Shields and ignoring the fact Spurs currently play there. It was so nailed on, I'll admit the train and accommodation was booked as soon as the semi-final draw was made. Not only have I now been to Wembley, I know the best way there, I know the London Underground line(s), I know the nearest hotels to Euston, the alternative places to stay within the M25, I'm already sick of Euston but still fond of the Euston Tap. If you're tired of a good pub, you're tired of life.

And it got me wondering to whether going to Wembley will ever get boring, will ever feel like a chore. Surely not, but eventually you just get used to it I guess. And never, as a child, could I have envisaged saying that in my lifetime. Though in those days I didn't know what envisaged meant anyway. And it got me wondering about Mauricio Pocchetino, and managing a club as a business concern rather than for the desire for your fan base to have as many magical days as possible.

Now I think Pochettino is doing an excellent job. He simply does not have the resources of City, and has built up an excellent squad that plays attractive football. A new stadium has only hampered his attempts at reinforcements even further. By slowly building he perhaps hopes one day to compete on all fronts. Nevertheless…..

Mauricio Pochettino may well be a fine manager, but he is wrong on winning trophies. Because winning trophies matters. It's the essence of being a football fan much of the time. I'm not saying that from a position of arrogance, claiming that winning make my club better than yours, that it's ALL about winning, but the hope that your club may persevere and have their time in the sun is what keeps many of us engrossed, keeps us going. Watching another club's captain lift a trophy makes me jealous. If you sat down a football fan as a child, or adult for that matter, and told them that the team they had just chosen to support would never win anything, would never get promoted, would never lift a single piece of silverware at any point, they'd soon change their mind. Change teams or follow darts or dressage instead. Sport is about winning as much as it is about taking part. If it isn't why celebrate a last minute winner, why celebrate anything? The managers whose only incentive is a top 4 place or to avoid relegation denies his club's fan base the chance of magical memories that last a life time. I understand the implications, mostly financial of finishing in that top 4, and the importance of Champions League football, but there must be more to life, to this sport, than this?

Trophies only help egos says Pochettino. What a bizarre comment. What they do is help mentality. They make your players want to stay. They make them endure sideways sleet on a February morning in Beswick. Winning breeds winners, by definition. And for City it breeds a mentality of success for the club after such a barren spell. The three previous League Cup wins carried their own importance beyond the trophy itself. Pochettino might not have City's resources, but if you're not going to try and win trophies, then what is the point? When you admit so publicly, how can you expect the players to perform? And as a fan who knows their manager is not invested in every competition you enter, where is the hope?
There is a reason that Spurs fans still talk about Ricky Villa's solo goal at Wembley, and not Peter Crouch's goal at the Etihad to secure 4th place in the league. There's a reason this week's defeat to Newcastle hurt more than just because of the level of performance. It hurts because it may be the difference between winning or not winning a trophy. A big trophy. Against a rival, or so they'd have you believe. The trophy, that as a fan lets you spend the summer strutting about due to something you had no control over.

Now City may suffer for trying to win everything. Could fatigue have played a part in this week's defeat when City have played four times since a Liverpool player last kicked a ball in anger? Maybe, we'll probably never know. But I wouldn't have it any other way. These cup runs, these chances for Wembley visits and your captain climbing the steps to lift a trophy are what it's all about, Community Shield excepted. It's the essence of being a fan. Last week a new ground ticked off. Next month, Wembley. The FA Cup, with one other big team left in it by the Quarter Final stage, offers a great chance of further glory. And City, a team that have never retained a trophy, need to ingrain a winning mentality into whoever wears the shirt, even after a glorious decade of more ups than downs.

I hope Pep never changes his principles.

FEBRUARY

Premier League: Manchester City 3 Arsenal 1

Another day, another must-win game. City needed to get back on track, and quickly.

It took ten minutes for the line-up to make any semblance of sense, and even then it was tenuous. There must be a left-back there somewhere, I'm just not reading the image correctly. Hang on, count the number of defenders again. Hmm, both Silvas, Fernandinho AND Gundogan. Is Fern playing in defence? Or left-back? Otamendi for Stones? Is this another Pep experiment, and is this the right time for one, in a must-win game against a side who split opinion but are still one of the "big guns", just. And would Sane not have had a field day against that defence and an ageing back-up right back?

These were questions I was still asking at half-time, but with the visitors failing to muster a shot in the second half and the visiting fans faux-fighting as if Adebayor had popped in our third goal, it all made sense in the end. Kind of.
(the real reason for the aggro in the away end – a coin knocked someone's couscous and aubergine salad out of a visiting supporter's hands, which then led to a fellow away supporter slipping on a cube of feta cheese)

Yep, this was Pep stretching his tactical muscles. Fernandinho was a defender and a midfielder, depending on whether City were in possession or not, full-backs were inverting themselves like the good old days, and Laporte at left-back had an assist within a minute. I'm still not sure the formation was necessary, against a fading power who are always compliant to attacking teams, but the fixture list has perhaps been taken into account here. City have a game mid-week unlike every other Premier League team bar Everton (naturally), and then there's the small matter of Chelsea and the Champions League.

The feeling was that absentees from this line-up were being punished for the horror show at Newcastle, but it's hard to tell sometimes how Pep picks a team. Danilo for example may just be burnt-out after the constant football he has played since returning from injury, and I cannot recall John Stones doing anything particularly bad that explains him flitting in and out of the team in the last couple of months. You always assume Otamendi is picked for his physical presence against physical teams, but you would hardly place Arsenal in that bracket and when they did have a set-piece, he made little difference. Not surprising really when you have got Raheem Sterling marking the goal-scorer, and City have conceded half of their goals from set pieces, which makes it something of a worry.

Anyway, it was all good in the end. Sergio's hat-trick (all legitimate, if you choose the camera angle that suits) was his 10th in the league, putting him just one behind Alan Shearer. City should have had more, and a penalty early in the game, but after more sluggishness after conceding, they turned the screw sufficiently in the 2nd half. The goal conceded was the first to be let in during the opening quarter hour of a match by City for over a year, so perhaps we shouldn't be too critical. A rare lapse so early in the game, a game in which the first 10 minutes had it all. And at the second time of asking, City put some pressure on Liverpool by winning first, though Liverpool will be expected to beat West Ham on Monday evening. Every game seems crucial now, and none of them will be easy.
So was this a good performance or not? It was good enough, and bizarrely that seems to be the theme for most of the teams near the top. Results are king, but it helps if you play well, you're more likely to win after all. Yet I repeatedly hear (and see for myself) about how Liverpool have played badly and yet won, and Spurs beat Newcastle this weekend despite being underwhelming. Perhaps the title will be won by the single team that really goes up the gears at some point. The pessimist side of my brain (left and most of the right) assumes that will be

Liverpool because they are fighting on fewer fronts. Maintaining a near-fit squad could be key for City.

With thoughts now turning to Wednesday, there will no doubt be a wealth of Everton fans hoping City defeat their team, as difficult as that is to admit. It matters not however, because the players themselves never think in that manner, as the disciplined, professional performance they put in against City when we won the league ahead of Liverpool in 2014 showed, so despite their poor form and questions being asked about their manager, expect them to once more raise their game and prove to be tough opposition. Everton too have proved to be susceptible to set-pieces this season, in fact they've been dismal at times, but this is not an area City would probably be in a position to exploit. The less said about our corner-taking prowess the better. But with this being a "bonus" game brought forward from cup final week, it bizarrely allows city to go top of the table should Liverpool fail to win at West Ham. I'm not getting my hopes up, naturally.

A final thought on the atmosphere. It was low-key once more on a miserable Manchester day, for a game that should be considered one of the bigger ones of the season. My left-field theory is this. We're spoilt as a fan base naturally, and that has led to something of an expectation to be entertained. Sometimes the football is so polished that a mis-placed pass is met with a chorus of groans and a release of pent-up frustration. But I think the fact that city are playing catch-up to Liverpool, and a fair proportion of fans fearing the worst at the end of it all, has fed into the psyche of the crowd, considering we were led to believe by many media types that City were going to dominate football for years to come and were killing the competitiveness of the league. Getting 100 points in the league would hardly dispel such a notion. So in a way this season has been a disappointment, and rather than gee up the fans, it's left us feeling a bit down, when really we should be thankful of our lot (imagine a rival fan reading about us moaning about our lot – from the outside it seems rather embarrassing).

If City had gone into the Arsenal game with a nice lead at the top, the crowd would have been a lot more patient.

The simple fact too though is that the sanitised world of modern football has just left a lot of fans (everywhere) cold, and great football can only heal some of the wounds. There is also just too much football, and it is a sport largely run for TV audiences.

Even a raucous, fiery crowd would be hard-pushed to create an electric atmosphere when it seems I am sat in my seat every few days at the moment - it would probably be cheaper for me to rent an apartment across from the ground. We pay a lot of money and we expect, not hope, to be entertained. It's just the way it is in modern football much of the time. If we ever let a single drummer into the ground to try and improve matters, then that's me done with football.

Anyway, three points, and Aguero's 14th hat-trick for City. He is getting adept at scoring in the first minute too. And if you're trying to recall how he completed his hat-trick it was the goal where he slid in and it *may* have hit his elbow on the way in. But probably didn't, though that failed to prevent days if squealing from opposition fans. It was ever thus.

Goals: Agüero (1' minutes, 44' minutes, 61' minutes)

And then, on the Monday night – West Ham 1 Liverpool 1. It may or may not surprise you to learn that Liverpool's goal was clearly – and I mean clearly – offside. WHAT ARE THE CHANCES???

And so after the despair of the Newcastle defeat, City could actually go top if they beat Everton at Goodison Park in a rearranged game on the Wednesday, though they would have played an extra game.

And that is precisely what they did.

Premier League: Everton 0 Manchester City 2

Is it safe to finally state that Everton do not have a hoodoo over City? I think so. The double completed, and a few demons put to bed.

It was once more tight, it was once more nervy, but City prevailed, though they could not relax until the death when the 2nd goal was popped in by Gabriel Jesus. This was the rearranged game brought forward, and its original timing left me nervous as hell, as it made for a tough, tough week. But having got through that week, its timing could not have been better.

City are top, on goal difference, theirs currently being 7 superior to Liverpool's. It was the first time they have been top since December 15th.

Aymeric Laporte met David Silva's free-kick to head home his fourth goal of the season, a belter, putting City in front just before half-time. That settled the nerves, but not totally, as Sergio Aguero and Raheem Sterling both spurned decent opportunities to extend City's lead after the break, before Gabriel Jesus sealed victory in stoppage time.

Bluemoon Podcast Audio Script

It started with a tweet. It always does. Sadly, this time it came from Barney Ronay. It read:

Sympathy for Liverpool last night, who don't have City's Special Sponsorship bottomless resources, who are missing three defenders, and who just looked a bit thin and stretched.

Ah yes, poor, poor Liverpool. Before I lose the plot at the latest example of journo nonsense, we should probably delve into a bit of context first. Of course part of this was simply Barney covering his back in the era of wild headlines and wild articles with wild claims that can be made to look foolish very quickly. Thus, Barney's proclamation that Liverpool would not freeze and let their lead slip last week looked on shakier ground once Liverpool then went and drew two games.

But what really baffles me, what that tweet, amongst others, highlighted is the lack of logic now utterly rampant in much of football journalists' thoughts nowadays.

Barney dug in and came up with this gem of a fact to back up his own arguments

They've spent 150m in five seasons. Man City have spent 500m in five seasons. These figures may or may not mean something, but at least know what they are.

Boy what a stupid, stupid argument.

Let's cut to the chase here. Net spend is utterly irrelevant as to how well a team should do. It's is staggering that I even have to point this out, though you blues listening to this have probably worked it out for yourself at least. If two teams are put together for £500m, as I pointed out to Barney, with no reply naturally, then they should have an equal chance or expectation of success. Where the money came from, be it a rich owner or sales is irrelevant. They cost the same, which in Liverpool's and City's case is a hell of a lot, and thus are not some plucky underdogs beating the system and winning against all the odds. You can stretch this point further. Cost in itself might be irrelevant too – perhaps value is a better guide. If Robertson is bought for £15m but is now valued at £50m, should we not expect him to perform as well as a City player bought for £50m? If James Milner lets his contract run down and moves to Liverpool for free, should we expect nothing of him because he cost nothing, or accept that the value is a consequence of the Bosman ruling and Liverpool have themselves a £30m player and thus he should perform accordingly, which he has? That's before we look at signing on fees, wages and many other costs beyond simple transfer fees. Such a piss poor argument. After all, if City had sold Yaya Toure and Samir Nasri for big bucks a few years ago, would Barney Ronay be now excusing our Newcastle performance because our net spend over the past 5 years was less? Yeah, right. And why 5 years anyway? It's just made up nonsense, and it's getting tiresome especially from journalists whose writing I enjoy and whose views I used to admire. I don't expect much positivity for City, considering the business model and the vast amounts that have been spent, but making Liverpool out to be the poor relative surviving and indeed prospering off cheap cuts and hand-me-downs is beyond the pale.

Another key point for me whilst navigating the daily Twitter grind is that your Barneys, Michaels and Miguels are never knowingly wrong. They make proclamations but never take on board dissent, differences of opinion or change their viewpoint. Which makes you wonder what the point of their tweet was. To educate us minions? Hey, we're probably all the same, entrenched with our particular views.

It's all so confusing. Liverpool fans if they fall short will no doubt claim they can't compete with City's resources, as some of the blinkered Liverpool press pack are already starting to do at the first sign of a blip, whilst spending all season telling us that they have the best left back in the world, and the best front 3, and the best central midfielder and so on. So which is it? I guess it must mean your manager is a fraud then. The sort of graceless fraud that would claim getting a big decision from a lineman cost his team. It takes cojones to come out with drivel like that. Anyway, what an interesting few days it has been, with many more twists and turns to come no doubt. Raheem Sterling, he's top of the league. Or as Liverpool fans would point out, joint top.

Everton was a stressful ninety minutes, no doubt about it. City, like their competitors, are not clicking through the gears with ease right now, and for all those at or close to the top, it feels like we are entering a period of attrition. Results are king from now on, and I suspect that plenty of points will be dropped from now on. The relentless pace of the first half of the season cannot be maintained. Therefore, every hard-fought victory is to be cherished – it could make all the difference,

Stressful it may well have been, but when you step back and assess City's victory at Goodison Park, you realise that the home team never truly threatened. With an XG (expected goals) of 0.1, they had one header I cannot recall, a few breaks that were snuffed out and a through pass anticipated and snapped up by the ever-proactive Ederson. City on the other hand scored two, missed an easy header, hit the bar and had claims (again) for a penalty. Statistically it was far more comfortable than it felt at the time. Like Arsenal at the weekend, the opposition was snuffed out and the defence did its job admirably.

But rather than discuss the ins and outs of the victory, my thoughts have turned to something else. The fact the game was being played on 6th February. You see, the moment the draw for the semi-final of the Carabao Cup was made, and City avoided Spurs and Chelsea, effectively guaranteeing another trip to Wembley in late February, a possibly important sub-plot opened up regarding the Premier League title race.

Firstly, Sky's plans went out the window. That random fixture list we all pine for in mid-summer had conveniently paired up a Manchester v Liverpool double for the same weekend, and Sky were all over it. Not any longer, as City have now got other plans that day, and thus the game was brought forward, and not back as most assumed, with no TV coverage in the UK as there was already an FA Cup replay being played on front of the cameras and a few thousand hardy souls at The Hawthorns. More importantly than Rupert Murdoch's weekend plans however is the effect this isolated fixture could have on the title race. And the effect was entirely dependent on the result. If City had lost, with Chelsea up next, the title race would have swung hugely in Liverpool's favour once more, many a blue bemoaning the placement of the fixture in between two other big, troublesome league fixtures. A draw? No sweeping conclusions would have been drawn.

But City won. City went top, for a few days at least. City suffered no injuries, even after Aymeric Laporte decided to run full pelt into an Everton player and knock himself out. The referee even allowed Fernandinho to tactically foul with impunity. It all went swimmingly. And now the placement of the fixture looks very handy indeed.

City will not win the quadruple, that much is clear to me. They may win nothing. But when we reach the business end of the season, the team could still be fighting on multiple fronts with two very winnable cup ties approaching. Should City or United progress through the next round of the FA Cup, and City really should, then the Manchester derby fixture will have to be put back until later in the season. With that in mind, the last thing City needed was a tricky game to play at Everton too, a situation that would push even City's squad to breaking point. And thus a fixture that originally looked very badly placed has proved to be a blessing in disguise. And whilst a week might be a long time in politics, it seems it's an even longer time in football, as Barney Ronay discovered just the other day. Things have just got very interesting indeed...

There was no chance in my mind that a depleted Bournemouth side that had lost endless successive away games could spring any sort of surprise on the Saturday, and that proved to be the case as Liverpool cruised to a 3-0 victory – and this time their customary offside goal probably made little difference, though it was the opener, so helped settle the nerves.

So onto another "must-win" game on the Sunday. Just one more good performance to go to round off a perfect week that many thought could end our title challenge. So how did it go again...?

Premier League: Manchester City 6 Chelsea 0 – Sorry Ball...

Ah yes. It went well.
Very well.
So well, that most podcasts the following week barely
mentioned City, emphasis instead on how badly things were
going at Chelsea. This was their heaviest ever Premier League
defeat, and their biggest defeat since losing 7-0 to Nottingham
Forest in 1991.
A game I watched on the couch, after my ankle refused to work
once more. Frustrating is an understatement, but a late 2pm
fitness test was sadly failed.
The run of City's "must-win" games continued, in the most
difficult of weeks – a week that was navigated with aplomb. And
another game in the run of Zinchenko coming of age as a left-
back. This was one of the stories of the season, his nailing down
of the most troublesome position. It would be a crucial factor in
City securing the title, and more.

Another game with Sane on the bench however, another story
in a season of stories. The recovery from the early season lull
seemed a distant memory. His exclusion did not seem based on
some specific poor performances, but it seemed it was due to
events off the pitch as on it. At the business end of the season,
Pep simply does not seem to trust him to carry out his
instructions right now. Consistency has never been his strongest
suit, but he remains one of City's most dangerous attacking
players. You hope this problem is short-term. The failure to sign
a new contract may be related to these problems, but this has
not and would not prevent Ilkay Gundogan from regular
football. Having said that, with Fernandinho hampered by
injuries at season-end, Pep had little choice.

Anyway, it may seem weird to say it, but this 6-0 win was a
weird game. City simply blew the opposition away for 25
minutes, before easing off and then having a taking advantage
of occasional opportunities to aid the goal difference even

236

more. Chelsea probably spent as much of the game on top as City did, but the clinical nature of the home side was planets apart from the sloppiness at both ends of the pitch of the shell-shocked visitors. Despite missing an early sitter, most chances stuck, and City were ruthless.

In the end, it only took 4 minutes for City to break the deadlock, Raheem Sterling slamming home a cross. The notable thing from this move was not the goal itself, but the synchronised goal celebration jump from Sterling and Bernardo. A 10.0 from the judges.

The mad first 20 minutes still found time for Aguero to miss an empty net from a sumptuous Bernardo Silva cross (how??), but thankfully it didn't matter. He rather made up for it in the 13th minute by slamming home the ball from over 25 yards out, so we'll forgive him, As we always must. And six minutes later Ross Barkley kindly set him up for another. Gundogan then hit another long-range goal that the keeper should have done better with, and somehow City were four up in twenty five minutes. They were both ruthless and ably assisted by a compliant opposition.

Bizarrely Chelsea then had their best spell of the game, and could easily have got at least one goal back. Or maybe it's not that bizarre for City to ease off after establishing a four goal lead. Either way, we should not forget a top class save during this period from Ederson from a Higuain shot that was on its way to the top corner.

The 2nd half was never going to be as frantic, but before City added two further goals, there was time for Sergio to slam a header against the bar. Then Azpilacueta fouled Sterling and Sergio slotted home to complete yet another hat-trick. Sterling added a 6th in the 80th minute from his usual spot and the rout was well and truly complete.

And as sure as night followed day, this result will have created considerable discussion over whether Chelsea would be whipping boys once more in the fast-approaching Carabao Cup final. I didn't feel this result told us much about how the final would go, despite the thrashing handed out, and for once I was right.

An extra note: in this book I talk about Pep, I talk about players, and that is about it. It's a bit unfair really, considering the tremendous job so many do behind the scenes. They too deserve a huge amount of respect and congratulations.
None more so than Mikel Arteta. During this game he noticed that Jorginho had lost his position and suggested changes to Pep that resulted in overloads and goal sprees. This is a common occurrence and his value to this setup cannot be underestimated. No surprise therefore that he is being touted as Pep's successor. He seems to possess all the abilities and character to do him proud.

FA Cup: Newport County 1 Manchester City 4: Things I Learned

<u>Manchester City are wealthier than Newport County.</u>

No, really.

This revelation was casually dropped into the commentary a few minutes into the game, and it fair blew my mind, I have to admit. Suddenly, it dawned on me why Newport, 15th in League 2, were 33/1 to beat Manchester City, reigning Premier League champions.

Once I delved further, the stats shocked me to the point of numbness. Turns out that the sink in Raheem Sterling's mum's house is worth more than Newport's entire defence. They never stood a chance. But then you'll never make it big if you name your ground after an Only Fools & Horses character.

<u>John Hartson needs a long lie down.</u>

If you watched this on the BBC and cast your mind back, this was the stand-out event of the night. John Hartson put in one of the most bizarre co-commentary performances ever committed to the big screen. Everything he said made little or no sense, everything he said was wrong. I didn't know whether to be annoyed or impressed by his staggering incompetence. It even managed to distract me from the actual game.

<u>City Roll On.</u>

This was no walk in the park from another strong City side, and the culture shock of it all would be nothing new in the FA Cup annals. But as always, City got the job done, eventually. The problem with games like this is not just the pitch or the physicality of the home team, but the inability to match the intensity of the really big games. It is understandable, and I accept it.

Newport, fresh from beating Leicester City and Middlesbrough, produced another strong display in the competition to hold City at the interval. They even missed the best chance of the first half, when Ederson produced a diving save to deny Tyreeq Bakinson's close-range header. It's fair to say I wasn't happy at half-time, in full woe-is-me mode, as I would be during many half-time breaks later in the season. I need to trust these guys more.

That's because two Phil Foden goals and strikes from Leroy Sane and Riyad Mahrez ended Newport's hopes and thankfully the second half belonged to City as Sane broke the deadlock from close range six minutes after half time. When Newport made it 2-1 late on, I wobbled once more, but this woke City up.

And again, it was great to see Foden on the pitch, and playing superbly. His time will come for greater match-time, but every little helps. His greatest asset is that at such a tender age, he looks like he belongs.

A Social Experiment: I Listen To Twitter For A Day: Part 1

If you're on Twitter, or a football message board, or ever venture online, you'll have seen it. The exasperation, the outright anger at another "hot-take" from a presenter that begs the eternal question, "why do you listen?!"

Yes, I am of course talking about Talksport. The station that seems to have a loyal swathe of listeners who hate everything about it. The radio station that drums up outrage and creates issues that don't really exist to maintain its business model of making money by getting people phoning its premium rate phone number.

Talksport's big cheeses will deny this, saying phone calls have no influence on profits, and judging by the number of adverts in any given day, I'm inclined to agree with them. The other issue of course is that the station is owned by the Wireless Group, whose parent company is News UK & Ireland Ltd, which is a subsidiary of News Corp, which naturally means this all leads back to Rupert Murdoch. Colin Murray famously quit the station after the takeover in disgust at the new owners, which was very noble of him, but as a consumer I don't expect people to make such lifestyle choices. A case of cutting off your nose to spite your face. I have Sky because I benefit from having it and my Virgin box was bobbins, so me cancelling benefits no one. Sky would survive my decision, I'd imagine – I've not even got a full package or fibre broadband.

Anyway, every day I see people getting wound up by the station's output, and I couldn't really comment as I have never, ever listened to it. Music is my medicine during the day, and besides, who wants to listen to a succession of men talking about football day after day, eh?! Talksport of course have numerous twitter feeds too, and a website used often so that presenters' views can be published as news stories, the sort of site used for nuggets like Kohn Aldridge to proclaim that Jordon Ibe is better than Raheem Sterling.

With all that in mind, I decided to take the plunge. I decided I would listen to Talksport for a whole day. A huge undertaking, not least because it would mean a 6am start. I had medication at hand, the kettle was full of boiling water and after 3 buttered crumpets and enough coffee to keep you awake through a Paul Scholes team talk, I was ready to be angry.

I guess the choice of day is important, but this was my day with little on (well apart from Tuesday, Monday, Thursday, last Friday, all next week...) so I plump for Wednesday 13th February, the morning after United are humbled at home to PSG. Pure coincidence, I assure you.

It's 6am, and we're off with the Alan Brazil breakfast show. I've no idea if anything comes before this show, and I never will. No normal person should be listening to the radio at 5am, unless James Stannage has gone on an extra-long rant. There's news, jingles, adverts and some early general chat with guest David Seaman, a pleasant voice and demeanour at this obscene time of the day. It is only by about 6:25am that I realise that the show is actually being presented by stand-in Ally McCoist. I'm not a morning person. They don't sound a million miles apart (apologies to any Scottish readers) when I'm still picking sleep out of my eyes, though there's less of a hangover twang from McCoist.

Talk is naturally about United and the sad passing of Gordon Banks the previous day. Plenty of good content and fair points made, and a nice tribute to Banks. There is an obsession over THAT save, but thankfully there is time dedicated to his wider career and life too. FYI, it's not the greatest save ever, I made a similar one in Heaton Park once, so it can't be.

What Talksport certainly does well it seems at this early stage is getting plenty of ex-pros and football journalists on the line to keep things fresh. Jamie Paradise, sorry Jackson, is first up and is a beacon of common sense, though falls into the trap that most have since last night of re-writing history by claiming that United really couldn't be expected to beat a superior PSG when most were trumpeting United to succeed pre-match, and when they were favourites with the bookies. McCoist and Seaman admitted that they had perhaps got ahead of themselves and their judgment had been clouded by results.

Alan is the first caller of the day at about 6:45am. Alan is a United fan and makes a fair point about the strength of the squad and the blame that must be laid at the feet of Glazers and Woodward, but I take the opportunity to have a poo. On my return we're back on adverts.

Jenny the newsreader is a part of the discussions too, and there's a long discussion on acne. No, seriously. And it's important to remember that this is TalkSPORT, and this is not a station dedicated to football chat. It helps if you like sport in general but prefer football above all else, as I do. So there's discussion on horse racing, and its return to the UK after the flu outbreak and a short look at England's victory over the West Indies.

So with an hour gone, has much actually been discussed? It's been an easy listen, but as is to be expected with a station that cannot fall back on music, it is rather padded out. And I remember why I turned away from commercial radio stations – adverts are so, so boring. I just don't need James Nesbitt telling me about BT broadband, at any time of the day. Rag.

It's 8:10am and Wes Brown is on the phone. I'm fully awake and now I am aware that the host is definitely not Alan Brazil. Wes Brown seems like a nice bloke and makes some pertinent general points, but adds little to the discussion if I'm honest. Sanchez's problems at United might be psychological. Well indeed. Wes hangs around for further discussions, including a call from Jason, a United fan who appears to be phoning in from a submarine in the Mariana Trench.

There's a bookmaker on the phone who notes that City are favourites for the Champions League. Bet responsibly guys and girls.

A quick look ahead to the Spurs game that night, before Wes Brown discusses some of his fellow players/managers. Then he's off, and I already can't remember anything he said. Sorry Wes. Not sure if I mentioned it, but I'm not a morning person.

It's 9am, I'm 3 hours in somehow, and I am already sick of hearing about Big Macs with bacon. This is not a station to be listened to throughout the whole day, unless it's background noise in an office, so I am already questioning my existence. It relies somewhat on repetition, like listening to The Fall on a loop. Still, we dig repetition, in the talk and the news, if not the music. I've got some tea leaves from Sri Lanka, so the kettle is near-boiled and I plough on.

Security cameras. Just Eat. James Nesbitt again. Jingle. The Times literary supplement (<raises eyebrows>). Tradepoint. Paddy Power with Rhodri Giggs. Cancer research. Zoom video conferencing. Van Monster. Jingle. Sporty news and non-sporty news with Jenny. Quick Fit. Three second weather forecast. Zelko. Normal sport news. Jingle. McDonalds (obvs). Just Eat. Tradepoint. James Nesbitt again.

That's ten minutes I'll never get back. I determine that future toilet visits will be on the hour, and leisurely. Might take Private Eye in there with me. Anyway, finally, we're back to Ally and Dave, and it's a proper look at Tottenham v Borussia Dortmund, and Ledley King is on the phone. Always liked Ledley. A short genial discussion and it's back to adverts, and 25 minutes into the hour, there has been virtually no original content. Referring to it as a proper discussion was probably being optimistic. The half-hour is saved with some banter on missed flights, after news filters through that Jadon Sancho forgot his passport before flying out to London. It's enjoyable listening, though David Seaman's stories are hardly rock and roll, being the consummate professional after all. What a lovely man though. More adverts, so I consider downing three pints of Vimto so that I can go to the toilet again, especially when I hear James Nesbitt's voice again. We're into the final half-hour of the breakfast show, after more sports news, and another staggeringly shit jingle for Tony Cascarino. There's chat about Sancho, then they replay snippets from Ledley King, and later Wes Brown. But at last, we get some hard-core analysis with Raphael Honigstein on the line. Honigstein was one of 97 journalists to have interviewed Sancho the previous week, and is always a good listen.

There's a quick recap on United's game that goes over old ground, then a joke feature about angling with Seaman that makes me queasy. It appears to be Seaman saying angling terms in a suggestive matter, before talking about bait. This is not a highlight of any day, fishing not really of interest to me. Angling is sport though, according to Wikipedia, so I can't complain.

And that's it for the breakfast show and part one of the blog. It's been a pleasant listen, though I knew when I started this epic journey that any fuckwittery would most likely come later in the day, and maybe Alan Brazil's absence hasn't helped in that respect. I've not looked at the schedules, so have no idea if Dean Saunders will appear with some hot-takes. If he doesn't, he may get a blog of his own. Anyway, it's time for a break. The key point about the first four hours is that over 240 minutes very little actually happened, but it all moved along swiftly with plenty of guests so it never occurred to me until afterwards. But boy, those bloody pointless adverts. Does anyone listen to them?

In Part 2, I'll look at the daytime shows.

Oh, and for no surprises, just everyday low prices, get to Tradepoint, or go to tradepoint.co.uk.

That's tradepoint.co.uk.

My Talksport Listen: Part 2

It's Part 2 of my day listening to Talksport, and it's Jim White and Simon Jordan, which has me shuffling in my seat uncomfortably. I'm onto my 2nd large coffee from my oversized sportsdirect.com mug (no idea where that came from) and I'm close to delirious.

Before writing this up I dip back into the breakfast show the day after my original review, discover they're doing a Valentine's Day Football XI and Dean Saunders is in the house, so thank my lucky stars at a bullet dodged. Dean is big on banter, but is also fumin' at Declan Rice now deciding he is English. Darren Bent and Sean "40-a-day" Dyche are on the phone, so it moves along swiftly again, for the 20% of airtime that is not adverts. I could murder a Big Mac right now. I'm about to switch off then Uwe Rosler is on the phone! His Malmo are of course playing Chelsea this week.

Anyway, onto the 10am-1pm slot. Simon Jordan I am not keen on, as he says mean things and looks like my definition of a cockney wanker, but I will try and approach with an open mind. Then fail no doubt. Is Jim dressed in all yellow? We may never know. Let's see how shouty he is.

Or not. Cos every presenter seems to be on holiday, and Max Rushden is standing in, and he is normal. I am not happy. Max gets an astonishing amount of abuse on social media, probably because he is safe and doesn't have hot-takes. Why this should be seen as a bad thing is beyond me. He's a host too, so surely his role is not to create controversy, but perhaps we will see a different approach later in the day. Bob Mills is around too, with a voice that makes him sound arrogant and superior, but I will keep an open mind. Bob's old school, but I can't remember if I like him or not. I recognise him, but can't recall his CV.

After Mpabbe's masterclass at Old Trafford the previous evening, initial talk is of quick footballers. And also, of how, as an opposition player, to deal with a player quicker than you. Talk turns to Solksjaer, and whether he has been tested and whether he should get the permanent gig. It's all listenable enough, and I am still not angry at any of Talksport's output. Simon Jordan makes a fair point about Solksjaer and I almost feel let down. Never mind, there's always an advert around the corner to wind me up. We're onto Compare The Meerkat I mean Market, and M & S now.

Oh, and there's been few callers on the shows so far today. It is clear early doors that getting people to call in is not key to Talksport's business model, unless they're paying £100 a minute.

Simon Jordan may be a perma-tanned rent-a-quote for some (not me, no siree, I take it ALL back), but he brings some perspective from that of an owner, not that his reigns were seamless, and makes some valid points about the likes of Alexis Sanchez, Ozil and salary scales. And, for the first time all day, someone actually speaks for minutes at a time with his opinions, and there is a proper discussion above the level of that of a banal ex-pro. I guess this is all deliberate and relevant to the time of the day. The breakfast show helps people get up and to work. This show has a very different feel and tone, and is much more listenable than the Breakfast Show because it has proper content. But again, time of the day and all that...

Jordan goes to town on ineffective ownership as shown by United buying Sanchez, and there is little I disagree with. Nothing in fact. Bob Mills and Max Rushden considering whether the fastest ever hat-trick (90 seconds, Ross County) includes the walk back to the centre circle is the first time I almost lose my shit. For fuck's sake guys.

After 6 hours of adverts, there's further discussion on United and Solskjaer. Simon Jordan is clearly the guy who does 90% of the debating on this show, and it is better for it. He is, quite simply, whatever you think of him, far more eloquent than Bob Mills, who is there for little interruptions and general trivia. A couple of United fans phone in, and the debate is good.

Bob Mills comes across as someone who has just stumbled in out of the rain and is just hanging around until he is dry again. He didn't contribute much to me I'm afraid, Jeff. In fact at one point Max even jokes about waking him up. He asks a few fair

247

questions to those on the line, but he does seem something of a spare part.

There's a run of callers, to ram home the change of approach of this show. The show rises or falls on the quality of these callers of course, so it's varied, but the quality on this occasion is generally good. Bad callers don't last long, it seems. The final caller stating that he would stick with Solskjaer adds nothing to the debate, so off he pops. And thanks for your call.

Danny Higginbotham is on, and he is great. The most erudite guest so far, very enjoyable. I missed a bit as I had a delivery of guinea pig pellets, but what I did hear was impressive. There's then a Championship watch. The "Moose", whoever that is. We aren't given a name, so I will assume it is twitter user @broadcastmoose, A.K.A. Ian Abrahams. Thus I am annoyed before he even speaks. If you have seen his social media output, you'll know why. If you don't let me explain – Ian's schtick, apart from having appalling opinions, is to get a photo with every footballer he walks past then call them his friend. He was 50 this week, so I imagine he had to hire Wembley Stadium for the party. Or a telephone box. He's only on briefly to complain about the fixture list, and then is thankfully gone. He may be great on radio, I may never know, but it's hard to get past his public persona.

We move on. Ed Aarons is on from the Guardian as we head into the afternoon. He is one of the 97 journalists that interviewed Jadon Sancho last week so there's another chat about him, like there was on the breakfast show with Raphael Honigstein. As always with any journalist interview with a footballer, it was amazing and the interviewee was humble and fascinating. Sorry, I appear to have suddenly become grumpy. Ed is good. At least the adverts have changed again. I haven't heard James Nesbitt's voice in hours, and Vanarama seem to have some great deals right now. Check them out. The f***king Just Eat adverts are incessant though. After another three second weather forecast (why?!), I'm back in the game, though news of a closed lane somewhere in Hampshire sends me into another spiral. Time for a break and a ham and coleslaw barm.

I return and there is a guy on the line talking about cricket. I don't know who it is, because I was making a ham and coleslaw barm. Talk turns to Joe Root, his sledging incident and talk of sport and homophobia. After another raft of adverts a woman comes on to talk about sportsmen "coming out" in sport, and talks intelligently on the topic. I didn't catch her name as I was distracted by a packet of salt and vinegar Discos I didn't realise I had. It's good to hear such a debate, which I will assume would not get such careful, considerate treatment on other shows on this station. It may well have been Chris Paouros, the co-chair of Proud Lilywhites. A welcome addition to the schedule anyway. As the show is close to the end, the cricket talk continues with an update on the case against West Indian cricketer Shannon Gabriel and a look at the England team's schedule, via another guest on the line. As a cricket fan it was interesting to me.

And so was the show. Simon Jordan was fair and interesting. If I listened for a week I'm sure he'd anger me at some point, but not today, and Max is an able host, with the added bonus of not being shouty. I like Max, even if he did say something stupid on Twitter last week (I forget what). He is also staggeringly patient and calm about his online abusers, calmer than I could ever be.

The 2nd part of the daytime schedule is where my greatest hopes lie. I've heard good things about Hawksbee & Jacobs, and am aware of their work, kind of. So let's see how it goes.

A disclaimer first. I don't know which is Hawksbee and which is Jacobs. I think Hawksbee always stands on the left, but I can't be sure.

Beginning with general genial chat about nothing in particular and by repeatedly telling us what is coming up in the show added to those sodding adverts (we're onto combi drills now), it is soon 1:25pm and nothing has happened. It was ever thus.

H & J start with more United chat, and Andy Mitten is on the line! Our paths have crossed before. And yours too I imagine. I am looking forward to this. Andy was happy with the 1st half, but admits PSG were better all round in the 2nd half. He manages to squeeze in speaking to Mata post-match. Calling PSG an elite club and admitting they have catching up to do is damning. Andy's tone is resigned - he can't even rally to mention empty seats at the Etihad. Still, he squeezes Citeh into the narrative when talk turns to Sanchez. Sadly the line then goes down, and the sadness ends.

H & B are more positive about United then most have been. Not sure why, they were outclassed.

Harry Judd from McFly is on about a golf documentary, and may well have been a fascinating chat, I wouldn't know as I go and do the pots as I don't care. I catch the end and he sounds like a nice chap. In fact I regret missing most of the section as he sounds interesting and genial. Dan Levene, a freelance football writer, is up next talking about Sarri, and it is a good listen, then Graham Hunter is on as thoughts turn to Ajax v Real Madrid. Graham is a footballing heavyweight in my opinion and even a one-time podcast guest. It's predictably an interesting chat, and Graham is almost moist when telling about Vinicius Junior. Good call as he stars later that night, so Graham can focus an article the next day on his role in Real Madrid's rather fortuitous victory.

Dexter Blackstock is in the studio talking about retiring at the age of 31 and life after football. He has taken a different route to many with a move into the pharmaceutical business. Another good listen. He pretty much fell out of love with football so packed it in, and his line of work is educating. Kevin Hatchard gives plenty of insight on German football, and then Tim Vickery is on from Rio, a man I have admired for a while, though he did big up Moreno when he moved to City, so a mark off for that. He has plenty of interesting stuff to say on Gordon Banks, the 1970 World Cup and the terrible tragedy at the Flamengo training ground last week. There's a man with a 200 year old golf ball, but I don't hang around to find why, as there's garlic to be chopped for a ragu. Apparently it has sold at auction for £5000 and is filled with feathers. Some people have more money than sense. My good fortune also sees me miss some boxing talk. Anthony Joshua is fighting in New York and people are angry.

And that is that for the daytime roster. Next up it's Drivetime, which I know will be less of a smooth ride. A quick power nap may be required. Either way, the day-time shows were better than I expected, the content often interesting. However, there's just too little of it, which is not surprising I guess for a station that must make money through adverts and has to fill every hour of every day with something other than music. Twitter interactions suggest I am avoiding a lot of the real dross, so perhaps I will do a sweep up after this day is complete. If I can't get angry at Andy Goldstein, then what's the point? As predicted though, Hawksbee & Jacobs were a pleasant, interesting listen, a good show to guide you through the afternoon. I'd still prefer some London Grammar or Arcade Fire though.

Right, time for a Big Mac and bacon, a combi drill from Tradepoint and to switch to BT broadband. Onwards and downwards.

Howard was speaking at a Tradepoint business fayre at Alexandra Palace as a proud company ambassador. For all your trade needs, go to tradepoint.co.uk today.

My Talksport Listen: Part 3

In Part 3 of my first ever listen to Talksport, it's the final, epic shift – Drive Time and beyond. I've had a lot of fibre over the past 24 hours so there may be gaps in the article, but I've already got Delia's chicken jambalaya on the hob, so fingers crossed for the journey ahead.

Yep, this brings me into contact with the fabled Adrian Durham, who of course I am well aware of because I have internet access. From what I know of Durham before venturing into his show, he is seen as an intelligent man paid to act stupid, essentially a poor man's shock-jock who likes to make wild statements to create controversy. We shall see.

Trawling his Twitter feed (@talkSPORTDrive) gives me a nice idea of things to come. After all, I am pretty sure he once suggested the Bristol clubs should merge as they never win anything. Nice one Adrian (if it was you). His feed is full of useless polls such as this from last week:

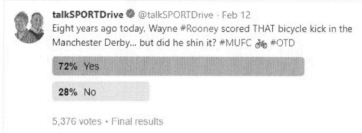

talkSPORTDrive ✔ @talkSPORTDrive · Feb 12
Eight years ago today, Wayne #Rooney scored THAT bicycle kick in the Manchester Derby... but did he shin it? #MUFC 🚲 #OTD

72% Yes

28% No

5,376 votes · Final results

Now this is not a poll based on opinion but fact. I mean, you only have to watch his goal to see it come off his shin, it's not a matter of debate, simply a matter of knowing how to operate a pair of corneas. This means 1505 people (and a quarter) can't even accept simple facts, which does not bode well whichever way you look at it. Hey, it's still a great goal – if I attempted that I'd be in traction and eating through a straw for months, but come on. An earlier clip from this week shows Adrian claiming Paul Scholes has taken the easy option by taking the Oldham job. It's just as well I don't suffer from migraines. Well not yet anyway. When his own club Peterborough aren't doing well he likes to pile in on the club too. He's probably the sort of weirdo that tweets players directly with thoughts.

Still, he is also supposed to have a soft spot for City, so we will see. I don't need presenters to have a soft spot for City I should point out – just to be fair across the board. Unfortunately, he is not on this occasion joined by Darren Gough. The talk on the street is that his presence would have finished me off for good. I don't even know if pig shit is thick (I've never handled any, thankfully) and I don't know if Gough is either. Open mind and all that.

Nope, instead Durham is joined by Matt Holland, who has always struck me as a pleasant chap. He may well be, but I have little idea of what is coming.

Durham gives us a taster by mentioning that he will be talking about Riyad Mahrez. Wonderful. I wonder what angle he will take?

Oh. Here we go. Shit just got real. Yes, as you may know by now, Adrian Durham is asking the question on everyone's lips. Is Mahrez the biggest flop of the season?

OK, I've got some Iburpfoen, let's do this. And to play devil's advocate, a lot of Durham's initial arguments have been mirrored by some City fans, none of whom are Algerian. But of course it's the leading question that grabs the attention.

"Was it worth it is the question," asks Durham about City signing Mahrez as he signs off into a break. Except that isn't the question you led with was it? That's a completely different argument. Already he has shifted the goalposts, because he is aligning some mixed performances with being an almighty flop. It can be the former without being the latter. And it is, in fact. Anyway, apparently this shit-show is coming up after 5pm. Matt Holland has already made some valid points in retaliation, but he's wasting his time to be honest. Durham is not for turning. In the meantime, there's some Championship and boxing talk, which seems ok to me, though there's too much boxing talk. Like, three minutes. I'd rather have an update on dressage. It's actually about ten minutes, so I zone out. And after the usual raft of adverts, news, adverts and weather, it's back to boxing.

Personal choice and all that, but this is of no interest to me. I go and clean the cupboard with all the spices in it instead. Been meaning to do it for months. Even found some mango powder at the back, six years out of date. Why on earth did I buy that? It's the 4:30-5pm segment, which as per all other segments has precious little actual content. Still, it's clear already that there is coverage of life outside the Premier League, which is good. There's three polls too. There's little more boring than three simultaneous Talksport Drive Time polls. Maybe four polls? Talk returns to the Championship, especially Aston Villa. Durham goes to town on the manager, but I cannot disagree with what he says as this is not a topic of expertise. A Villa fan is on the line, and makes some valid points. Talk turns to the FA Cup and Durham argues that the Doncaster player that faked a head injury after handballing a cross should be done for cheating. And he's right, he should (though where do you draw the line on cheating?).

We move on. There's no putting it off any longer, as it's now after 5pm, so it's time for the Mahrez discussion. Now, as already alluded to, no one is claiming Mahrez has been a runaway success so far at City, but Durham's arguments are tiresome. And whatever your views, it's all tabloidesque creating and then discussing a topic like this, not that that is something I should automatically raise my nose at. Discussing if he has been successful is a valid argument, and that's essentially what the two discuss. But framing it in this way is clearly done to get a reaction. And how Fred does not win the title is baffling (is he alive?), but then Adrian Durham would never hold a discussion on that, it's not reactionary enough. And apparently Mahrez is a bigger flop because the set up at City is better than elsewhere and thus it was easier for him joining the Centurions. There's a slither of logic in there, but the basic argument is piss poor – the competition is also stiffer, after all. Holland on the other hand talks total sense.

Anyway, it gets people calling in. Of course the station is not reliant on such calls. Calls cost 44p a minute, and a friend informed me over the weekend that even if you phone in and never get through, you are charged. Makes sense. Four City fans phone in to generally agree that Mahrez has not been a success, but, and I'm sorry for repeating myself – ASKING WHETHER HE HAS BEEN A SUCCESS IS NOT THE QUESTION THAT ADRIAN DURHAM FRAMED THE WHOLE PROGRAMME AROUND.

So let's move on. There's talk of Scott Brown getting a 2nd yellow card for over-celebrating a late winning goal. I don't say this lightly, but Durham's argument against Brown is probably the flakiest, shittiest hot-take I have ever heard, though I'm still to encounter Dean Saunders. F***ing hell, the crap coming out of his mouth could fertilise whole continents. Hawksbee & Jacobs seems like a lifetime ago. Essentially Durham argued that as a captain he has a responsibility to not show passion and get on with it, and because Celtic had been rubbish the previous game, he has added responsibility not to go over the top. I'm paraphrasing his drivel, but you get the gist. He basically should not show any passion after a late winning goal, especially as it was deflected and against Kilmarnock.

"Over celebrating the games they should be winning whilst sweeping the garbage like against Valencia under the carpet."

Sigh. Why am I doing this? I am getting the creeping realisation that Durham is playing a character here, and we're all falling for it. Hey ho. A couple of Celtic fans call in, but I'm too annoyed to have to listen to Durham repeat this drivel. I water a plant, and make a hot Vimto.

There's Chelsea chat, which thankfully avoids controversy. One caller hopes Chelsea get thrashed as Sarri is a stubborn old fool and needs to go. No true fan wants their team to get thrashed. Unless it relegates United I guess. The final half hour I skim over as my mind is made up.

So that's the show done, thank god. For the first time I get the feeling that the show is structured to get people to phone in and text (50p plus charges). As a result, it is immeasurably poorer for it. And what a waste of Matt Holland to spend 3 hours arguing against a succession of Durham's hot-takes. He deserves better than this. It's fair to say I won't be listening again, ever. There's little titbits that are interesting enough, but otherwise little of merit, because Durham predictably dominates. Compare to the 10am-1pm slot when Max Rushden was understated and allowed Simon Jordan to put his points forward.

The evening is filled with coverage from Stamford Bridge, so I will skip to after that. The coverage during live football is supposed to be good, as you would expect, as it is standard sports reporting rather than opinions, and is something I may dip into if travelling in the future. I don't require live football on a radio if not.

Last up is the Sports Bar. It's on until 1am, gulp. It is hosted by Andy Goldstein, whose avatar suggests he thinks he is in Oasis in 1995. Goldstein presents himself as an MBE, which I imagine is some staggeringly shit attempt at banter. Wikipedia tells me he uses the nickname Galeforce. If I make it to 1am there should be a statue of me erected in St Peters Square, perhaps next to Emmeline Pankhurst. Maybe of me slumped over a desk, crying. But as always, I listen with an open mind. Dazzle me Goldstein. Having said that, Goldstein, from London, is of course a United fan, so after their victory at Stamford Bridge, this could be very painful.

This is a call in show too, which I hate. Still Danny Higginbotham is in the studio, so there is hope. And hey, you know what? It's alright. The start is more a discussion where Higginbotham dominates and he makes lots of good points. He's not actually in the studio, but at home in his jimjams, but you wouldn't know. There's just one caller in the first 25 minutes, who only repeats what has already been said. Loads more calls thereafter, which concentrate more on Chelsea's problems than United's resurgence. I can't disagree with most of what is said. Talksport employee Jason Cundy, a Chelsea fan, has had a strop so hasn't called in, so Goldstein rather lamely gets callers to leave messages on his answer phone. The key thing here is that for some baffling reason he plays canned laughter as the messages are left, which makes me want to tear my ears off. Please stop. But otherwise it is fine, and Goldstein is not as smug as expected. Well not the bits I heard. Again though, as with all other shows, at least half of the airtime is not original content. The second hour has more United calls, with some discussion about Pogba and Lindelof. Naturally the odd Irish accent is apparent. Keith Hackett is on the line to discuss contentious issues from the weekend. I'll assume he called everything wrong. There's a good discussion on the rules on offside and handball though.

Darren Lewis is on next, from The Mirror. Goldstein has got the canned laughter out again. It's appalling. Lewis sounds like me on my first foray into radio – either stoned, or has just woken up. Anyway, he looks at the upcoming Liverpool match. There's nothing wrong in what he says, nor is there much insight. There's a look at the back pages too.

Next up, and Ian Abrahams is back. Great. I consider going to bed, but let's see what he has to say. My mind remains open for my good friend The Moose. He is clearly on fire from the off, asking that if there has had to be a whole new law created after the Leeds Spygate fiasco, is Danny Higginbotham not surprised that there wasn't a points deduction? Well no Ian, because the law wasn't there before to deduct points off them. Jesus Christ. Go to be Howard.

Credit to Goldstein to pointing this out – there was no actual rule they broke, so the fine is a joke. Anyway, there's some Championship talk thereafter which is fine.

We're into the last hour now. It's thus past midnight, there's European football coming up, more boxing talk (yay!), more Danny Higginbotham, and clearly this is not just a talk-in show as I assumed. I should do more research in future. There's a feature called The Midnight Train To Madness, which means calls about anything at all that's not sport, and there's not a chance I'm staying up for that. I go to bed.

So that's it. The journey is over. I have apparently avoided some of the worst output, so may revisit in future. Or perhaps never listen again, for my health. And overall, the output was patchy but ok. The best quality was clearly from 10am-4pm, and the worst clearly followed just after. There is plenty of good content to dip into, it just amuses me that so many are drawn towards the shows they know will antagonise them. For me, the lack of content is the biggest killer of all, but is a necessity I guess, for the business model to succeed. Overall, it was not as bad as I expected, with one exception, but for now I'll stick to music – no adverts, and I know what I'm getting with Hans Zimmer and Wolf Alice. Try it, you'll thank me for it one day........

Champions League: Schalke 2 Manchester City 3: Some Thoughts

Well that was interesting. A roller-coaster ride ending with another magical late Raheem Sterling winner, and City are strongly expected to now progress to the quarter finals of the Champions League. No easy draws from now on if they do, eh? Obviously the score line barely tells the story on another eventful night. Controversy reigned, and we learned that VAR most certainly will not temper post-match debate. Last night it did the opposite.

So where do you start? Well with Pep, I guess. City persevered, which allowed Pep to swat away controversial topics in the post-match press conference. Maybe he would have done anyway. City made harder work of a game against what appeared to be average opposition (do we judge them on league position or cup exploits?), but there were multiple reasons for that. Questions will again be asked about City's performances in away games in this competition, as they seem intent in making life difficult for themselves, and their manager will be scrutinised too. After all, Pep has not made a final for eight years. Did he over-think his line-up again? Not really, once John Stones was absent. The bigger question was the lethargy and cruise control applied once more once a lead was obtained.

Nevertheless, it was a successful night. Brilliance sealed it in the end, and you would not have known as a newcomer to the last twenty minutes of the match that the visiting team were a man down. And despite my disappointment before the late goals, I was not that down. It just seemed like one of *those* nights, and from what I had seen, I was confident that City would win the 2nd leg comfortably, as long as they didn't shoot themselves in the foot again, which can never be discounted.

The question that arises once more is the lack of intensity of this team when they have the lead and when a game is there for the taking. Schalke looked poor and lacking in invention. What they did do was keep numbers in the box to make life difficult. Were City players cruising, managing the game, or fatigued? I don't know, but they may need a greater intensity than this when the harder games arrive. Perhaps this is a consequence of fighting on four fronts.

As for VAR, which I am generally in support of, it was an absolute shambles on the night, but that is as much down to human error as much as the technology itself. I support a fully functioning VAR, even if it can strip the emotion out of celebrating a hotel. However, what we had last night was not a fully functioning VAR.

To over-turn the initial award of a corner, the UEFA rules set down for VAR in this competition were essentially ignored and this broken. And you wonder why some of us hate this competition? Not me, but some do, and nights like this don't help me embrace it. The rules specify that the referee must make the final decision, but he couldn't, as the screen by the pitch side was broken. In that case, VAR should not have been used. End of.

I could almost understand it if it was to overrule a "clear and obvious" error, such as a City player punching a Schalke player, but it wasn't. It was used to make a subjective decision that many cannot agree with anyway (including me - that should not have been a penalty) and was used using slow motion replays which should be banned. If you can't see an error at full speed, then there's your answer. There wasn't one.

Still, there was no long process for the 2nd penalty. Strange that, considering two Schalke players were interfering with play whilst offside. The argument may be put forward that they are not interfering if the ball does not reach them, but I'm not convinced. The ball was heading their way and it influenced Ederson's actions. I cannot be convinced that Fernandinho's offence came first. But VAR wasn't interested in that.

As for our Brazilian maestro, Fernandinho's yellow card could be a blessing in disguise if it gets a suspension out the way in a game City should sail through with or without him. His concession of a penalty does raise another point however. My relentless fear that this team lacks the cuteness or nous to go all the way, because it takes a rather different approach in Europe, with these match officials and fine lines between success and failure. Perhaps too with Fernandinho, a player who likes the odd "tactical" foul and plays on the edge more than any other City player, it is best he stays out of the penalty area after recent weeks. The hybrid defence/midfield role brings its own risks.

Individual efforts won the day rather than a shift in the game dynamics. The best team won though, of that there is no doubt. With 15 minutes to go it seemed like the typical City of old, losing a match in which the opposition had not fashioned a proper chance. City did do certain things well – Schalke are undefeated in their last 9 European home games, or they were – City restricted them to any meaningful chances away from the controversies.

Anyway, there are few better feelings than winning a game in that manner. Winning every game comfortably would soon get rather boring after all. For Raheem Sterling, this was his 12th goal since the start of last season that has been scored in the 80th minute or after. Five of those goals were winners and one an equaliser. His worth just rises with every passing week, as does his composure. As for Sane, it was the greatest of free kicks, Ronaldoesque, in the days when he scored free kicks regularly. The only surprise was that he did not start, as he returned to the club that made him.

As for Aguero, he has now scored in seven consecutive European away games, a first for a player of any British club.

Other players still give some cause for concern. David Silva is struggling to justify his selection despite his awareness to break the deadlock, and we're still not seeing the Kevin De Bruyne of last season.

Pep will no doubt still go strong in a few weeks, as there is still work to be done after all. But Schalke need, probably, to win by two goals to turn this around. Unlikely, as long as City do not give European referees the opportunity to make decisions against them. Otamendi should have realised this once on a yellow card, as should Fernandinho as soon as he touches a Schalke player in the penalty area. Ah well, little damage done in the end, an next up, the small matter of a Cup Final. Exciting times....

Carabao Cup Final: Manchester City 0 Chelsea 0: City win 4-3 on penalties

Told you we wouldn't thrash Chelsea again!

So for the first time in their (eleven year) history, Manchester City have retained a trophy. Hopefully this would be the season they would do it twice.
A nice early start as always at Piccadilly station, and a good trip down, to be greeted by summer weather in February. T-shirts for a Carabao Cup final – whatever next?
Liverpool were busy drawing 0-0 with United, which put me in a good mood, as dropping points could only be seen as good news.

This was not the game most were expecting though. Perhaps Pep though that Sarri would be stubborn and not compromise his beliefs again, playing into City's hands, but that was not the case. Chelsea defended far better than they had a couple of weeks previously, and retained the threat in attack. They had the best chances over 90 minutes.

So probably best not to forensically analyse the match. What lingers in the memory is City's adeptness once more from the penalty spot, but even more, the bizarre events just prior to it. Kepa Arrizabalaga refused to be substituted, something I don't think I have seen before. I wasn't complaining – the script had been written that Caballero would come on and once more be a penalty hero, against his old club. I was happy to see Kepa stay on, and his week attempt at an average Aguero penalty in the shootout was vital in City crawling over the line.

So not the best performance, but City got away with it. It is always good to accumulate trophies, however important we consider them. And the dour match and nature of the competition led to the poorest atmosphere I have experienced at the ground, though at least no one was fighting this time around. It's logical really. We've been here 15 times now, it's not a novelty, and this cup final is not the biggest prize, by a long way. That's just how it is. It's the most arrogant statement, but this was just another visit to Wembley!

Of greater concern was Fernandinho limping off as full-time approached. He will soon turn 34, and the concern is two-fold – we need a replacement for him soon for the long-term success of this team, and also the concern over the immediate impact on City's results. Enter Ilkay Gundogan, a different type of player, but one easily capable of filling in during the Brazilian's absence, even if he does see his ideal position as further up the pitch.

Anyway, well done Raheem Sterling, who I admit I was not confident was going to score the winning penalty. But he did and what's more, he hit it TOP BINS!

City's Good Fortune – A Bluemoon Podcast Audio Script

It's the sign that City have arrived. That we're one of the big boys now, whatever rival fans say now. Yep, if you ever wondered why David Gill used to jet over to Monaco to watch a cup draw he could have watched in bed, or why Txiki does now, then it's all become clear. One quiet word from Txiki and it's Schalke in the knockout round. A personal call from Pep asking Darren Fletcher if he is well and before you can say microwave ping it's Swansea in the quarter finals of the FA Cup. We've arrived. Our balls are warmed not cooled. There's no stopping us now. We're Manchester City, we'll play who we want. OK, that may be a tad tongue in cheek. After all, I'd gladly travel to Monaco for the opening of an envelope. But have City really been lucky in draws? Well that depends on how far you spread the net.

In the FA Cup, the draw has certainly opened up for those left in it. One of the key factors was teams like Liverpool not prioritising the competition. Klopp's record in the competition is poor, which is hardly City's fault. Another big factor is not so much City's good fortune, but other team's bad fortune. Namely, big teams meeting each other, which was statistically unlikely, meaning of course one of them had to be knocked out. United have thus done for Arsenal and Chelsea. It's harder for City to get a tough draw when the draw is weak. In previous seasons, the luck has been average, and nothing that stands out. After all, if we look back further, our 3 semi-finals this decade have been against United, Chelsea and Arsenal.

Since City last won the FA Cup, prior to this season, they have had 12 of their 24 ties against premier league opposition, and none against a team outside the top 2 divisions. In that time, in both the domestic cups, it's 30 premier league opponents in 48 ties. In percentage terms, we are 2nd of the top 6, a slither behind United, in the percentage of other top 6 teams drawn in cup competitions.

Remember that in the 3rd round there are 63 other teams in the competition still, so the law of averages states you should avoid a Premier League team in at least 2 in every 3 years. Of course the tiresome conspiracy theorists would have you believe that even a tie against a mid-table Premier League team is still some sort of fix. We all remember of course the long run of away ties City received in cup competitions, even if this season has been kinder than most. Before this season only 7 ties in the last 23 of the two domestic cups haven't been against Premier League sides, and only 1 of them was against a team outside the top 2 divisions – Wigan, who were top of the 3rd tier at the time, and of course have a powerful spell over us. Right now United have had a tougher run in the FA Cup than city, but it would need a recency bias to say we've been lucky for a while.

And then there's the Champions League. Funny isn't it that City got a better draw by being champions, as per the rule change over 4 years ago. Win the league Liverpool fans and you should too, cos you're guaranteed being in Pot 1, not 3. Funny too that City got an easier draw by winning their group. Maybe Liverpool should have tried that too. After all, it worked for them last season, winning 5-0 in Porto. Less so for Jose Mourinho's United against Sevilla, but, you know, Jose Mourinho...
Of course the likes of United would much rather have a seeding based on historical data so that they are assured top seeding, even if they do finish behind City in the league six seasons on the row. But this newer system is fairer, and is not for city to defend anyway. It can't always ensure the top 8 teams in Europe are in pot 1, as sometimes 2 of the 8 are in the same league, but it is fairer than relying on ancient history. Should city Get past Schalke, there will be no easier draws left to have anyway, I would imagine.
As for just this season, it has been a fairly kind run in luck draws, even after we take into consideration the options that were available, seeding etc.
The stand out piece of luck was probably drawing Burton in the semi-final of the Carabao Cup, but City would have been clear

favourites whoever they drew. Still, I wasn't complaining. Earlier in the competition, it sometimes matters little whether you draw a big team or not, considering the weaker line-ups picked by the big boys season after season. City have been adept at just doing enough to be successful in this tournament. Let's hope that trend continues at the weekend.

So In conclusion, City have had some luck recently, but over time it has been nothing more than average. The key piece of luck may not be the favourable draws, but the timing of them. City will not win the quadruple, you can take that as read, but whilst they continue to fight on four fronts, every favourable draw is a bonus, as it helps keep the squad fresher than a run of tough games. When the season ends, that may be a key factor for Pep's Centurions.

Premier League: Manchester City 1 West Ham United 0

How many times have I said "job done" in this book? Twenty? Thirty?

But yet again, that is the phrase that first popped into my head when considering this match. City laboured, and needed a fairly soft penalty (but still a penalty in the modern game) to collect all three points.

Early doors and everything seemed fine. City flew out of the traps, and a goal seemed inevitable, but it did not arrive. David Silva turned Kevin de Bruyne's cross on to a post but West Ham soon began to frustrate the home side. Maybe Pep regretted leaving the likes of Sterling, Bernardo Silva and Walker on the bench. Bernardo replacing Sane in the 57th minute changed the game. It was Mahrez's first league start of the year, and he did not grasp the opportunity. His form has been a concern for a while, but let's not write him off just yet, as some are keen to do. His problem for me revolves around decision making, and believing he belongs. Maybe he too needs a year to adjust to the unique demands of a Guardiola system.

As for the penalty, it was soft for me, and the replays suggest some contact. But if it had not been given, I doubt there would have been much of an uproar. For all the luck we claim Liverpool have had this season (and they have), we have to note this one down as a tad fortunate too.
Of course this is not to say that without the penalty City would only have drawn. It does not work like that. Without it they would have pushed harder, but with the goal they saw out the game and took what they had on a difficult day.

Finally. 76% possession. Such figures barely register any more. This is the true mark of Pep. Opposition teams just play dead much of the time, suffocated by City's system, and its players use of the ball. This game showed though that a well organised low block can still frustrate even if City have all of the ball.

As it stands, City got over the line and Liverpool retain a single point lead at the top with ten league games to go. This could go to the wire.

Bluemoon Podcast Audio Script – Superstition

I consider myself a logical person. Despite social media often being a soap box for the cesspit of humanity, it has taught me a few things, one being not to take everything I see at face value. It may surprise some to learn that words written over an image are not automatically true. I've learnt, partially, to accept alternative views, though I have a long way to go on that score. If Michael Cox proclaims that Eden Hazard is the best Premier League player this season then I accept his opinion and give it some thought, before throwing my TV out the window. And I now realise that footballers are human beings, and should be judged as such. Poor form for example can have many underlying causes. We've all underperformed at work, and so do they in their job.

But in one area of my life, I act like a man stripped of all logic and reason. I do stupid things that serve no purpose and make no sense. Because for football matches, and only for football matches, I am deeply superstitious.

In an attempt to pad out this piece, I googled the definition of superstition. It is defined as an excessively credulous belief in and reverence for the supernatural. So essentially I am attributing supernatural powers to myself. Sounds legit.

Anyway, my match day routine would have psychologists wetting themselves, perhaps questioning whether I had a difficult childhood or had a knock on the head when younger. Now I think about it, I did once fall down my gran's stairs and head butt a cupboard at the bottom, before being sick in a bowl. It's all starting to make sense.

So here's my match day routine. The same superstitions too, never varied, otherwise City will spiral down to the 3rd tier of English football again, Pep will leave, the oil will run out and Jadon Sancho will lead United to 8 successive Premier League titles. Or even worse, Virgil Van Dijk will lead Liverpool to one. Left sock on first, left leg of jeans first too. Adidas St Petersburg trainers on, even though I don't like them anymore. Shut bedroom door before leaving. Always keep certain valuables in left pocket – wallet, bank card, confetti. Keys and phone in right pocket, plus Anadin Extra if a long day is planned. Cross Brooklands Road at the top, at the lights, not immediately after I exit the house. Tram ticket, if needed, in right rear pocket. Tear up the credit card acknowledgement the machine prints out and place in platform bin. Then I am free of superstition until I reach the ground, apart from having to enter the pub by the main door, not the side one. Always enter the far left turnstile, always walk up steps one at a time, never arrive in seat too early, though that may be just to avoid boredom.

Anyway, it's working quite well. You're welcome. And what thanks do I get from the club for maintaining this winning streak? None. Nothing. Not even a Cityzens training top or an inflatable banana.

The superstitions are similar but modified for away games. For away games I am not at, which is most, there are lucky pubs and unlucky pubs. There are also lucky seats within lucky pubs. There are cursed friends' houses too, places where I have never seen City win on BT on a Tuesday night in February. We're never going back there, however many snacks are provided.

I don't need to point out to you that none of my actions are having an effect on team results. You're probably intelligent and sensible enough to have already figured that out, unless you're one of those people that equates footballers' wages with those of nurses and soldiers. My match day routine was carried out prior to a home defeat to Crystal Palace, plus the defeats to Leicester City and Newcastle United and yet I ignore that and carry on with the same routine for no apparent reason. Of course that was just due to me forgetting to do one of my superstitions, or perhaps a temporary glitch in the matrix.

271

And how did they originate? Where did they come from? I've absolutely no idea. At what precise moment did I decide that walking to the top of my road was helping my football team to win? They're just randomly made up without reason and yet still I persist. I can't even link them to famous victories like many can do.

And outside football, I am devoid of such stupid rituals, apart from being unsettled by stepping on cracks in pavements. I even walked under a ladder once, and it's fair to say my life has been a spectacular success ever since.

Footballers have superstitions too, which also will have little effect, but are more understandable. After all, at least footballers can influence the result, so if they believe in their superstitions, it can aid their performance, like some sort of placebo effect. David James' ritual involved not speaking to anyone, going to the urinals, waiting until they were empty and then spitting on the wall. Johan Cruyff used to slap his goalkeeper Gert Bals in the stomach while he was at Ajax, and then spit his chewing gum into the opposition's half before kick-off. When Cruyff once forgot his gum, in the European Cup final of 1969, Ajax lost to Milan 4-1. The coach of the Zimbabwean side Midlands Portland Cement sent his squad of 17 players into the crocodile-crowded Zambezi river in a ritual cleansing ceremony, intended to restore their harmony ahead of their next game. Sadly, only sixteen of his players emerged minutes later, so probably best that he knocks that one on the head or he'll be transitioning to 5-a-side football pretty soon. Anyway, a quick search shows that so many footballers' superstitions revolve around urine, so perhaps it's best we move on.

I am not alone though, I know that. There should be support groups for us. There are those that thought that City tweeting about their long undefeated run against Newcastle United was somehow tempting fate. Maybe Rafa Benitez printed out the tweet and posted it on the wall of the home dressing room. Somehow I doubt it though.

A quick Twitter poll reassured me that I am not alone too. I say quick, it was anything of the sort. I had no idea what fellow fans were going through. Gaz Warrington turns his back on penalties – and if it's good enough for Pep, it's good enough for the rest of us to do that too. Listening to the Charlatans, specifically The Only One, is also compulsory, and watching Jimmy Grimble pre-derby. Joanne Jackson calls at the same McDonalds with the same order on the way to the game. That's some sacrifice. Dancity9 never predicts the score of a game, which I am fully on board with. It pains me to do the same, though nowadays I consider it bad luck to predict a defeat, which thankfully with the current team is not much of a problem. Karl F must always enter the stadium before his dad, and sit to his right. Kay Arrowsmith has a morning brew in a City mug, the match day scarf is never washed mid-season, and City cannot be watched on holiday which seems harsh. Having said that, when I was in Turkey last year, City put in two bang average performances against Everton and Bournemouth. I apologise for watching them. It all turned out OK in the end.

And the list of superstitions just kept on coming. I can't even list 10% of them, so apologies. Specific squirts of a specific aftershave, unknotting scarves before kick-off, not shaving pre-match, walking on certain sides of the road, lucky socks, lucky underpants, not washing lucky items of clothing, which must be fun for those sat around you, keeping feet in the same position as when a goal was scored, entering the ground in a specific order as a group, going to the same chippy and ordering the same thing, counting ducks on canals, drinking a specific energy drink pre-match, wearing plain socks, eating scrambled eggs and toast, wearing the same jumper for 20 years, the jumper now possessing its own twitter account, rubbing a Sun Jihai footprint pre-match, wearing specific shirts, specific toilet routines, walking up Peel tower and knocking on the door 22 times, drinking only Old Speckled Hen, which is surely the ultimate sacrifice, and many, many more. You bunch of utter weirdos. Welcome to the club.

And the left turnstile seems to have popped up with a few of you. And I've just realised that despite using the left turnstile, I always head for a right urinal. Our group is even convinced we score more goals when our mate goes to the toilet mid-half, as he has a habit of missing a lot of goals. Hashtag early leaver.

Do City's owners even realise the effort we are putting in to make this team successful? I doubt it. I doubt Sheikh Mansour even has a lucky scarf, the amateur. When they do eventually erect statues for the likes of Sergio Aguero, David Silva and more, they should erect one for us too. The superstitious fans that powered this club to glory, and kept them there. And when we are all gone, and that day will come, the baton will be handed over to future generations of weirdos to carry on the traditions. Using a specific hover board to get to the match, that sort of thing. So come on City, recognise us. We're not weird, honest. We're just committed to the success of our football club.

We've put in the hard yards, unknotted a thousand scarves, queued at a thousand left-sided turn stiles and dressed to the right just for your benefit. A new City top will do as thanks – but not a 3rd kit - I've heard they bring you bad luck.

MARCH

Premier League: Bournemouth 0 Manchester City 1

Another tough game, unexpectedly perhaps, another three points gained nevertheless.

Pep Guardiola said City's win at Bournemouth was "one of the best performances we've ever played" as the centurions overcame injuries to Kevin de Bruyne and John Stones to go two points clear at the top of the Premier League, with Liverpool still to play. I think he was being serious too.

To be fair, Bournemouth did not have a shot on target the whole match, so in many respects it was a complete success. In front of goal it was a different matter though. Substitute Riyad Mahrez's possibly sliced shot in the 55th minute was ultimately the difference between the two sides. Bournemouth never threatened, they rarely entered City's half, but it still felt like a nervy last half-hour.

Any season, even the best ever, will have days like this. That old adage of results like this being the stuff of champions. I'm not sure they really tell us much, apart from the fact that a team cannot be devastating on tap. Take the three points and run.

The injuries on the other hand are a bitter pill to suffer. The impact of them may hurt as much as dropped points would have done. Only time will tell, but I am already hoping for Kevin De Bruyne to have his greatest ever season starting in August. He must have a lot of pent-up frustration. No surprise therefore that he told his wife, who recently gave birth to their second child, that she now had to look after three babies.

Bluemoon Podcast Audio Script

It's a long, long road - with many a winding turn, as Liverpool fans are discovering this morning. Manchester City are not merely joint top of the Premier League, but alone at the top by a solitary point after Liverpool's draw at a windy Goodison Park on Sunday afternoon. Many a Liverpool fan's arse has gone (figuratively speaking), and as a pessimist fan I know that feeling well. It's not that the title has slipped from Liverpool's grasp – of course it hasn't. It's more the disappointment that the team is putting the fans through the wringer when they could almost smell the polish on the Premier League trophy just a few weeks ago. There was no need for this stress.

Of course it is stating the obvious to point out that this title race has many more winding turns to provide in the remainder of the season. After all, City were accused of destroying the competitiveness of the Premier League in August, decades of domestic dominance seemingly lying ahead. Last week Phil Thompson mused that the title was Liverpool's if they were victorious at Old Trafford.

Liverpool were not victorious at Old Trafford.

As you will know, Liverpool have had their chances to build a sizeable lead in this title race, but have wasted opportunities. And now, for the first time since December 7th, it is back in City's hands. When the top two met on January 3rd, Liverpool were 7 points clear. Victory would take them 10 clear and essentially seal the title. City won, just, and the gap was back to 4. When City surprisingly lost at St James' Park on 29th January, Liverpool had the opportunity to build a 7 point lead again at the top at home to Leicester City the next night. They could only draw, but 5 points was healthy enough. We should also note it was both snowing AND windy, so they can be excused that one. The defeat at the Etihad has been Liverpool's only one in the league this season, but draws can be almost as costly when the pace is so relentless. That's why some may argue that attaining

100 points in the league is every bit as impressive as going the whole season undefeated. And they'd be right.

The bookies make City clear favourites now, with Liverpool over 2/1 for the title. Bookies are rarely wrong, but those odds look skewed to me. This title race is still in the balance. Whilst analysing fixture lists can often be rendered pointless, Liverpool probably have the easier run in, though it is marginal. City have their own away derby, plus a tricky trip to Selhurst Park, and welcome Spurs to the Etihad, a team surely not ready to cave in just yet, a team with a superb away record. Liverpool welcome Spurs too, and Chelsea, and the final date at Wolves could be tricky if the home team are not already dreaming of sangria and sand in their flip flops.

With Liverpool's Champions League participation hanging in the balance too, fighting on one front may help them. All eggs in one basket and all that, but City have shown that fighting on multiple fronts can bring its own benefits, whilst Liverpool's warm weather training does not appear to have achieved its aims. City could have told them that, once crashing out of the FA Cup at home to Middlesbrough after a jaunt to Abu Dhabi.

What's more, there is only a solitary league game remaining until the end of March. For City this is both an advantage and a disadvantage. If you believe in momentum, then it is definitely with City right now. They have ground out the results in a week where 300 minutes of football was played and no goals were conceded. With that in mind, you'd think a run of more league games would be relished to drive home the advantage as Liverpool flounder on a bank of draws. That said, City need a rest and a rare football-free midweek is well-timed. The raft of injuries to key players means a lack of league games should be welcomed, as should the international break in the horizon, and I never thought I would say that. The levels of performances from both teams tells us little at the business end of the season, but the grit shown from City players this week, a belief that victory would come has certainly boosted my confidence for the remaining games.

But Liverpool's games over the past week were not easy. Drawing away twice in two of the hardest remaining games is no disaster. The form and quality of performances may be the greater concern though. But if we must hold up a draw at Goodison as evidence, we must also present the 5-0 demolition of Watford, a team in good form who many thought would pose the hosts a problem.

In the end, April may well be decisive, as April often is. City are now fighting on three fronts, but the FA Cup could prove vital. City's involvement in the competition means the postponement of the derby in 2 weeks' time, and this allows Liverpool to get back in front and apply pressure. They can even build a 5 point lead due to how the fixtures fall. I don't readily accept the notion that there is an advantage playing first over a weekend, but Liverpool fans will feel better with points on the board. And with the delayed game against United, City will be a game behind for over a month, which is not ideal. They will be expected to get past Swansea in the quarter final of the FA Cup to, which means further fixture congestion.

Either way, with the premise that points are dropped in the most unlikely places (as City have already demonstrated this season) and if we assume calm weather for the next two months, then this title race is clearly far from over. One result can change everything, including the narrative once more. The road ahead is neither short nor straight, but one thing is clear – it could be one of the best title run-ins of the Premier League era.

Premier League: Manchester City 3 Watford 1

Another three points, after Raheem Sterling hit a 15 minute hat-trick in the 2nd half to see off a stubborn and determined Watford side. But this did not come without some controversy. With the game goalless at the start of the second half, Sterling was challenged by Daryl Janmaat as he ran on to Sergio Aguero's flick and the ball cannoned off him and into the net. Sterling was clearly offside when Aguero chested the ball into his path and the lineman's flag went up. But, after a long discussion with his fellow official, referee Paul Tierney overruled his decision, to the disbelief of the Hornets players.

I'll take any goal, but Tierney got this one wrong. You see, if Raheem Sterling had made no attempt to play the ball as it came his way, he is not, strictly speaking, interfering with play. But in this instance he swung at the ball, thus making him active. It should have been disallowed.

So a nice bit of luck for City, and after a frustrating first half, it spurred on the team. Raheem quickly added another two goals before Deulofeu replied with what thankfully turned out to be a consolation goal.

The match was a nice distraction however, as news broke during the week of various investigations into City's affairs, news of which would haunt the side for the remainder of the season. As for Watford, they were one of many teams to play dead against City. I can't blame them, and this is just something City will have to deal with increasingly in the future. City go four points clear but only because Liverpool have a game at home that I fully expect them to win. And even though Burnley made life difficult for them for a long while, win it they did.

Champions League: Manchester City 7 Schalke 0

Well that was rather easy. After the 1st leg dramatic comeback, I was quite relaxed for this one, As I could not see how City would not score at least a couple of goals. I did not however envisage us scoring 7 (seven).

So just to recap, here's how the scoring went: Agüero (35' minutes pen, 38' minutes), Sané (42' minutes), Sterling (56' minutes), Bernardo Silva (71' minutes), Foden (78' minutes), Gabriel Jesus (84' minutes).

In a season of records, you've probably forgotten most of these goals pretty quickly I imagine, as City qualified for the last 8 with ease. Schalke provided stiff resistance for a short while, but once the barriers were breached, the floodgates really opened.

It is tempting to suggest that City truly belong in this competition now, but Schalke really didn't tell us much. It's also easy to forget that Manuel Pellegrini somehow took us to the semi-finals of this competition.

If you needed something to be annoyed about though, this match provided a talking point via VAR, the constant checks taking the enjoyment (almost) out of a scintillating performance. I am an advocate of the system, but it has to be used better than this, as it was during the World Cup. We surely have the technology to check offsides within seconds.

And on a night where it was great to see Sane pick up three assists, it was also great to see Ilkay Gundogan in sparkling form – and was a timely reminder that a summer exit would be greatly detrimental to City's cause.

City have scored at least two goals in each of their last seven Champions League games; the longest such streak by an English team in the competition.

And so the draw for the next two rounds, which was made simultaneously. I hate that. This was a nervy one, as United and Liverpool could await, but in the end City got Spurs, then Ajax or Juventus. I was happy with that. It seemed a better route than Liverpool, who despite having the easiest of the quarter-finals, against Porto, would probably then face Barcelona. Or United.

So Barcelona then.

A Look At The Run In

It's that time of the season, the business end, the time when nerves are shredded on a near-daily basis for some football fans. For me, basically. It's amazing where you can find new grey hairs.

For Manchester City fans, the impossible dream remains a possibility – the quadruple. The word that they dare not say, and a word that refers to an achievement that is not that plausible, despite City's band of merry men being closer than ever to immortality.

The reason a quadruple is not really plausible is not down to talent or attitude. It's the simple fact that going for multiple trophies is a draining experience that is very difficult to pull off and usually ends with failure somewhere along the way. We're probably past questioning how good the players are now. We need fitness, mental strength and a bit of luck along the way.

Firstly, biology is rather important. It does not matter if a footballer is on £20 a week or £200,000, they remain a human being. And sports science is quite clear on the matter of regeneration, namely that the human body needs four days to recuperate fully from acute physical activity. When Bernardo Silva covers 13.7km in a single match, as he did against Liverpool in January, he needs recovery time. Even Ederson does, kind of.

Sadly, many of City's players will not get the luxury of four days' rest. Manchester City have a minimum of 11 games left this season. They may have up to 15 games though. That's after many of them have played a couple of international games, after which they have to fit those 11-15 games into a 6 week period. You do the math.

Now of course, should Pep Guardiola manage to maintain a largely fit squad between now and May, not every player needs to play every match – not even the key players have to. And that may be the key. A few injuries, and those remaining will have a huge strain put on their bodies. And the strain is both physical and mental with so much at stake. With so much to win, and so much to lose.

The key is how a brutal April schedule affects this team. Momentum can build or momentum can be lost. One of the four trophies is in the bag. City have only one domestic cup game remaining before the Premier League ends. Their challengers for the title, Liverpool have one less league game to play (and City's game in the hand is the small matter of United at Old Trafford), but will be expected to progress to the semi-finals of the Champions League, so will have to manage their squad too.

When seeking to assess whether City can manage this fixture list, thoughts naturally turn to past occasions when teams have swept up a multitude of trophies in a single season, and United in 1999 seems an obvious place to start. For me though it is not really comparable.

The reason it is not comparable is due to the luxuries United were afforded in their league campaign. United won the league that season with 79 points. Liverpool already have 76 points this season, whilst City would have 77 should they win that game in hand. United won the league by a single point, and were pushed to the end by Arsenal, but could afford to draw four times in their final 8 games, from April onwards. City have no such luxury – we cannot accurately predict how many points Liverpool will finish the season on, but I doubt City can afford to drop points in more than a couple of games. United had rid themselves of the League Cup too by 2nd December 1998.

Now United's treble in 1999 was of course a wonderful achievement, but was characterised by many a close, nervy game decided by a moment of brilliance, a bit of fortune and the fine lines that big games often bring. That is not to downgrade their achievement, but merely to suggest that if City are to pull off immortality, similar days may lay ahead, games where crucial moments make the difference between success and failure. FYI, Juventus finished 6th in Serie A That season,

Inter in 8th. United's double winners of 2007/08 surrendered both domestic cup competitions at home to Portsmouth and Coventry City, before John Terry fell on his arse and had a little cry. Fine lines.

The Arsenal Invincibles? Well not quite – they went out at the semi-final stage in both domestic cups and to Chelsea in the quarter final of the Champions League.

Basically, the situation City now find themselves in right now is of course not normal. In fact it is unique, for the English game at least. No English team has completed a clean sweep of competitions entered in a season. Apart from those already mentioned, Liverpool won the league, League Cup and European Cup in 1984, and a cup treble in 2001 (which included the UEFA Cup). Little wonder then that Pep wants to temper any talk of the "q" word. It has even turned a United-supporting friend towards hoping Liverpool win the league, as the thought of a City quadruple is too much for him to bear. If you think the next six weeks will be stressful for City fans, imagine how United fans are feeling.

There's no room for manoeuvre in the modern game, in the big matches. Maybe there never was. A drop off of just a few percent by just a few players can have disastrous consequences. Any fatigue can render a world class player ineffective, can risk the chance of a season-ending injury.

Pep will have to make full use of his squad. A player like Fabian Delph may have burnt bridges during the Swansea match, but he may be needed. Pep will have to trust him to discover his form of last season. He may need Benjamin Mendy to finally reach full fitness and remember how to play football. Big players will have to produce big performances and big moments. When a trophy rests in the balance, someone will have to stand up and be counted. But hey, this is a team that has won 18 of its last 20 games. In one of the other two games, they won a trophy anyway. They've stood up and been counted so far. Take a deep breath, because ahead lays possible immortality. Whatever the wealth of the club, whatever the investment, the team right now is in a special place. It's up to the City players to use the situation they find themselves in as a positive, rather than let the weight of history destroy a chance for the greatest legacy of all. Soon we will know……

The other factor is of course the Liverpool narrative. I will avoid further discussion on this in the book, as we'd all had enough of it by the end of the season. It was one of the main reasons why we HAD to win the league. Why large swathes of the country needed us to win the league almost much as we desired it. It has been overwhelming, their seeming expectation that destiny would deliver them their first Premier League title, because it meant more to them (it would if you have never won it before), because their club is unique (spoiler alert – all clubs are unique), or because their club just deserved it more because of their history (another spoiler – all clubs have a rich history). It was impossible to deal with the relentless torrent of Liverpool propaganda, and let's not deny the fact that many media outlets knew the importance to their business model in Liverpool being successful, and acted accordingly.
Day after day after day. More fans, bigger club, means more, we're special, it was like Waco all over again, but without guns and fire. Well so far anyway.
By the end of the season I think I preferred United fans, and would rather United were successful than Liverpool. This is where we are as a human race. The shame.

And that is where my future match reports came from. I snapped. Enough was enough. They deserve it. All of them. All should become clear later.

FA Cup: Swansea 2 Manchester City 3

Well, that was different to how I had envisaged it. A crazy game, and City benefitting for once from some poor officiating. Mark this date down in the history books.

OK, not really, I'm not that paranoid. But this was far tougher than expected, and it was only a sleeping linesman that got City over the line.

Well, we'll never know. The assumption that City would have drawn if Aguero's goal had been correctly disallowed is pure speculation. City may have still gone on to score a winner, we will never know – after all, for the first time in the game, City were totally dominant by that point, and it felt like a winner was coming.

Credit to Swansea, who went toe to toe with City and were a joy to watch at times. I am no sure City helped themselves however. I have commented in the past that City have triumphed in the League Cup despite their efforts, which naturally a times have lacked the intensity of Premier League or Champions League games. And in the FA Cup this lack of intensity has showed, with some disappointing campaigns since that 2011 victory. You sense Pep wants to add this trophy onto his CV, but this game did not further his cause. City woke up eventually and turned the screw, but they walked on thin ice, and of course needed help.

Of course, as per last season, Fabian Delph did not help matters. There was simply no need to commit to that tackle in the penalty area, and the result was wearily predictable. The second goal I simply applaud, because it was really beautifully executed, and sometimes you just have to applaud an opposition goal. Pep won't see it that way of course, and will bemoan the swathes of space available to Swansea players. And naturally it was an ex-City player that had to stick the knife in.

But the old City may well have buckled at this point, but this team is better, and made of sterner stuff. And thus they came back in the 2nd half and rescued the most difficult of situations. Because when you have the likes of Bernardo Silva on the pitch, anything is possible. His finish for the first was one of the cleanest strikes of a goal-laden season. The penalty awarded for the equaliser was correct, in the modern game, but soft. It's given every week though elsewhere, so was hardly controversial. The winner was, but hey, City got a break. Onwards and upwards!

There was more luck to be had though. Aguero's penalty hit the post then rebounded back onto the keeper and in. Fortunate. The fact is that Aguero is not one of the best penalty takers we have had, and it is a slight problem. It would prove costly too later in the season. Penalties would have a key effect on the season.

Let's not forget though at least two other occasions where it's hard to work out how City did not score, one in each half, including a great double save from the keeper in the second half. City did enough in the end to win, but the way it happened will of course trigger great debate.
With none of the traditional big boys left, United falling at Wolves, City would be happy with whoever they got in the semi-finals, though Brighton was probably the best option of all. Rival fans can moan all they want about City's easy draws, but it's hard to draw the likes of Liverpool, United and Chelsea when they get knocked out. Jurgen Klopp threw the FA Cup to concentrate on other trophies, so quit your tiresome whinging and conspiracy theories.

And so to one of the highlights of the season on Twitter – the absolutely serious suggestion by a journalist, by referencing the 20th anniversary of Arsene Wenger offering to replay a cup tie against Sheffield United, that perhaps City should offer to do the same with Swansea City, because Sergio Aguero's winning goal was offside.

To repeat – a journalist suggested Manchester City should offer to replay a game because they scored a goal from an offside position.

I've literally nothing to offer after that. Nothing.

Anyway, no time to rest, because we once more got the joy of an international break – YAY!

Bluemoon Podcast Audio Script – Back In The Bunker

Hello? Hello? It's me again. Back from the future. Not sure what year, I forgot to decide on that, you just make one up for yourself. Maybe 2023? As the UK is already close to a post-apocalyptic wasteland, I didn't have to travel that far back in time.

But anyway, it seems I have to warn you foolish City fans again. It's becoming a bit tiresome this. But here we go, nevertheless….

You see, there's a new threat. It's not City dominance any more, or Liverpool dominance either. No it's something even worse. It's the attempt to rewrite history, and when you try and do that, the ramifications can be disastrous.

This time around, it all started in the middle of March 2019. Manchester City had sneaked past a lively Swansea City in the FA Cup, to reach Wembley yet again, where they would play Brighton. 2nd home and all that. Talk turned once more to the possibility of a quadruple – after all, no team had ever got this close in English football. Naturally, for those of a non-blue tint, this would simply not do. So history was rewritten. Step forward a certain Adrian Durham.

You probably only know Durham as the shock jock on a crap radio station, but he's now the Tory backbencher MP that proposed bringing back corporal and capital punishment last month - and the abolition of income tax for red heads. He started all this shit.

He questioned whether, because City got a soft penalty and scored the winner from an offside position, that the tie with Swansea should be replayed. Ben Rumsby of the Daily Telegraph mused that the Swansea game reminded him of when Arsene Wenger offered to replay a match against Sheffield United 20 years previously. SiriusXM (no, me neither), asked if all four quarter finals should be replayed as VAR was not used consistently in all matches? And so it began.

Well, not really, as this was nothing that new. Mainstream journalists such as Barry Glendenning had already suggested that City's achievements would have to come with an asterisk next to them, due to claims of FFP irregularities, transfer bans and the like. City's reputation was tarnished, as you already knew. This was exacerbated with the fear that city could win an unprecedented quadruple. Now history had to be rewritten. The possible achievement was downplayed, starting with City's generous run of cup draws that season. City were suddenly fortunate for getting kind draws after winning the league and topping their Champions League group. City were suddenly lucky for progressing through two domestic cups when other big teams drew each other or didn't take the competitions seriously. In conclusion, City were nothing special, though for the money they had spent, they should be anyway. But they weren't.

But then it really got serious. Because City had already won loads of stuff, and that really couldn't do. The rest of the footballing world had had enough. They wanted a return to the old days, a level playing field where United could organically dominate once more.

This feeling only got worse when for them, the thing they dreaded most happened. City won the quadruple, with almost 54000 fans turning out on Deansgate to greet their blue-shirted heroes. But soon after the transfer and CL bans kicked in, and it was then that past achievements came under scrutiny. Under pressure from the likes of Liverpool and United, the Premier League and FA looked into whether City's trophies were legitimate. It may not surprise you to discover that they were not.

The reclassification process went in chronological order. The FA Cup of 2011 was the first to go. A committee comprising of Mick Hucknall, John Aldridge, Paddy Crerand and Bobby Charlton's comb-over decided that the red card for Paul Scholes in the 2011 semi-final was a tad harsh. What's more, Dimitar Berbatov was put off by a light reflecting off someone's watch when he missed a good chance in the first half. The score was reversed, and it was assumed that United would brush aside Stoke City in the final with ease. The committee returned after a light lunch to consider the 2011/12 season. Needless to say United won the league too, after it was considered unfair that United's final game at Sunderland finished before City's. Thus, only goals scored until full time at The Stadium of Light counted. United were champions once more.

A new committee was sworn in to look at the 2013/14 season. City were allowed to retain the League Cup as it was only Sunderland they had beaten, but the league was a different matter. A committee of Dean Saunders, David Gill, James Nesbitt and the band Cast pored over the evidence. I think you know where this is leading. Gerrard's slip was considered unfair, and another result was reversed. For the 2017/18 season, the middleman was cut out and the title was deemed illegal due to financial doping. City were also relegated four divisions. The committee made two final decisions. City's badge was changed, to contain a hundred asterisks. Secondly, it was made public record that the club was established in the year 2008. City got two minor concessions – they could continue doping and The Paris Angel would be allowed back on Twitter, for a probationary period.

And that was the beginning of the end. Crowds naturally dwindled, players left, Sam Allardyce had a brief stint as manager before the Venkys bought the club out and installed Glenn Roeder in the hot seat. City never recovered, and eventually sealed a ground share deal with Stockport County. Still couldn't sell out.

But United and Liverpool fans were still not happy. They bemoaned the lost years, years they lost due to City's financial doping and cheating, so they claimed. So City fans, the few that were left, were pariahs. They were held responsible, for allowing it all to happen, for cheering as it did. This was Brexit Britain, where law and order had already broken down. The Men In Black roam the area as I speak, picking off any blue citizens they encounter.

Thus I hide in this bunker with a steady supply of monster munch and pukka pies and DVDs of the good old days. I've even got a VHS of Back In The Big Time, with Shaun Goater on the front. Younger listeners should ask their parents about what VHS is, and whilst you're at it, the joy of a season ticket book. So, I hear you ask, what do us City fans need to do to combat this? Well I'm afraid to say, that the answer is nothing. There is nothing you can do. This is one challenge too gargantuan, too massive to complete. You cannot fight a tide, and you cannot fight this. We're pariahs now, and the club's achievements count for nothing. They remain only in our memories, and one day those will go too, and history will not have recorded the great City side of 2011-19.

I send you this message simply to inform, and to implore you to enjoy that quadruple before the house of cards collapses. The summer is yours, so make the most of it. It's a scorcher by the way, though I should point out most of East Anglia is under water nowadays. Don't worry, they moved mustard production elsewhere in the nick of time. To Singapore in fact, after Brexit kicked in.

I digress. The wonderful journey is about to end. So whilst you can, drink it in. History will not judge City kindly. One day, you may find it easier to support someone else instead – perhaps go back to Chelsea or FCUM. That is up to you. Just know that openly being a City fan is too dangerous now. There's no glory to be had, Pep is managing United and Salah has three separate religions based on him. The cult has not weakened, nor will it ever. But don't be sad – we had a good run. We had the Aguero moment, and no other fan will ever experience anything like that. And we had the quadruple – the league sealed with a 93rd minute winner from Ederson at Brighton, the FA Cup sealed with ease and the Champions League final against Liverpool won with a 98th minute offside, handballed winner from Raheem Sterling. History makers, never to be repeated. Enjoy, because it was one hell of a ride... I'll see you all in 4 years, bunker 2347 just outside Basingstoke, free entry to anyone who can recite the Bernardo Silva song. Until then, good luck, and keep the faith....

Bernard Halford

On 26th March, the sad news emerged that Bernard Halford had died at the age of 77. Bernard spent nearly four decades working as the club secretary at City before being named as the club's life president upon his retirement. He was Mr. Manchester City, an integral part of the club's history, a lovely man who cared as much as anyone for his beloved blues during a rollercoaster history. He would certainly have some stories to tell over the decades he spent at the club.

Pep Guardiola, who visited Bernard whilst he was receiving treatment in hospital, said: "It is such sad news to hear of Bernard Halford's passing. It was an honour and a privilege to meet and talk football with him and his knowledge of this football club was amazing.

"He was a great man, but moreover, he was also a great football man with a complete understanding of the game from grass roots level up. His whole life was dedicated to the game, but mostly to Manchester City and we were lucky to have him."

At the end of season trophy parade, Pep would wear a flat cap that Bernard's wife had given him for the occasion.

Rest In Peace, Bernard.

Raheem Sterling & His Fake Redemption

What must it feel like to score a hat-trick for your national side? I couldn't begin to imagine. Raheem Sterling doesn't need to imagine, after firing England to a 5-0 win against the Czech Republic at Wembley. He lifted his shirt after scoring to reveal a tribute Damary Dawkins, a Crystal Palace youth team player who had been fighting acute lymphoblastic leukaemia for four years. Damary died last Sunday, aged just 13. As Rob Harris pontificated on Twitter the ramifications of his tribute, under FIFA law, Sterling spent the post-match period celebrating his hat-trick and the Wembley crowd's standing ovation by spending some time with Football Beyond Borders, a charity that uses the power of football to change the lives of young people. Raheem signed his England shirt, and donated it to charity.

Raheem Sterling, encapsulated perfectly in one single evening. The first City player to score a hat-trick for England in a competitive match, just a stone's throw from where he grew up (if you are particularly good at throwing stones). The stuff dreams are made of. As Jadon Sancho commented after the match: "He is a great player, as you can see on and off the pitch. He is a humble guy and I am just so delighted I am sharing the pitch with him and obviously I look up to him as a role model and especially starting with him was a great feeling."

48 caps for England, 6 years in the Premier League, 46 goals for City in 124 appearances, a Premier League title, 3 other trophies, and currently pushing for an unprecedented quadruple, all by the tender age of 24. And suddenly, Raheem Sterling is finally appreciated by the English public in a fairly low-key qualification game. Strange that. The backtracking from the public and media alike for many months has been something to behold, the hypocrisy now reaching new levels. Perhaps this appreciation is due more to his transformation with the three lions on his shirt. Admittedly he has rarely reached the heights for England that he has for his club sides, but that is nothing new for an England player. His role in the

World Cup was not best suited for his skill set, and i would say the same for the likes of Kane and Alli. Only one player got the bulk of the criticism though in a summer filled with sunshine and good will. You almost understand why United fans use to sing Argentina when you look at the detritus of social media responding to an England game. Now he fits the national side too, in a 4-3-3 formation, and a swathe of uneducated bigots have awoken from their four-year slumber and decided to wipe the slate clean. How considerate of you all. But England are at last fun to watch again, and that may be Gareth Southgate's greatest legacy. Sterling is a big part of that.

There was one word however that kept cropping up however as the match reports filtered in on Friday evening and Saturday morning.

Redemption.

Raheem Sterling's redemption.

Yep, that's right folks, City's star player had "redeemed" himself in the eyes of the footballing public.

How fucking dare you.

Redemption from what? Redemption because a group of pot-bellied middle-aged privileged white males took offence at a tattoo he'd had for a year? Redemption for having some nice cars? Redemption for buying his mum a house? Redemption for the horrific hatchet job endured for wanting to move to a new club? Redemption for being booed by opposition fans at every away game he played in? Redemption for his extensive charity work? Redemption because he missed a few chances on a football field in the past, the first to ever do so? Redemption for not being white?

If you are one of those people that think Raheem Sterling has found redemption, then kindly fuck off. And when you've fucked off, come back and then go and fuck off all over again. Sterling has nothing to apologise for, nothing to prove to any of you out there. The problem was never with him, and it never will be. It's not about crediting him now, as it is about it suddenly dawning on large swathes of the population not to blame him for things that aren't his fault, and never have been. You know his story by now. The weight he has carried on his shoulders for years not just due to his coverage in the media or how he was perceived, but for all players that have been victims of a barely concealed racism in the public and in sections of our wonderful press. The strength he has shown has not only been admirable, it has been staggering. Strength shown by him from a very young age.

Raheem Sterling could easily be playing in the lower leagues now, largely stripped of his precocious talents, his confidence shot, his footballing brain redundant. Instead he is finally talked about as a world class player. And because of everything he has been through, Raheem Sterling should clean up every Player of The Year award going this season. Now, Virgil Van Dijk has been majestic, and like Mohamed Salah last season, when once more a City player and a Liverpool player went head-to-head for the major individual awards, you could not, in normal circumstances, begrudge him winning the players' and football writers' awards, especially when we consider how often defenders are overlooked. But these are not normal circumstances, and this is about more than mere ability and performance levels. This is about much, much more. Perhaps you think such awards should only be about performances, and that's fine. But it would send out a powerful message to reward Raheem Sterling for what he has done, what he has achieved, over the past few years and especially this season.

You see, Raheem Sterling has created feelings in a footballer I have not experienced before. When I look back at this golden generation of City players, whilst being force-fed rusks in a care home, I will shed a tear for the likes of Sergio, David, Vincent and more. It was an honour, a privilege to watch them. I almost feel blessed, in a weird atheist sort of way. I cannot thank them enough for what they gave to us City fans. But with Raheem, there's a new feeling.

I've no need really to feel protective of Raheem – he's far stronger mentally than I could ever hope to be. But the desire to protect, to man the barricades, is natural for City fans. And I feel protective of him like no other footballer that has ever donned a sky (or laser) blue shirt. And he has consistently, repeatedly, made me proud to have him represent our club. And now, and only now, do rival fans begin to appreciate what we have, what our club has.

One day he will probably play out his end game and move on to pastures new, probably Real Madrid, and City fans will stoically wish him the best whilst desperately trying not to act like Liverpool fans. I hope we are simply thankful for watching him grow as a footballer, and as a man.

You hope a corner has been turned in this country now. You hope that people think twice about how they talk about and treat footballers, human beings, in the future. That may be me being optimistic. In fact I know it is. But Sterling changed the narrative, altered the conversation and forced us to take a long, hard look at ourselves, whilst simultaneously doing the business on the pitch too. I don't believe that footballers should be seen as role models, but if you must have one, if your child is looking for someone to admire, someone to aspire to be, you could not choose a better man to look up to than a certain Raheem Shaquille Sterling.

Manchester City's Greatest "Alternative" Moments

We know about Manchester City's greatest moments – they've been well-documented after all. Since the takeover, it has been a glorious chapter in the club's history, and we've lived through it all. The 2011 FA Cup*, the 2012 league title*, three more League Cups* and two more league titles*. But what about those alternative great moments? The little things that still played a part in City's recent history because, quite simply, they were bloody funny. Bonus points for winding up rival fans. Here's those greatest moments, in no particular order. I've only included incidents since 2008, when the club was founded.

Dzeko feigning death on the Goodison pitch.

It's May 2014. It's my 40th birthday. I'm drinking shit beer in Courtyard, and there are balloons with my name on them (thanks Rochelle and Lou). I couldn't care less about that though (soz), because I have rarely been this nervous about a football match. There's a league title on the line. The balloons and vodka liqueur with glitter in it can wait. As for the match, you know the rest. City go behind to a Barkley wonder-strike, score three, then see out a nerve-wracking finale after Lukaku halves the deficit with 25 minutes to go. What is often overlooked is Edin Dzeko's epic role in seeing out this game. Yeah, he scored two goals, but that's only half of the story. On 79 minutes, Dzeko falls to the turf, clutching his face. At this point he is probably trying to avoid a yellow card following a challenge, where he tried to pull back an Everton player as he broke, perhaps just wanting to stop the attack. I prefer to think it was in fact one of the greatest time-wasting efforts in modern football. Unfortunately for him, the referee is not interested in his near-death experience. It is at this point it becomes a battle of wills. Referee Lee Probert is not impressed, but Dzeko has committed himself to being injured, so it's a case of seeing who blinks first. Within a short while it becomes clear that Dzeko is not going to get up, perhaps ever, so Probert is in a difficult position. He is pretty sure Dzeko is faking injury, but what if he isn't? One day as a referee he'll ignore a genuine injury and be reffing in the Beazer Homes League the week after. If that was still a thing. Probert refuses medical attention, and waits, yellow card in hand, as a succession of players from both sides put forward their cases. Dzeko is face down all the while, blocking out the world, perhaps his embarrassment getting the better of him. He eventually blinks first, looking up at Probert, who remains unimpressed. Eventually physios are allowed onto the pitch, and even a stretcher, which we all know will not be needed. Dzeko is pretending by now that he has dislocated his shoulder and eventually rises, to be carded, throwing in a limp for extra effect as he departs the pitch. He stoically finished the match, and the delay probably didn't help the City team to be honest. Bloody funny in hindsight though.

Adebayor goal celebration

I used to sit in the corner of the Etihad next to the away fans. The year is 2010, and City are locked 1-1 in a tight game against Arsenal. Then, Emmanuel Adebayor rises to plant an excellent header into the back of the net to put City ahead against his old club, and the rest is history. The goal was at the other end of the pitch to the away fans, and me, so I was somewhat surprised as Adebayor got closer and closer to where I sat. Then the knee slide started and the vast majority of the ground bent over double laughing. I turned to my mate immediately, wiping the tears away from my eyes and said "he'll pay for that!", but it was probably worth it. In fact it definitely was, despite its juvenile nature. The true joy from the incident though is not the long goal celebration run and knee-slide, but the faux outrage of the Arsenal contingent as they pretended to get to him on the pitch whilst simultaneously having no intention of getting to him on the pitch. At one point you can see a single nonplussed steward holding over 50 of them back.

Arsenal fans seem to have mastered the art of hating players for daring to leave in order to supposedly better themselves, and are also masters of signing the type of player who cannot move on and shrug their shoulders at the abuse. It creates the perfect storm, repeatedly.

In the end, Adebayor escaped with a £25,000 fine and a two-match ban, which was suspended until December 2010, following a personal hearing at Wembley, and a feeble attempt at a public apology.

Inevitably someone somewhere on Twitter then commented that if he'd done that on the streets, he'd have gone to prison. And scraped the skin off his knees, I imagine.

Time wasting at Old Trafford

Now we're talking. Kyle Walker had already warmed up for this majestic two minutes by repeatedly throwing away the ball handed to him by a ball boy, before trying to dob in the child to the referee for his own actions. But before Ederson allegedly threw milk over Jose Mourinho (semi-skimmed), City's winding down of the clock in a corner at the United end is majestic stuff, piss-taking in the extreme, and a nice analogy for the power shift in Manchester football. What makes it all the better is watching Ashley Young desperately try not to self-combust as the home team desperately try to get hold of the ball so they can try and attack for an equaliser.

It all starts as the clock approaches 89 minutes. Raheem Sterling holds the ball in the corner before Ashley Young kicks the ball out for a throw-in, before shouting at no one in particular. Kevin De Bruyne has not read the script and takes the throw-in quite quickly, to Bernardo Silva, who passes to Sterling, who immediately moves back towards the corner flag. He doesn't reach it though, as Ashley Young, who by now is really losing his shit, fouls him and is booked. By the time de Bruyne lays off the ball to Sterling, the 90 minutes is almost up. Sterling resorts to holding the ball in the corner, and wins one, as the board goes up with 4 minutes on it. By now Jose Mourinho is arguing with the 4th official, in which time Sterling has won another throw-in. He throws it to Bernardo Silva – he breaks free, and he could be in on goal! And this is where it gets really funny. Bernardo simply turns round and takes the ball back to the corner flag despite a clear goal-scoring opportunity, before winning another throw-in. De Bruyne throws it to Bernardo, who hits it off a broken Ashley Young for another throw-in. De Bruyne throws it to Bernardo, who hits it off Lindelof for another throw-in. De Bruyne throws it to Bernardo, he returns it, and finally the strangle hold is broken as De Bruyne hits the ball out for a goal-kick. 150 seconds of pure belly laughs, and a couple of minutes later the game was over and City had won at Old Trafford once more.

Pep Guardiola v Stan Collymore: A one-way spat

A classic case of an intelligent, classy man clashing with a spiteful, dumb buffoon with enough chips on his shoulder to keep Lou Macari in business or decades. To recap: Pep Guardiola was asked, by a Spanish journalist I think, a question about Stan Collymore in a press conference, no doubt after Stan had been once more instructing Pep how he could do his job better, having questioned his management. Despite what many may claim, Pep was clearly confused by the question, hence his reaction. It is quite clear if you watch the clip that Pep just does not understand why he is being asked the question, or does not want to discuss it in a press conference. And that's it. Pep is just not the sort of man to dig someone out in public anyway.
But oh no, not for Stanley Victor Collymore. He took the simple misunderstanding as a slight, as Pep disrespecting him, pretending that he didn't know who he was. Cue a 2 year+ meltdown, and a succession of pitiful Daily Mirror articles whereby Stan had little digs at Pep, laid out what he had to do to be considered a success, beginning with this staggering piece screenshotted below.
Of course Pep Guardiola has continued to do his job and live his life none the wiser at Stan's weekly servings of tripe and insecurity, all started by Stan not having the intelligence to interpret an innocent situation in a press conference. Still, at

least he's got loads of articles out of it.

Now of course Collymore has suffered terribly from depression for much of his life and has been refreshingly candid and open about his struggles, struggles which should always be taken into consideration. But still, strip that away, and you're still left with a grade A ****.

So man up Stan (about Pep), and get a grip. He's made you look like a fool ever since you started your grudge. It's probably time you moved on. Pep did within 3 seconds. Then we may be spared less of shit like this in future.

Zinchenko knocking over the PL trophy

Back to the trophy, rising cult star Oleksandr Zinchenko is jumping up and down celebrating winning the league, as footballers are wont to do in such circumstances. But then he gives the Premier League trophy, sitting proudly behind him on a plinth, a little nudge, and gravity does the rest. Now this doesn't quite rank up there with the likes of Sergio Ramos throwing a trophy under a bus, but is absolute comic gold for the dawning realisation of what has happened on Zinchenko's face as he turns round. And also the reaction of staff and fellow players. It even seems to have floored Yaya Toure.

Of course, as celebrations go, it cannot quite match Martin DeMichelis and his erotic (not my words) dash with the trophy after winning the league in 2014. Drink it in...

Mario Balotelli tales

Where to start? Where to end?

I'll be honest, I was never truly on board as a full member of the Mario Balotelli fan club. If I was detached from the club, I would have been, but I always felt he was a hindrance much of the time, for a team aspiring to be at the top. His personality allowed him to get away with things other players would not have done. Of course football does not have to be deadly serious all the time, and Mario brought some light relief to proceedings. He brought character to a sanitised world. He was unfairly targeted during his time at City, but boy he did not help himself.

Anyway, it's hard to pick one moment from his stay. This is especially so considering how many false stories swirled around the true ones. His friend destroyed a bathroom with a firework, not him. Did he really drive round Wythenshawe handing out Xmas presents? Are any of the stories true?

The greatest alternative moment should really be a serious one – his solitary assist being the one that set up Aguerooooooooooooo. But there you could choose any of his penalties, THAT T-shirt, the shouldered goal, the grass allergy, a training ground scrap with Mancini, winding up Rio Ferdinand after a victory, throwing darts at a youth player, his inability to put a bib on and numerous acts of philanthropy. But I'll stick with that assist, thanks.

Last I heard, Balotelli is available on a free this summer. Just saying.

Kolarov Xmas Carol

City's media output is generally excellent, but I pay little attention to their stuff to be honest. Just want to watch football and all that. Nevertheless, Aleksandar Kolarov has always fascinated me, perhaps because left-backs generally do, that being my position of choice. My right leg is merely for standing on, after all. His Christmas carol certainly lives long in the memory, probably because of its chilling nature. It's Jingle Bells performed with menace.

Have little doubt, Kolarov has SEEN things. I would not want to mess with him.

Aguero v the police

I appreciate the job our boys (and girls) in blue do, usually, but the football fan often gets a rum deal. So it was nice to see one of our own stand up for a bitter bertie during testing times. It is early in last season, with none of us capable of comprehending what lay ahead in the league. A tough game at Bournemouth was heading towards a dull draw when up popped Raheem Sterling to bounce in a late, late winner. Cue understandable pandemonium in the away end, a ridiculous red card for Raheem and one City fan being forcibly restrained at the edge of the pitch by a steward. Sergio took offence at this and went to the aid of the fan, got involved in an argy-bargy (sorry) before a couple of policemen blocked his route to the steward. You can see in his eyes he is genuinely fumin'. Hero status further reinforced.

The steward later claimed he had been assaulted, dollar signs flashing in his eyes, before soon realising he was on a hiding to nothing.

Mancini laughing at 1-6 and just taking on Ferguson

As Edin Dzeko slotted in City's 6th (SIXTH) goal at Old Trafford sometime in 2011, Roberto Mancini was not the only person laughing at the madness of it all. By this point I had stopped celebrating goals and was doubled up in laughter, such was the astonishment at what had just happened. Mancini sat on the bench having a good chuckle, scarf immaculately tied, and I've never loved him more. Well almost, because here was the guy that took on Ferguson, and knocked him off his fucking perch. And there was no greater sight than Mancini going at it with Ferguson on the touchline. Followed by a City victory, naturally. Magnificent.

I noted with Mario Balotelli that a person's personality can have a huge bearing on how they are perceived and treated by a fan base, and Mancini was a clear example of this. Obviously he deserved adulation for what he achieved, but he retained tremendous support even when everything deteriorated. This was partly because he helped changed the balance of power in Manchester football for the first time on over a generation. But also, he was just a handsome, suave bastard that made fawning all too easy. I'm proud to have been part of that fawning.

There's a reason I never wear scarves, because if you can't carry one off like Mancini, then what's the point?

Mancini's QPR meltdown.

Hey, we can all laugh about it now. Due to football's greatest sliding doors moment, we are allowed to view history rather differently, by which I mean the 2011/12 league season. City of course need to beat a struggling QPR side to win their first league title in 44 years. It was all going ok at half-time, but then somehow City contrive to concede two goals, because, you know, City, and this is against 10 men after Joey Barton had his own personal meltdown. More on that shortly.

Cue the meltdown. It's understandable really, because at this point, there is not much Mancini can do apart from some canny substitutions. This is on the players really. And so Mancini stood on the touchline, basically shouting swear words randomly at his players, and no one could really blame him. City were somehow contriving to mess up their title push, and the unthinkable became a distinct possibility.

Thankfully, it all turned out alright in the end, and Mancini's leftfield approach to rally the troops is one little footnote on a day of a thousand stories.

But as alluded to, a shout out must also be made to Carlos Tevez, and perhaps another contender for one of City's greatest alternative moments. For there was a reason Joey Barton got so irate, apart from the fact that he is Joey Barton, and that is the fact that Tevez definitely has a swing at Barton before he retaliates. It could easily, and probably should have been, two red cards. Thankfully the referee did not see what started the eventual mass brawl, as Barton tried to take half the City team with him. Perhaps it would not have made any difference. City would still have dominated, and Tevez did not have one of his best days. For that moment though, he perhaps deserves a statue outside the ground.

Premier League: Fulham 0 Manchester City 2

For a change, my day involved getting a steam train up to Ramsbottom to watch this match, because – well, why not? Fulham are not my favourite team right now, as they have made a lot of people look stupid. I tipped them for a great season, and they have been quite appalling. I saw them a couple of weeks previously against United, and what struck me was their nervousness on the ball – they made mistakes that United seized upon with glee.

And it was a similar story for this match. City scored two goals in 25 minutes, could have scored many more, then took their foot off the gas and managed the game to cruise over the line. Bernardo Silva and Sergio Aguero supplied the goals on this occasion, and it was as leisurely an afternoon as you could hope for.

And there was no better illustration of that by pointing out that Fulham became the latest side not to register a shot on target against City. It was cruise control throughout against the most compliant of opponents.

Oh and needless to say, City had a clear penalty turned down. It's beyond a joke now.

If any proof was needed that City would have to win every league game remaining to retain the Premier League title, it came at Anfield the following day. Yet again Liverpool were gifted a victory in a game they deserved to lose to Spurs, as Sissoko blazed over with the goal gaping and a player to square to, before Lloris decided to palm a weak header onto his own player, and Liverpool had a late winner. This will have to be done the hard way.

APRIL

Premier League: Manchester City 2 Cardiff City 0

I had planned it meticulously. The comedian Rhod Gilbert was touring for the first time in 6 years. I love his live shows. He was playing three dates in Manchester too, so I checked the fixture list and chose the date where City could not possibly be playing. That is until the fixture was moved to the same night. This is not the first, or even tenth time this happened to me.

Ah well, I was not missing the gig for Cardiff, so had to follow via my phone.
Thankfully City scored before Rhod had even stepped onto the stage, and this was another procession capped with a nice Sane goal and then yet more game management that it requires little analysis.
A chance late on for Cardiff could have made for a few nervous moments, but it was squandered and City had another easy three points.

Not quite the thrashing that some may have expected, but in a season when the team would score 159 goals, let's not be too down-hearted.

FA Cup Semi-Final: Manchester City 1 Brighton 0

The cost of being a football fan has finally caught up with me. For the first time, I declined to make the journey to Wembley. I simply could not afford to, and the decision was made easier by the strong opinion that a semi-final shouldn't be at Wembley anyway. At least the empty seat counters had a fun day, as I was clearly not alone.

Let's be honest, I did not miss much. I don't want to sound blasé at a semi-final victory and another FA Cup final appearance, but this was no classic. City scored early with a nice goal, and then seemed to ease off as if they felt they had bigger battles ahead. They have in a way, but it was a dangerous tactic, and only a great goal-line clearance from Aymeric Laporte in the 2nd half saw City through.

Still, it only took 4 minutes for another timely reminder of why we miss Kevin De Bruyne. His perfect cross was expertly headed home by Gabriel Jesus. And as goals go, that was it.

There was still time for a dust up between Kyle Walker and Alireza Jahanbakhsh. It was much ado about nothing, but in the modern game it was still idiotic of Walker to move his head up when in the face of the Brighton striker. VAR didn't see a problem but I could easily see a red card being doled out for that. There's no need, whatever the provocation, the Brighton player perhaps raking a foot down Walker's leg as the ball was shepherded out. A loss of composure could cost us the chance to win a trophy though. Stupid.

Anyway, despite the lack of an attacking threat, City were rarely in danger and repelled Brighton's physicality. And with the other semi-final providing a tad more entertainment, it is Watford that City will face on May 18th in what will hopefully be their attempt to secure a unique domestic treble. Fingers crossed.

And of course there was still talk about the quadruple. Which may explain the lacklustre performance, as there was no rest before another match in London as City faced Spurs.

The Era Of Cult FC's Match Reports

After Liverpool's rather fortunate late winner over Spurs last week, I was forced to read a piece on the site of a rather well-known podcast/writing site attached to Liverpool. You may know to what I am referring. The sickly prose that made me want to scratch out my eyeballs was replicated by me below. And then in a couple of subsequent match reports.
So with that in mind, I decided to write my own Liverpool match report. Picture the scene...it is late July 2019, and we're all ready for a new season...

We've travelled so far yet not travelled at all. We've climbed the tallest mountains and descended into the deepest valleys. We've seen things no mere mortal should. We've had experiences most could only dream of. Yet here we are.
Gigg Lane, on a cloudy August afternoon. For some an inauspicious start to the season. But not for those of us crammed into the small paddock behind the goal. We sing YNWA. The home fans sing it with us. They get it.
Beg, steal, borrow. Do what you can. This is football, yet it is not football. It is more. It is always more, even when it isn't. Which it is.
It's the haze of red smoke, the billowing flag, the stowaway on the ferry desperate to smell Andy Robertson up close. It's Shankly, it's the King, it's Salah's delicate kiss of the turf. It means more to the family. Red men. Red children. Red elders. Firmino is my strength and my song; he has given me victory. This is my God, and I will praise him - my father's God, and I will exalt him.
Klopp's smile says it all. He is ready. Ready to fight the good fight once more. He transcends his sport. He transcends his profession. Those teeth could tell some stories. Maybe one day they will.
One day.
But not yet, not now. There are other duties to attend to. Sharpen those warriors' legs, get them fit, get them rampaging

across the land yet again. This is our time. This is your time. This is the time of kings.

Hammer time.

The heady aroma of cheap pies and stale beer. This is real football, away from your sanitised television set. This is reality and it smells great. The flags pass over, and for a few short moments I weep in my little bubble, under fabric woven by generations across our fair city.

Five times.

I've travelled across land and sea yet I always end up back here, back where it began, back with these men and these women, doing what we do. The best of times, the worst of times. Sometimes Liverpool are too good. Sometimes. And yet they are in generous mood too as the sun breaks through on a calm yet chaotic afternoon. Later it will sink under a sullen horizon. The shakers saw a crescent, but we saw the whole of the moon. These lads are our lads, and there are 11 of them, no 20, no there are millions of them. All wanting the same thing. To pray, to worship, perchance to dream.

Because it means more. They could have won, they could have embarrassed their opposition, but there are bigger forces at work here. Mystical forces that tell those in expensive boots and freshly-cleaned linen to forget results and just be themselves. On this occasion it was not to be. Not today, but hopefully next time.

We'll be there too. I like to think that Liverpool did not lose this match – they just didn't win it. Or draw. Think Tom Cruise shaking that cocktail mixer. Kevin Costner in his field of dreams. That big guy being electrocuted in the Green Mile. Liverpool's redemption is less Shawshank, more destiny.

Hey, James Milner being substituted in a pre-season game will never garner more than a small footnote in the history books. But he's our James Milner, not yours. As he solemnly and respectfully left the pitch, unaware that at that precise moment his house was being burgled, all I could sense and hear and smell was time halting, standing silent, like a solitary boat in a calm sea. In that moment I was at peace, and so was the rest of the away contingent. Where do we go from here, apart from Lyon in the Continental Cup next Thursday? There will be other days like this, and there will be no days like this. Breathe it in, all of you. For these are special times, and we are special people.

Final score – Bury 2 Liverpool 1.

Champions League: Tottenham Hotspur 1 Manchester City 0

Feel free to skip ahead to the next game. I wouldn't blame you to be honest.

This was the game that was dissected more than any other during the season. The debate resurfaced over whether Pep was abandoning his principle sin the tournament once more, over-thinking, making concessions when he wouldn't in any other competition. And it's hard to disagree with much of that. There's a second leg to put this right, but this was a frustrating night.

It was not the team that was the problem but the approach. With Zinchenko not available, Delph slotted in and continued the poor form we have seen when he occasionally reappears. The inclusion of Mahrez perhaps raised more eyebrows, and he could not impose himself on the match, whilst Leroy Sane once more sat on the bench. And then to compound matters after the goal, Sane and De Bruyne were introduced with only minutes left which served no purpose. Pep was clearly by this point worried about the prospect of conceding a killer 2nd goal, so decided to quit whilst he was behind.

But the key aspect of the game was the caution that he applied to his team. He seemed scarred by previous campaigns, both in Monaco and at Anfield, and it was the template used at Anfield this season that shut out the hosts that he turned to. On another day we'd be applauding the approach, seeing the wider picture of a tie with two legs and giving his team the chance to attack in the 2nd leg. Aguero should score a penalty, and this becomes a different match report. It becomes a report that mentions that City scored an all-important away goal, and who knows what effect the early goal would have had on both sides. The fact is, Aguero just ain't a great penalty taker, but I thought the award was fairly soft, and Guardiola can't base tactics on the hope of getting handball decisions. Managers will always be judged on results, and what really annoys is the feeling that Tottenham weren't even that good. This was not the same as Liverpool the previous season. They were there for the taking.

And it was Delph in the end that cost us. He switched off, Son Heung-min did not, and with 12 minutes to go, with City slowly turning the screw and getting on top, Spurs were ahead. Ederson was slow to get down to the shot, but was perhaps hampered by a hip injury he had picked up not long before. Maybe I am being clouded by the result. Once Harry Kane went off, with an injury he only had himself to blame for, City were gaining control. But goals change games, and they may have changed this tie. City did not create anywhere near enough opportunities, and I feel that the rule I hate more than anything is going to bite this club on the behind again – the failure to get an away goal could prove costly should Spurs score in the 2nd leg. And you'd fancy them to, as losing Kane has not greatly affected them in the past.

So a frustrating night as the fabled quadruple hangs in the balance, but at least the team gets the chance to put things right next week.

Premier League: Crystal Palace 1 Manchester City 3

This was better!

A 9th straight win for City, and another two goals for Raheem Sterling. He's top of the league. In what was a potentially tricky match, City navigated it professionally. The nerves returned as Palace got a goal back with 9 minutes to go, but City snuffed out any chance of an unlikely comeback and the home side could not muster another chance, before Gabriel Jesus sealed three points late on from a slightly offside position.

And Raheem Sterling once more showed mental resolve, scoring a superb goal shortly after a quite shocking miss with the goal gaping in front of him.

72% possession, 20 shots. Just another normal day for a team that are rewriting the rules.

And a welcome return for Benjamin Mendy to fill that troublesome left-back spot. He was rusty as you would expect, but City got three points and got him match time, so it was in many respects a perfect day. The key now is to stay fit. Likewise for Kevin De Bruyne, whose battles with injuries meant his assist in this game was his first in the league for 336 days.

So the win moves City back to two points behind Liverpool, with a game in hand. That game being at Old Trafford of course. Stay calm everyone.

Because next up was a biggie….

Champions League: Manchester City 4 Tottenham Hotspur 3 (4-4 on aggregate) – Tottenham go through on away goals

What just happened? Seriously, what?

When I step back and write this now the dust has settled, if it ever does, I can appreciate I witnessed one of the greatest, most crazy games of my lifetime. A game that had it all, literally. Except perhaps a managerial punch-up but you can't have it all.

It had atmosphere too. It is well chronicled how City fans have not embraced this competition, but they were up for this. And like Liverpool last season, the early goal followed. A beauty from Raheem, and it was game on, with the scores level on aggregate.

But then City did the worse thing possible, and temporarily imploded. Two goals from Spurs, meaning City needed three without reply. At that point it was game over for me.

And the defending was woeful, from the most unlikely of places. Aymeric Laporte was having one of his first ever bad games, and the timing could not have been worse. Son did not need an invitation to score on current form. He probably could not believe his luck.

But then City got three goals. The first had an element of fortune, but the impressive thing was that even at 2-1 down, the players' heads did not drop. They still believed even if I didn't. Raheem was on hand to put City ahead on the night, before Sergio stepped up on the hour to put City ahead on aggregate. A crazy game, the first Champions League game to ever have 5 goals within 21 minutes.

And then City threw it away again. And we are forced to talk about VAR yet again and I am afraid, for quite a while. I can accept the goal – it seems to have brushed an arm, kind of, and maybe it could have been disallowed. What I cannot accept is that a referee that clearly went to a monitor to look for a handball was not provided with all the angles to show him just that. I don't believe in conspiracies, but tell me anywhere else this has happened? Just one occasion?

And so City had it all to do, and then the biggest celebration of many a year followed by the biggest comedown. The decision was correct, Aguero was just off, but VAR destroyed the emotion that is the essence of what being a football fan is about, but it also ensured Spurs did not go out to an offside goal, so we could argue over it for years without coming to a satisfactory conclusion. That sinking feeling when I realised it was being referred and then when the decision was made will stay with me for a long while.

And who knows, without VAR perhaps the linesman would have flagged at the time? VAR allows officials not to make a decision knowing that video referrals will deal with it. It also leads to false celebrations, and fans will have to adapt in the future. Goals, big goals, trophy-defining goals, will be celebrated or bemoaned via an announcement on a big screen. I am a VAR supporter, but this doesn't feel right.

So what a game. Astonishing stuff. Such a shame that I was on the wrong side, and for Pep and City the Champions League dream dies for yet another year. The quadruple is off, but I never gave it much thought anyway. I always assumed City would stumble at some point, they just had to.

I've heard fans bemoaning this tie weeks later. How I will judge it depends on what happens from now on. Because if City win a domestic treble, I couldn't give a damn about this. Because if you have just had your most successful season ever, you do not complain about not winning everything on offer unless of course you're seriously spoiled. This was cup football, there are no guarantees. And just to ram home the point, City did not lose to Spurs over two legs – they scored the same number of goals, just as they did against Monaco two years ago. It's just we have a stupid, illogical rule that rewards attacking over defending, in away games. I'm not trying to make excuses for City, both teams knew the rules, but it's still a stupid, stupid rule.

But the fact is that in the end, Pep paid for that 1st leg. And for a missed penalty. Hopefully a missed penalty won't have similar costly effects in the league.

So City must regroup. There is no time for rest. There is no time to reflect or feel sorry for themselves. They will be tested now – not just their skill with a football, but their mental strength. At the start of this week City were on for a quadruple. By the end of it they could be looking at no more than a domestic cup double. This is not the time to let it slip.

Bluemoon Podcast Audio Script

Is it enjoyable this football supporting lark? Is it supposed to be? What is the life of a football supporter supposed to be like? Cos if it's always going to be as stressful and fraught as the last week, I'm not sure I'm long for this world.

Imagine not liking football, commented Richard Osman on Twitter last night. Indeed. But there are many days when I truly wish I didn't. As I left the ground on Wednesday night, not quite sure what had just happened, not quite sure what I felt, I yearned for a quiet night with a pizza and Line Of Duty on the telly. Not this. Anything but this. Dazed in the tram queue as a man whinged about people pushing in, then the announcement of delays, and a rising tension. That electric atmosphere and Raheem sterling's curled shot into the net seemed a lifetime ago. That tam trip home gets longer every time we lose. The single trams get busier. Twitter gets harder to read.
Football, sport, can do this to you. But it rarely does that much to you on one night. Sadness, disappointment, pride and frustration all rolled into one. Questions will be asked about our players and our manager, and I'm not ready to answer them for a while.

And VAR did not help, on the night. City always seem late to the party – when we needed it last season, it was nowhere to be seen. This season it knocks us out. Don't be surprised if the away goals rule is shelved soon, but too late for the 5 previous times it has knocked us out of Europe. And that what really annoys me about the game this, week, just like Monaco 2 years ago. The opposition were lauded for being better despite not scoring any more goals than City over 2 legs. And video refereeing, something I've always been in favour of, in varying degrees, robbed me of possibly our greatest moment as a supporter since the QPR match. It made me wonder what being a supporter will be like in the future, when half of all goal celebrations are put on hold until we are permitted to celebrate via the big screen.

But anyway, I digress. When your team is gunning for glory on all fronts, the stress is relentless, and there is more to lose. The worry is that by going for everything, we end up with very little.

The Crystal Palace game three days previous certainly brought back memories. It has been 5 years since I have been that on edge for a league game. We all know what happened that season. I wasn't confident then, which may surprise you, and I'm not now. City's fixture list makes me think we'll fall one result short. Win the next two however, and it should be ours.

My problem is this, and it always had been - I invest too much in City's fortunes, and their results define my mood. That's not healthy on any level, even if you support the centurions. Every time City are in a title race #i tell myself, as a mantra, that if we just win this one then I'll die happy. Just this one. But every time there is a new reason why a win is so, so important. After knocking United off their perch, it seemed vital in 2014 that the history cult be prevented from winning the league again. The added incentive was the desire to see Luis Suarez cry. Mission accomplished. And now we find ourselves in that same situation, except the consequences of them winning seem even worse. And I want us to retain the league, to cement the team's place in the pantheon of greats. Next time there will be another reason. Liverpool again, united even, Pep's legacy, who knows? There's always something.

But the last thing we want is a replication of the Scottish league, not that that seems remotely likely. Liverpool have ensured that talk of City's domination of engulfs football was a tad premature. And to quote a cliché, without the lows, the highs would not be so enjoyable. I dread derby days and wish they did not exist, yet imagine how many unbelievable highs we would have been denied in the last decade if that were the case?

But the last few weeks have brought the stress levels back up. Even got a weird rash as a memento. Many fans relish situations like this. City were on for an unprecedented quadruple, and for now, are still on for an unprecedented domestic treble. And I'm an absolute wreck much of the time. Others though love every minute, and I'd pay good money to find out their secret. When you write and talk about your club too I feel the stakes are raised. I can't just walk away from a bad result and do other things. There's articles to be written, debate to be had, podcasts to record. Not like the old days, when football was a release, rather than all-consuming.

But deep down, we know we wouldn't have it any other way. Because, one day in summer, I'll be sat at home munching on some scampi fries. Afghanistan v Bangladesh will be on the telly in the cricket World Cup, and there will be nothing of interest to do. I'll be putting off that 4 mile trek round Ikea for a coffee table, and it will suddenly dawn on me how boring life is without football. The sun is out, there's holidays and alcohol still and camping trips and lots to do and it's still not ok. There's a void, something missing. The highs and the lows that I have no control over, they actually gave structure to my weekly life, rightly or wrongly.

We all need football, even if it gives us nights like on Wednesday. We've travelled over land and see and stood squashed on a thousand trams, watched dross season after season for the other days and nights, when it all goes right, as it often does now. To see 154 goals and counting, to see David Silva in the flesh, to reap the rewards on spending every spare penny on events we cannot control. Despite how the Spurs match turned out, I'll always have the memory of Sterling's shot hitting the back of the net, the elation of Aguero's 4th, the buzz off the red-hot atmosphere, that moment when I thought we had got through to the semi-final deep in injury time It's why we do it, for moments like that. And Richard Osman is right – life would be pretty boring without this roller coaster ride. And there's so much more to look forward to.

Doctor's Notes – Patient Number 3007

Howard has started scratching his left cheek, and also staring into middle distance vacantly mid-conversation. His tone seems slightly more aggressive than usual. Asked me which team I supported, and looked at me suspiciously when I commented that I wasn't really into football.

Stress level: Similar to getting to the final episode of a series you like and realising you haven't recorded it, and it's gone from the On Demand section on your Sky box.

Premier League: Manchester City 1 Tottenham Hotspur 0

They've done it again. Four to go.

This might have been the nerviest of the lot. It was not a compete performance, far from it, but they got over the line again. This really is going to the wire.

Pep surprised us once more, throwing Phil Foden into the starting line-up, a big call in such a big game. He repaid his trust within minutes, but to be honest never really imposed himself on the game. He wasn't the only one though. And to get his first Premier League goal is a momentous event in itself.

It's a repeated mantra that at this time of the season the result is the only thing that matters, and after the Champions League exit only a few days ago, this was especially the case. The big, big question was how City would respond to the heartbreak of midweek. I predicted incorrectly that it would be all or nothing for City - they would either be brilliant or terrible, an empty shell of the old team.

But they were neither really. They were quite good at times, average at other times, resilient, but dependent for once on their keeper for the points, especially in the first half.

And this was Ederson's game. Son is, as we know, on fire right now, and he was no different during this game. He also saved well from Christian Eriksen and Lucas Moura. Son was also denied by a magnificent tackle by Aymeric Laporte.

A part of me hoped that their midweek endeavours during the week would mean they would switch off for this game, which meant more for city than them. That was not the case. Spurs still have a top four fight of course, but perhaps they could afford to play with freedom too. And they do not seem to suffer when Harry Kane is absent either.

The second half was a more composed affair, but City could not get that second goal, and time moved very slowly. Raheem Sterling had City's best chance after the break, only to be frustrated by the outstretched leg of Spurs keeper Paulo Gazzaniga. But Spurs could not fashion the chances that they did in the first half as City once more went into their game management mode.
And thus, City retain a one point lead at the top of the table with four games to go. Quite a big game up next, but then they all are by this stage.

Phil Foden

You may or may not have noticed that I have not spoken in depth about Phil Foden in this book. This may disappoint you, but I, quite simply, don't want to. There is nothing I can tell you, and I just want to enjoy watching him develop, without over-analysing.
So that is what I will do.
After all, we have all witnessed what he can do – his poise, grace, and energy are there for all to see. He turns 19 as I write this, and the future is whatever he wants it to be. The only issue this season has been playing time, but it is a manufactured issue. No other 18 year old that I am aware of has ever been discussed so vehemently over playing time. Pep is playing it perfectly for me, and as long as Phil's playing time (fitness-permitting) grows exponentially, that is fine by me.

Phil Foden. He's one of our own.

I've no idea what exponentially means, but it seems to fit.

Doctor's Notes – Patient 3007

Howard has begun tugging at his grey hairs, and his beard has become rather unkempt. Mutters quite a lot about an unknown "cult" and doesn't appear to have showered for at least a couple of days, possibly longer. Claims the last series of Games of Thrones is the "best one of the lot".

Stress level: that of someone who has locked themselves out of their house just prior to a holiday, as the taxi pulls up outside.

Manchester United 0 Manchester City 2 – My Cult FC Match Report

Veni, vidi, vici. It was the best of times, it was the worst of times.
Acclaim them. Love them. Commune with them. Drink with them. Greet them. Smile at them. Wear signed shirts of them. Be prepared to bleed with them. But be part of their brilliance and have them be part of our need. Time has accelerated around us. And at times it has slowed down. The rules have changed.

There are no rules.
Not with this team.

A theatre of dreams. A team of nightmares. Twisted blood, tired legs, blue-shirted heroes straining every last sinew for you, for me, for football.

Because football won last night, and in a way, we all did.
Never has a crowd deserved a football team more.
It was more, it was less. It was all of us, it was none of us.
Breathless.

Jumpers for goalposts. Egg on toast with tommy k. Scratched knees. Innocent childhoods. Adulthood. Responsibility. The cool breeze on an autumn day at Pontins, Skegness. The soft touch of a labrador's paw. Three shredded wheat.

This is what this team does to you. Takes you back, to more innocent times. To buying cassettes in the Arndale, falling off your bike in Heaton Park, scratched knees, a broken Spectrum 48k, to your first taste of Boddingtons, or the advocaat at the back of your parents' cabinet, to becoming a man. Your first kiss, your first love.

Neil McNab.

Snowballs.

One thing is clear. I'm not going to be the man I'm expected to be anymore.

Or woman.

However you identify.

City started nervously. They were collective nerves. Vinny was booked, Rashford looked keen, too keen. Flustered, pressured, on the big stage. Was this the day dreams came crashing down? Was this the day that eight months of perspiration and inspiration counted for nothing?

We've come so far and yet we've not even moved. We've loved, we've lost, we've laughed, we have cried. This is what it feels to be us, a family like no other. This is how it feels to be Citeh.

But the counting has not stopped.

Not yet. Not now. Not ever.

Out of nowhere, time speeds up. But before that it was Bernardo Silva. It was all of them. We should resist attempts to reduce any of us to just one thing. And Bernardo is many things. He is ours, he is theirs, he is the world's.

Acclaim him, acclaim us.

Jumpers for goalposts.

And then.
And then.......
There is a murmur. The murmur becomes a roar. He is stripped and ready on the side line.
Leroy Sane is coming on. Before long, the net bulges lewdly, and the deed is done, and we are done too. It was superstar stuff. It was Frank Sinatra performing My Way, it was Elvis's comeback gig, it was Jupiter aligning with Saturn, it was a chippy tea when you expected beans on Birds Eye potato waffles. It was Leroy Sane.

Destiny is ours now. Maybe it always was. Maybe nothing has changed. These guys have always been there for us, representing us, projecting, performing, sweating.
Profusely. All in the blink of an eye.
Our eyes, your eyes. Sergo Aguero's eyes. Pep's eyes.
Acta deos numquam mortalia fallunt.
Raheem Sterling wins a header with Paul Pogba. He grows in front of us. Literally and metaphorically.
And spiritually.

It's time for honesty. I'm dumbfounded at the clarity of these things.

Ginger Rogers had Fred Astaire. Yoko had John. Dempsey had Makepeace. We get them all. We are them, and they are with us every step of the way. This crazy journey that we strip down to call the Premier League 2018/19 season.

Three more games. We get to see their box of crayons, a Benetton spectrum of brilliance and charisma or something. Time to lift something up blues. A trophy, but also our hopes, our aspirations, our journey. Hold it up to the world. Smell it. Cherish it, like you would a new fragrance from Chanel No. 5. Because it just means more.

Manchester United 0 Manchester City 2.

Ok, perhaps I should talk about this match in a serious manner too. When I look back on this season, this will surely be the day that almost broke me. The stress of a title race where in your mind (correctly, as it turned out) you cannot drop any points at any time takes a serious toll. If it was a race against someone like Chelsea, I imagine I would have been a tad more relaxed about the whole thing.
But it was not. It was against Liverpool, and all that comes with that.
And a lot comes with that.
So with that in mind, the day really dragged. Work was fleeting and probably of a low quality. Time slowed even more between the time of the line-up announcement and kick-off, because by then you just want to get on with it.
Of course this was a rearranged game due to cup exploits, and after it, there would be three games left for both sides, and the path ahead would be clear for both City and Liverpool.

I think I am right in saying that United had never been such long odds for a Manchester derby at Old Trafford, perhaps anywhere. That just made me even more nervous. This is a derby, anything can happen, as we know all too well. This was not the type of game we really needed with a league title on the line.

Well, I was right in a way. The first half was cagey and those hopes you had that City would fly out the traps and put this game to bed like they have before in recent years at Old Trafford soon faded. United were full of energy, and Rashford was causing Vincent Kompany, picked again for another big game, all sorts of problems. This was not a day for our captain to play on the edge.
Thankfully it did not last. City managed to wrestle some control back, as United started to run out of ideas. But the visitors were

over-elaborating a tad, and half-time brought us yet another goalless score line.

But I needn't have worried. I do not know what happens with Pep in that dressing room at half-time – watching that documentary makes me wonder if some of the players understand a word he is saying – but it seems to have the desired effect a many times more than it does not. City were better in the 2nd half, they were clearly the better side, even if David De Gea gave us all a helping hand or two.
And it was almost fitting that City's most consistent player this season, Bernardo Silva, was the man to break the deadlock. God, what a rush when that ball nestled in the back of the net. And I don't actually blame De Gea for this one. There is still an obsession with goalkeepers not being beaten at their near post, but I am not sure why. The key to this goal was Bernardo hitting it early, and catching De Gea by surprise.

The nerves were still there of course. But it was only 12 minutes before they eased off a tad. Sane added a second, De Gea sluggish reacting to his shot, and City had breathing space. And whilst it was not game over, this was clearly a United side that had no idea how to respond, a pale shadow of past sides. There was one fleeting chance at 1-0 when Lingard missed the ball completely right in front of goal, distracted by an acrobatic attempt at a clearance by Kompany, but that was all they had in the final hour of the game. City killed the game once more, and were worthy winners.

This was a huge hurdle cleared. Huge. With each game that is won, the hearts of Liverpool fans must sink and sink. They would rightly have expected a stumble somewhere along the way in a series of games that were all challenging in their own way. But City have not stumbled, yet. And the games are running out.

As for United, I'm almost at the stage of pitying them now. Almost. I mean, I'm more beach-body ready than Manchester United's Player Of The Year. Crazy times.

And the simple fact is that there is nothing they can do this summer to catch City next season. Nothing. They appointed a manager on sentiment alone, and because no doubt he was a cheap option. They could, and should have waited until the summer to decide whether Ole was the right man for the job, but they placed him at the wheel before then and have paid the price. A man that has no track record of managerial success, cannot rule on spirit alone, and it seems he's lost that now anyway. They stumble from one disaster to another – having finally realised, sensibly, that they need a director of football, they are now thinking of appointing the likes o Rio Ferdinand or Darren Fletcher. It is incompetence on a global scale, but as long as the money keeps rolling in, the owners won't really care. I never thought I'd see the day that City lorded it over their city neighbours to this extent, whilst the likes of Republic of Mankunia is reduced to screenshotting trophy parade crowds to his loyal band of dim-witted followers. What a time to be alive.

Raheem Sterling, at the age of 24, in his 7th season in the Premier League, wins the PFA **Young** Player of the Year.
This is a process that clearly needs reforming, especially when you consider that Bernardo Silva was also nominated, a player who turned 24 on the opening day of the season.
Sterling is not the first to be in this position. Milner won it when he was 24, Hazard won it when he was 24, Kane won it when he was 23? But now because Sterling has won it at 24 (when rules state 23 at start season which he was) there is outrage. And I am obviously happy to see him get the recognition. But I'd rather the award went to a young, breakthrough star. And the rules mean someone like Wan Bissaka at Crystal Palace, who had a stellar season, was not even nominated.

No prizes for guessing who won the senior award. I'm actually fine with that too. Defenders do not get enough recognition for their endeavours, and the player of the season award should not be swayed by the success of the team, though Liverpool may still be very successful anyway.
Still, with key games to come, it is weird that in 2019, with the technology available at our fingertips, we are still asking people to vote during the season. Still stuck in the dark ages in many respects.

Doctor's Notes – Patient 3007

Howard is now very distracted most of the time and has developed a significant facial twitch. Startled by the smallest of things, such as a pigeon flying past the window or any sudden movements by me. Claims that a shadowy cabal are monitoring his emails and keep sending him his favourite takeaways each night. Has put on weight.

Stress level: similar to that of Jose Mourinho when discovered hiding in a laundry basket, or Alex Ferguson when Edin Dzeko slotted home the 6th goal at Old Trafford.

And with another game comes the tedious pre-match coverage. And the endless narratives. The method of choice right now seems to be to drag opposition players out to talk about how they'd love to spoil City's party, because they support Liverpool or are partial to a bowl of scouse. God I need this season to end, whatever the result.

Premier League: Burnley 0 Manchester City 1

Two to go. Just two. A nervy, hard-fought 1-0 victory at Turf Moor saw Manchester City hit 92 points and return to the top of the Premier League. Sergio Aguero's shot crept 3cm over the line, and that decided the game, despite a raft of chances and a strong penalty claim in an improved 2nd half. Here's five things I learned.

The stress of a title race

I'd forgotten what these levels of stress brought on by a football team felt like. I can't say it is pleasant in any shape or form. With a bloodstream swimming with pale ale and gin, sleep on Saturday ranged somewhere between fitful and non-existent. Sunday morning saw time slow down to a crawl, much like early

Wednesday evening. I was even reduced to watching Formula 1 at one point to try and fill time, but that simply slowed it down even further.

Is it worth it? If they win, then yes. Every second of stress is worth it for the outpouring of relief, elation and much more when that final whistle keeps blowing. But it is taking a lot out of me, eleven players kicking a pig's bladder around a piece of grass and synthetic turf. Ridiculous. I crave a summer of cricket and mountain walks. But the players get two days off, and we get seven, and one way or another, it's almost over now. And if City won the league by 19 points every season, that would be pretty boring, right?

Sergio Aguero cements position in pantheon of greats

Sergio Aguero has not been firing in the goals recently, but his overall performances have been as good as ever. Just look at his fired-up face after blocking a United clearance on Wednesday to see how much he is up for this. He is putting in performances for the team, when they are most needed. And with his scrappy goal against Burnley, he joins a select club, a club containing only Alan Shearer, in that he has scored 20+ goals in 6 different seasons in the Premier League. Considering much of his time at City has been hampered by niggling injuries, that is an even more impressive statistic.

City fans already appreciate what this guy has brought to the club, and the day he departs will be devastating. But only when he has left will the rest of the footballing fraternity truly understand his contribution to the Premier League's history. Truly one of the greats to grace the English game.

As is Vincent Kompany. You fully understand his inclusion in such games, the enormity of the match calling for leadership, but of course the physical aspect of the home side also demanding his appearance.

And he delivered. You may miss the likes of John Stones passing through the lines, but you game someone who instead held the back line together and prevented the home side having a single shot on target. He won 6 aerial duels in all, cleared the ball 9 times, made 2 interceptions, 2 tackles, and perhaps most importantly cut out a through ball right at the death. A timely reminder of what he has brought to this football club over an 11 year period.

Fine lines in an astonishing title race

The best team always wins the league, so I repeatedly read and hear people say. When a team wins the league by 19 points, it's hard to argue. However, there is no concrete evidence of this when title races are so, so close. If Aguero had missed his shot on that fateful day in 2012, would that have meant United were the best team that season? I can assure you they were not. What is more certain is that this campaign will be decided on fine lines. If City are ultimately victorious, you can look at the 29mm over the line that Aguero's shot ended before being kicked back out. Or the millimetres short of a goal Liverpool found themselves in January before John Stones scooped the ball off the line, through the onrushing Salah's legs.
If Liverpool are victorious, there is of course a long line of rival goalkeepers assisting them in their campaign. Or the various penalties that, whether valid or not, seem to be given far easier than if an opposition player against City bats a shot away with his arm. Fine lines indeed. One free kick, one mistake, and City's season could have collapsed close to the line yesterday. Thankfully, for now, the players are holding their nerves, when few around them are.
With City and Liverpool, we are witnessing two of the greatest league campaigns ever. Unfortunately for one of those teams, they will receive scant reward for their efforts, except glorious failure. Talk of bottling and failure can be assigned to history's bin now, as neither team could have done much more, neither team blinking in 2 months. This has been something special.

With so much at stake, nerves are to be expected

I've already mentioned my own nerves, but what of the players'? Well I cannot claim to be an expert in body language, nor be in a position to get inside the minds of players in this sort of situation. But in the two recent games, it appeared to me that there was a nervousness about City's play in the early stages of both games. In the United match it seemed to last about 25 minutes before they began to take control of the match and their slick passing returned. Against Burnley, it seemed to last an entire half, before orange segments were no doubt thrown around the visitors' dressing room by an enraged Pep Guardiola. Maybe I am misreading things, but if they are nervous, can we really blame them? Of course these sort of situations are where we expect these highly-paid athletes to step up and be mentally strong, but they are still human beings at the end of the day. They know what is at stake, and they must assume that Liverpool will win all of their games, so any slip-up could prove fatal. With that in mind, the way they have seen out close games has been admirable. They are not putting themselves in a position whereby the opposition sniff an opportunity.

Anyway, for City, the stats continue to stagger. Three league goals conceded in 3 months, another team vanquished who could not muster a single shot on target. Burnley are far from alone. Twelve league wins on the bounce. City's goal record already broken by the end of the United match. The bar just keeps getting raised. And even if City fall short at the final hurdles, they have easily mounted the strongest attempt to retain a title in the past decade, and amassed a points total that in most other seasons would have seen them coast over the line.

Games last 90 minutes

This may be quite the revelation to some of you. At half-time in Wednesday and Sunday, I was not in a good place. The league was lost, woe was me, life was crap, I wanted the ground to swallow me up. You get the idea. By full time in both matches, I was doing knee slides across cheap laminate flooring.

In the first half against Burnley, exasperation levels reached new highs. The left side of City seemed shambolic, Zinchenko and Sane operating in different time zones, every misplaced pass taking another few hours off my life expectancy. But they responded, and that's the important thing. In hindsight, perhaps the 1st half wasn't that bad, or perhaps the knowledge that we ultimately prevailed has clouded my judgement. Either way, City were focused in that 2nd half, and should have won by more than a single goal. The penalty was stonewall, Jesus had one cleared off the line in spectacular fashion, and there were other opportunities not taken.

City ultimately suffocated Burnley as they have so many other teams. As mentioned twice already, Burnley could not muster a shot on target, but almost as importantly, they could not even win a single corner, their danger from them obvious to all. City did their job, and now must do it two (or three) more times to achieve immortality.

No pressure lads....

For all the talk of fine lines though, yet again City were denied a clear penalty. You wonder what the referee, who had a clear view of the incident, was thinking. Nothing it seems. Now as you may know, I do not like to see a penalty given easily for handball. But this was blatant. The arm moved away from the body, the shot is heading towards the goal, it's an easy decision for the referee. And if he didn't see it, how can the linesman also fail to spot it? Just bizarre.

Sterling then announced as FWA player of the year, with over 60% of the vote. Nice one.

Bluemoon Podcast Audio Script: Mental Strength

I played badminton on Monday night, as I always do. I lost the first game. I wasn't very good. I'm not sure I'd recovered from the stress of the previous day. It's taking a lot out of me. Anyway, my game regressed further, before I finally won a game at the 6th attempt, mostly due to my partner having a good smash shot. My confidence was shot for most of the time, as is often the case when I lose the first couple of games. I am the ultimate confidence player. Sometimes I feel invincible. Sometimes I am happy to get the shuttlecock over the net more times than not. Apart from many other obvious reasons, I could never be a professional athlete, because the mental side of things would need too much work, and there isn't enough time in the world.

But it's a topic that has been on my mind a lot recently. Not because of my badminton woes, but because of Manchester City. Mental strength is something that will surely be a key factor in who wins the premier league this season, especially when the bar has been set this high, again. Because if I as a fan cannot handle the stress of this title race, god only knows how the players deal with it.

When the going gets tough, the tough get going, as Billy Ocean once opined. He knew. So does Pep. He talked about mental strength after the Burnley game, commenting on the mental strength to react with the problems we have had without Kevin [De Bruyne], Fernandinho, important players. He added: "Every press conference I say the same but from the deep of my heart it is incredible."

The world is littered with players of immense talent playing in lower leagues or even not at all. It's also littered with players of modest talent who reached the top because they had the drive to do so. Players will have been conditioned to deal with situations like this. They will all have their own ways of coping. But until you're in the heart of a race like this, where a single blink can prove fatal, how can they really be sure how they will react?

Retaining a title takes mental toughness – it takes the desire to play with the same intensity as the season before. That may explain why no team has done it for over a decade, though poor recruitment by successive champions hasn't helped. And now, at the fabled business end of the season, this run of games is a strain mentally as much as physically. We are talking about players who have been playing football non-stop for a long time – for some, it's approaching 2 years of near continual football. There is, as always, talk of bottling the title race. Or there was. It's not the first time, it won't be the last. United bottled it in 2012. Liverpool bottled it in 2014. Spurs bottle everything, all the time. It's an easy narrative, that suggests that football teams can't just lose a game of football, they must be weak to do so, especially if they do so from a previous position of strength. We're thankfully past that point now. Two teams who have amassed over 90 points have bottled nothing. The only bottling is going on behind them, the race for the top 4 resembling a city coach driving through Liverpool's back streets.

But what must be clear by now is that if - IF - City win their final 2 league games this season, mental fortitude has to have played a part. Whatever a club's budget, whatever their financial might, that alone does not win you 14 league games on the bounce.

And here's where Pep comes into the equation. Any football manager is more than just a manager of football matches. He, or she, is a manager of people too. Success depends on firing up the players. Look at United under Mourinho and now Solskjaer. There was and is more than tactics at play there, just as there was the previous times Jose poisoned whole football clubs. The mental side of the game may well be a key reason why Pep was always adamant that a quadruple was not a possibility. He knew he had the talent and the players to do it, but fighting on four fronts takes more than fresh legs and good ball control. The strain mentally of game after game would always take its toll. For him, it was inevitable.

And it's not long since sports psychology was mocked and derided by Fleet Street's finest, the old boys' brigade that still think footballers should get pissed when they want to and wonder how footballers can be depressed when they earn so much money. Psychology is key though, as is how you handle being a professional athlete. A tennis player who draws level by winning the 4th set is more likely to win the 5th. A penalty scorer in a shoot-out who celebrates wildly is more likely to see his teammates also score subsequent spot kicks. A team that is 2 goals down and looked dead and buried suddenly scores a goal, and immediately the whole feel of the game changes. Momentum, and psychology.

Gareth Southgate is one person who is well aware of the importance of mental strength. Perhaps this explains England actually winning a penalty shoot-out under his tutelage. The FA hired Pippa Grange, a psychologist who has been tasked with improving the team's "psychological resilience", and they are one of the very few football organisations – be it national teams or domestic clubs – who are alive to the opportunities that analytics offers in the sport. As Southgate said early in his tenure:
"I think there are things we can work on with the team to help develop mental strength. I think mental resilience is generally a product of the experiences you've been through, so we have to tap into those.

So come next Monday, and the Sunday after, City players will step onto the field knowing so much is at stake. More at stake than there is for Leicester, and hopefully more at stake than there will be for Brighton, who I hope will be safe by then. There's more to gain too though. I've sensed nerves at the start of the past two games, and Leicester are dangerous, but they have come too far not to be focused now. They won 12 league games on the trot to get to this point, they won at Old Trafford, they beat Spurs, they won a penalty shoot-out at Wembley, they have passed a lot of tests. So it's over to you lads. Up to you to show why you are not someone like me, who gets nervous when a labour councillor knocked on the door yesterday, worries that a bout of rain will cause all our foreign players to hand in transfer requests, or fears an opposition goal every time they enter our half. You're thankfully not like me, so good luck, and bring it home.

Doctor's Notes – Patient 3007

Howard now lives exclusively in one room of his flat, and only
ventures out for emergencies.
Comes to appointments wrapped in tin foil. Claims that a
network of referees are conspiring to deprive his football team
of success. Muttered talk of moustaches, bitter berts and
paranoia leads me to suspect this team is Manchester City.
Howard's guts have now totally given up the ghost, and he must
remain close to toilet facilities at any given time.

Stress level: similar to that of winning a jackpot winning lottery
ticket. Then forgetting where you bought the ticket, or what
your name is. Whilst also forgetting where you put the ticket.

Premier League: Manchester City 1 Leicester City 0

One to go. Just one.

I'm committed now. I said weeks ago on a podcast that
whichever team was leading the Premier League going into the
final day would win the league. That team will be Manchester
City. 13 league wins on the trot. Astounding.

Of course City had to win this game. Saturday was my birthday,
so I walked up a mountain in the Lake District, with no intention
of watching Newcastle v Liverpool as the sun disappeared over
the horizon. It came as no surprise that they won, and of even
less surprise that Fabinho blatantly cheated to help secure a late
winning goal. Good luck with VAR next season.

Enough of the small talk. There's only one topic of conversation.
Should City beat Brighton on the final day of the season, then
tonight we witnessed a historic moment in the club's history.
Vincent Kompany had gone and done it again. With the nerves
jangling, with the clock speeding up and time ticking away, he

step-up and delivered. I mean, how do you explain (to your grandchildren etc) that your inspirational captain rocketed the ball into the net from 25 yards out to possibly win his team the league? This was one of those moments you never forget, this was a goal celebration for the ages. This was everything.

There was one last act in this play though, Kelechi Iheanacho hitting the ball horribly wide from an excellent position. A moment of fortune for City, but no different to the Liverpool-supporting Morrison diving under the ball virtually on the line then wrestling Salah to the ground needlessly to concede a penalty in the Cardiff match. I am naturally past caring now. Past caring about offside goals, moments of luck, who deserves it more, net spends, wanting it more, history, fair play, dives, cheating, destiny. City won, and are close now, so close.

But let's be honest, Iheanacho knows better than to ruin City's party. Once a blue....

But yet again City win 1-0, yet again we had to wait until the 2nd half for the breakthrough. We're seeing a different story of team in recent weeks under intense pressure. Cautious, cagey, but proficient.

A detailed analysis of games like this Leicester one seem pointless. I doubt you care by now about inverted full-backs, half - spaces or whether Sterling should be on the right, if you ever did anyway. Whatever team Pep picked it would be good, better than the opposition, and this was now about focus and application, and not choking with the finishing line in sight. But to be VERY brief – the first half was tight, with few chances. I thought City improved in the 2nd half and pinned Leicester back, but chances were still hard to come by. It required a moment of brilliance, a moment of genius, and that is precisely what we got.
And a word about Leicester City too. They were excellent. That squad is peppered with talent, and this bodes well for next

season, if they can keep the top talents there. It's easy to mock Brendan Rodgers and his tremendous character, but he is a good fit for the job. There are interesting times ahead for them. A drink was had in City square afterwards, the utter relief of getting the result almost draining me of the energy to finish it.

And so a six day gap until the final game. Part of me wants to play the game immediately and get it over with, but part of me is also glad of these breaks. My body needs it.

In the meantime we all got to watch two nights of astonishing Champions League football. The two teams I wanted to lose ended up winning. The two teams in question had to engineer amazing comebacks to do so. I should by rights be bitter. But it was something of a watershed midweek for me.

Perhaps the knowledge my own team could win a domestic treble had softened me, but amongst the constant vitriol that has surround this title race, you sometimes forget that at the end of the day we all have something in common – we just love football. And these games proved why – sometimes you just have to acknowledge amazing matches not involving your team, and accept that other teams can have success and amazing nights too, not just your team.
Still, with that in mind – come on Spurs!
(that feels so, so wrong).

Doctor's Notes – Patient 3007

Patient has now become delusional and claims that a cabal of giant lizards control Western governments. And Thailand's. Also claims referees are biased against Manchester City. Dresses entirely in purple and diet consists mostly of bacon wheat crunchies.

Patient has had to be heavily sedated having tried to seduce a potted plant in reception. Thinks Pep Guardiola is a bald fraud and refuses to converse with anyone from the Liverpool area. Offered to drive Fabian Delph to the airport himself and believes the club will raise his season ticket by £10 shortly, just to personally wind him up. Twitch has developed into a series of spasms.

Stress Level: Similar to having to move house on the day your dog dies and your divorce is finalised. F**k you Sharon.

Premier League: Brighton 1 Manchester City 4

MANCHESTER CITY ARE THE 2018/19 PREMIER LEAGUE CHAMPIONS

I repeat….

MANCHESTER CITY ARE THE 2018/19 PREMIER LEAGUE CHAMPIONS

YESSSSSSSSSSSSSSSSSSSSSSSSSSSSSSSSSSSSSSSSSSSSSSSSSSSSSSSSSSSS!!!!!

They bloody did it. How could I ever doubt these beautiful, beautiful people?
Lesson learnt.

Of course the team had to give us a bit of tension and anxiety to spice up proceedings. I knew Liverpool would win, it was 2012 all over again as far as I was concerned – we had to win, and that was the sole issue of the day. I also knew though that Sky love the "as it stands" league table, so when Liverpool inevitably scored quite early the butterflies returned, and they took over my body when Brighton then scored. The doubts were creeping in.

And weirdly those doubts were under control before the match. This made no sense, but I think I worked out why in the end. You see, when I was tense for previous matches, I knew that even with a win, I'd have to go through the whole process again. This time, I knew that whatever happened, at least by 5pm it would all be over. No more torture. And Brighton should, I hoped, prove easier opposition than any of the four teams that city had previously played.

When we look back at this season, and the crucial moments that shaped this momentous achievement, there will be some obvious candidates. Sane's goal against Liverpool, and perhaps to a lesser extent John Stone's goal-line clearance earlier in the game. Kompany's winner last week. Any of the goals in those collection of 1-0 victories. But surely Sergio Aguero's equaliser against Brighton is right up there. Now if City had not got back on level terms that quickly then yes, there's a fair chance they would still have gone on to win this game. But to score within 90 seconds of going behind was crucial for me. To restore parity quickly removed a lot of tension and focused the minds of the City players. Further goals then followed.

In fact you could present a case for any of the goals being crucial moments in the season. Laporte's robust header put is back in control, back top, further removed tension and nerves and gave City a much treasured half-time lead. Mahrez gave the team real breathing space, killed off Brighton resistance, limited as it was, and was the point that I believed the team had done it. Gundogan sealed the deal, and that was the point celebrations could really begin. Pep knew it too on the touchline. It was over, it was done. His players had delivered the title, with a 98 point haul.

And some redemption too for Mahrez. We can finally stop talking about that bloody penalty miss 7 months ago. And for Gundogan too, to a lesser degree. Astonishing that there are still fans out there that cannot see his worth as a player. The news after the final that he is considering reopening contract talks is great to hear. Let's hope he signs on that dotted line soon.

The evening will live long in the memory. A lot of hugs, much back - slapping, too much Jack Daniels. The stress just spirited away. Watching the fans at Brighton celebrate with the players and Pep. Watching Vinny lift the trophy again.

Anything after 8pm is not clear in the mind, and the best morning I awoke with a massive grin on my face and fried chicken scattered around the flat.

14 league wins on the row. One of the greatest achievements by any Manchester City team, perhaps the greatest of all. Neither Liverpool or City blinked after 3rd March. Madness. These two teams will surely compete for titles in the coming years. And credit to Liverpool, who irrelevant of decisions, luck or whatever (every team has some), showed they are a great team too, and will not be going anywhere anytime soon.

All that was left was to make more history. The team seem really good at that right now.

And so back to that fateful game in early January. For Liverpool, it means that the defeat to City stopped them being champions, stopped them being centurions and stopped them being invincibles.

Tough luck, losers. *does L sign on forehead*.
And how fitting for Liverpool that their final goal of the
domestic season, the 2nd goal against Wolves, was offside.

But when it boils down to it, should they triumph in Madrid,
both sets of fans will spend the summer feeling pretty pleased
for themselves.

Which is more than can be said for Manchester United fans.

Brighton 1 Manchester City 4: The Alternative Match Report

We've toiled. They have toiled. They sweated. We sweated.
We saw what they had to offer, and we liked what we saw.
Their sacrifices were real, but ours were greater.
And now, the end is near. They did it their way.
I wandered lonely as a City crowd.
Just 11 human beings kicking a ball around on grass? No, so much more.
The madness of it all.
One step beyond.
A long journey. A necessary one. How was it for you? Erect but beaten. Warm but moist. Tired but alive. Elated but wary.
We are us. And he is Pep.
I am reminded of older times. Of being young, and being alive. Buses on Canon Street. The 50 bus to Burnage. The little zoo in Heaton Park. Woolworths Pick and Mix. Juicy Lucy lollies from Mr Whippy. The latest album release by Climie Fisher. A Belinda Carlisle teenage crush.
The journey.
These players represent us, and they are us. They are better than those before. They believe, they eat, they perform.
Five shredded wheat.
And now they go again. These blue-shirted warriors with ice in their veins. There will be highs, and there will be lows. There will be a sea of blue in Piccadilly Station at 8am. There will be shared memories and tears shed. For this is what we do.
Bald men. Hairy men. Women, and children too. Some thin, some fatter. Hairy women.
Size is abstract, as is the time that fleetingly progresses through a ninety minute match.
Some in shorts, some sporting scarves. All with stories to tell.
Flags to wave. Questions to ask. Lives to be lived. And live them we did, and will continue to do so.
This is what we have always done.
I've loved too many people, but I haven't loved enough. Can I love these guys too? I think I can now.

I think I can.

But the day itself was never going to be straightforward. We don't do straightforward. News filters through that Liverpool are in front.

Inevitable.

Then City are behind. I am tense. We are tense. I think of better days and depths of despair.

Not today.

Sergio, for it is he, quickly calms us. Aymeric caresses us, and we are now on a high. Riyad comes of age, as we knew he would, then Gundo seals the deal. Beautiful. Art in physical form. Brush strokes and a palette of a hundred colours, creeds and cultures. We are blessed.

They bless us.

Gesundheit.

The players celebrate, as they should. They celebrate with us, for us. Their box of tricks was too much for a forlorn Brighton side, whose manager departs for good soon after. They won a battle, but lost the war.

They were not pooping this party.

Not now, not ever.

You held me down, but I got up

Already brushing off the dust

You hear my voice, your hear that sound

Like thunder, gonna shake the ground

Sergio, David, Kyle, the others. They represent us. They are there, in spirit if not in actual human form, when we experience life. There when we marry, we grieve, we suffer the effects of an over-spiced curry. They share this journey, be it in the ground, waiting for a tram, or bent over a toilet bowl.

They are us, and we are them. We share the joy and we share the despair.

We've come too far not to. We've suffered too much. We have

experiences to tell our grandchildren, and stories will be told.
Books will be written. And there will be poetry.
Endless poetry.

For if you can meet with Pogba and Jones,
And treat those imposters just the same,
If you can sit in half-empty crowds and keep your virtue,
If neither @simplyfirmino69 nor loving friends can hurt you,
If you can fill the unforgiving minute
With sixty seconds' worth of distance run,
Yours is the Earth and everything that's in it,
And—which is more—you'll be a Man City fan, my son!

Endless
Poetry.
Back to back Champions. Drink it in blues.
Drink it in.

Bluemoon Podcast Audio Script

Hello there. How's your week been? Celebrating the greatest title win ever, whilst looking forward to another cup final and the chance of an unprecedented domestic treble? Or maybe instead you've been on social media and it feels like we were relegated on Sunday. More on that later I guess.

Anyway, the great narrative died, the dream of large swathes of the media. The trophy parade bus, rusting since 2014, if not longer, reverses back into its garage in Liverpool for a few weeks at least.

And have no doubt, this is the greatest Premier League side of it all. Try and debate otherwise as much as you want, not that we would, and you'd be wasting your time, or more accurately you'd be still desperately trying to convince yourself that it's all about money, Pep's a fraud who should try managing Oldham Athletic, and Liverpool were the real winners, on their shoestring budget, getting by on hopes and prayers and the odd loan signing.

It probably didn't surprise you therefore that Liverpool still got more coverage even though they fell short. Even though a premier league team retained the title for the first time in a decade. Even though City have averaged 99 points over the past 2 seasons, thus dropping a total of 30 points in those 2 years. But why be surprised or even bothered?

The media has changed over the past decade beyond recognition. Print is dying, and we consume much of what we read online, though a vast array of sources. Football used to be about going to the match, getting the football pink, reading a report, then reading the odd transfer rumour or opinion piece before the next game. Now every second demands a new story, a new angle, a new hot take.

Quite frankly, and this is not a dig, but a sign of the times, we don't need football journalists any more. They are not our portal to news and reports and their opinions matter not one jot when we ourselves have access to all the information, all the action, and can develop our own opinions. Of course I am using a bit of hyperbole there, as breaking transfer news will always be consumed, and a well-written opinion piece will always be appreciated, on any topic, and there are some great scribes out there. We should always be open to alternative opinions and take on board new information. But without sounding snobby, much of what is out there is not even good for holding fish and chips. Not that you can anymore – it's health and safety gone mad.

But really, their standing is not what it was. And they know it. They have to find new ways to stay relevant. Like we all do. Juvenile retweets, twitter spats, hot takes, we're all part of the machine. But imagine needing the validation of a football journalist to back up your point of view on a City topic. You don't anymore.

But news outlets need to survive. And in 2019 that means clicks as well as print sales. So of course they will produce more stuff on Liverpool. Of course certain articles such as that in the New York Times will be timed for maximum effect. It was always thus. That's how the industry works, and it is logical.

I just think the last few weeks may be a watershed for many of us on social media. To walk away and spend more time elsewhere. It is destroying us, and it is serving no purpose. We won the league on Sunday, with 98 points, having won 14 games on the bounce to do so. There's the facts laid out in front of you, and I don't need a glossy pull out in the Guardian to validate that achievement, nor clarify what happened. We were there, we experienced it all, we drank it in.

So walk away. Go to the park. See the world. Walk up a hill. Go to the pub. And forget the detritus of twitter discussing plane songs, net spends, human rights or anything else that takes your fancy.

And laugh. Laugh at John Aldridge losing his mind because his precious little Liverpool couldn't compete with oil money City, chuckle at the faux outrage at a song on a plane and calls for apologies and reprimands. Snort at Tony Evans suggesting asterisks next to our achievements, because he thinks possibly we may have broken some rules he doesn't really understand on where one small section of our sponsorship money came from five years ago.

Wonder too why there was no similar outrage at Lingard chanting about City beeping off home. This, two days after a terrorist attack in Manchester was hugely insensitive, at a time that the city had never been more united in peacetime, but there was rightly no outrage because all footballers sing songs like this, let off steam and celebrate trophies in this way. So it wasn't really worth dwelling over.

And that's the key to being annoyed over a song on a plane that some unknown players may have song parts of without really knowing what they were doing. Unless of course we assume someone like Sergio Aguero has forensically deconstructed the chant before singing it with glee. Footballers more than anyone have been in the heat of battle with Liverpool over the past 12 months. They live in a bubble and cannot say anything. They have won the title, and are letting off steam – get over it. It happens in every dressing room in the land. It's just this one became public. And was on a plane, not in a dressing room. Or if you can't get over it, bore us all to death by analysing every football song in the world, because footballers will always sing fan songs, and it's usually endearing to hear them do it. In that situation, a single person sings a song, probably a member of staff, and some players join in with the catchy allez allez allez bit – hanging's too good for them, eh?

Now that's not to say any song is fair game. The song, which I hate personally, has a couple of words that have obviously drawn focus. Maybe the players will have to be reminded of responsibilities or something, but let's not go over the top here. The singing of a sing containing the words battered and victims will obviously lead to questions being asked. I'm just not sure it requires fifteen articles and counting on the disgrace of it all.

What also leaves a nasty taste in my mouth is how the incident has been used to further the cause of others. Sean Cox has been through hell, and so has his family. To use them for gain in a campaign to denigrate Manchester City football club is beyond the pale. Yet not a word of criticism will exist online for such actions. Nothing. We all know the song is about Kiev. You are entitled to have the opinion that the players singing the song is wrong – but stay on topic please.

Of course a fan base will always dig in and protect their own. We don't need to. I am not responsible for the actions of footballers or staff. Nor are you. We're not their guardians. Nor was I responsible for City's accounting in 2014 and 2015. If mistakes are made, then those responsible should be held responsible. We do not have to defend everything our club does. We certainly don't on our own message boards, so why disagree if a football journalist says the same thing you did in the pub the previous day? Get out the trenches. Nevertheless, and I say this even as a left-leaning thin-skinned liberal, the pathetic overreaction and forensic deconstruction of everything that happens in the football world is so tiresome. Even more so when led by a single fan base who can't take defeat with an iota of grace, because of some cult-like delusion that they are and always have been the best, even if actual football results do not back up such an assertion.
So with that in mind, this is my own pathetic little call to arms. Enjoy your trip to London on Saturday. Enjoy the whole day. Hope for an unprecedented domestic treble, and enjoy that possible achievement with fellow blues, because the rest of the world don't matter. What they'd give to be in our shoes, to have walked just a mile in them. These are the best times of our lives, so never forget that, and have a great summer.

FA Cup Final: Manchester City 6 Watford 0

They did it. They only bloody did it. 6-0 in a cup final, and Manchester City, little old Manchester City, become the first side to complete a domestic treble. For a club with no history, they seem remarkably adept at creating it in recent times.

Another fun day was had in the capital. An early start, and for the first time the pleasure of first class travel. It's another world. I mean, they even gave me a smoked salmon and cream cheese wrap. For free!

The key issue of course was whether to travel with coat or without. First world problems. The temperature was such that this decision could make or break the day. I opted in the end for a T-shirt with hoodie on top, as this dealt with the issue of all Virgin trains having a core temperature greater than the inside of a volcano. I called it perfectly.

And the pressure did feel off. We were all desperate to see the team make history, but after last weekend, it felt more like a free hit then it actually was. And the team largely played with that same feeling too.

The team itself was something of a surprise too, with big names missing. But then it dawned on me that this was Pep rewarding those that had got the club to the final. Fair enough. And whilst I later bemoaned some of the absentees not getting on the pitch when the game was in the bag, I saw the other side of that too. Foden was the player I most had in mind, but you could argue that those that came on had just as much right to step onto the hallowed turf. Pep does not manager on sentiment, and I am fine with that.

Done with ease in the end, Watford really troubled City at times in the first half, but it couldn't last. The first goal dimmed their spirit, and it was killed off with each subsequent goal.

And Watford lost 6-0 because they played a suicidal high line in 2nd half against a superior side and abandoned principles of 1st half that had served them fairly well. It's got fuck all to do with the death of football, as some would have got believe in the media.

I didn't want us to score a 7th though. I just wanted to win, secure the treble, and enjoy my summer. The players are ruthless, but there is little too gain by running up a cricket score.

Anyway, the argument that many hacks immediately brought up about the death of competitiveness in English football is a relevant one. There are many elements of truth in it. But to be honest, tough shit. City are simply taking advantage of a system they did not create. They did not distort the market or get us to where we are today. The real problem is that City got in before the drawbridge came down on a system designed to protect the traditional elite. New money was not supposed to be capable of doing things like this. City knew this – Brian Marwood spoke many years ago of the accelerated spending spree due to the knowledge that Financial Fair Play regulations were approaching. Without it, spending may have been more tempered and structured.

Let's also not forget that this was the first season that a Premier League has been retained for a decade. Before this season, City had never retained a trophy. They only won the Carabao Cup on penalties, and also had to beat Leicester City by the same route, only won the league by a single point and could easily have finished second, and this is only the club's 2nd FA Cup triumph in 50 years. So let's not start planning football's funeral just yet. It's up to the other clubs to compete – City got to where they are with vast resources, but also due to one of the greatest managers the game has seen.

There was an incident after that match that perfectly brought this into focus. Long after full-time, with medals collected and confetti strewn across the pitch, Pep could be seen in an intense discussion with Raheem Sterling. It turned out he was criticising his play, as he later commented that he was not happy with his first-half performance. And that is Pep. Any other manager would be naked (or fully clothed) in the bath with a bottle of champagne, but Pep was still obsessing about individual performances that irked him after the joint-highest victory ever in the history of the FA Cup (*clinks glass with Bury FC*). He is something else. He is unique. He is ours.

Of course a lot of this hatred comes from darker places – the source of the funds, the methods in building the squad. United dominated for many years. Many City fans claim on Twitter there was no outrage then. Was there? Probably not, but then there was no Twitter, and media was consumed in a different way. And I'm not sure anyone can really remember whether there was or not, it's just a hollow claim.

I personally would love a level playing field – the sort of field that allows a team like Nottingham Forest revisit past glories. But I also want to ride to work on a unicorn, and that's not going to happen either. This is where the appalling idea of a European Super League comes from, as it would at least be more competitive than many domestic leagues (as I type, Bayern Munich have just secured their 7th successive league title). The owners of all of Europe's biggest clubs, including city, are not interested in a level playing field, so forget it. They are all about PR, influence, power and money. The game will eat itself, and there's little we can do – City are not to blame for all this happening, but are certainly part of the problem now.

No hat-trick for Raheem, so Stan Mortensen remains the only player to score one in a cup final, for Blackpool.

And bravo to the hearty renditions of "allez, allez, allez" at half-time. Oh how we laughed.

Doctor's Notes – Patient 3007

A remarkable improvement from the patient. Waltzed into reception whilst whistling the theme tune to Bonanza.
Presented a bouquet of flowers to the receptionist. Gave me a hug on entering office.
Skin is clear and twitch has disappeared.
Appears to be wearing a fragrant cologne and new Adidas trainers.
Hair has ungreyed itself.
Patient has decided to go back to university and study ancient history, after taking a year off to do charity work in Asia.
Not seen him this happy since he won a box of Wheat Crunchies on Twitter.
Clean bill of health.

Stress level: Zero.

2018/19 Season: Player Ratings

Handing out marks is an impossible task, and lacks nuance, but I've done it anyway.

Ederson – 9
Absolutely superb. We know what he can do with his feet – essentially as much as some international midfielders can. But we never really knew if he was at the top of the tree as a shot-stopper, as he had so few shots to save. He is probably not quite at the top, but at the end of the season, he proved his worth. The multiple saves against Spurs in the league game probably made the difference between 1st and 2nd, and his save in the FA Cup final allowed City go on and dominate the game. But when he did a Cruyff turn on his own goal-line at Southampton to evade Charlie Austin, you know you're dealing with a rather unique talent.
Stat: It may not surprise you to learn that Ederson played the most minutes of any City player – 4980. Laporte was 2nd with 4352. Ederson started 55 games.

Aro Muric – 7
When called upon in the as the Carabao Cup keeper, performed to a high standard throughout. Five games, four clean sheets, and some penalty heroics thrown in for good measure. It's far too early for me to judge him as a keeper, but he is very highly rated, has shown maturity beyond his years and is definitely one for the future.

Bravo – 10
His best season at City.
But to be serious – his injury was no laughing matter, and I hope he can get back to playing football next season and get his mojo back. I just doubt that will be at City, where it just hasn't worked out.

Vincent Kompany – 8

He only fails to score more because he is not a regular, and never will be now. But still, what an impact, from someone I thought was finished two years ago, his ageing body ready to give up the ghost. Vinny himself was not ready to however. What a way to go out, what a player, what a man. And he proved that even at 33 and with his injury record, he still has plenty more to give. I'm thankful we got 11 years of service, and I am thankful he went out with the biggest of bangs.

Nicolas Otamendi – 7

Didn't really do anything wrong, but was relegated down the pecking order after making the PFA Team Of The Year last season. When he did play he did fine, and rarely let down the side, one error against Burnely aside. But his frustration at not playing more was well-documented and thus began the rumours that he will leave this summer, perhaps to Atletico Madrid.

I hope he stays, as he has been a consistent, tough performer over the past two seasons, and with Vinny leaving it would prove problematic to lose him too.

Aymeric Laporte – 9

Absolutely peerless performances all season from the guy whose name was always first on the team sheet. Pep realised quickly that he was key to the defence, playing him virtually every week, rotating his partner on many occasions, even utilising him at left-back every now and then too. The fact that he remains without an international cap is staggering. A classy act whose rare poor game was costly against Spurs in the Champions League, but no player is perfect. He has been Mr. Consistent, putting in classy performances week after week, and most of the season was a case of Pep picking Laporte + 1 in defence.

John Stones – 6.5

A surprisingly downbeat season for Stones, and I am not sure why. He just seemed to be one of those players, like Sane, that Pep stopped trusting, yet had not put in any terrible performances that spring to mind. It's none of my business, but he had a relationship break-up and perhaps he had other things on his mind. He is human after all. Am hopeful we see a lot, lot more of him next season, as assumed him and Laporte would be our 1st choice partnership for many years to come.

His lack of match time is even more surprising when you consider that Stones had the highest average pass success rate (94.2%) out of all the players to feature in the 2018/19 Premier League.

Kyle Walker – 7

I spent a lot of time trying to score Walker, and essentially failed. This was not a stellar season for the full-back, but after dips in form, I felt he recovered well to put in some strong performances in the run-in. He is certainly beginning to split fans however, if social media is anything to go by, and perhaps it should not be. There were lapses in concentration, but what frustrated me more was his reluctance to overlap and provide a real attacking threat. Low on assists, low on great crosses, I feel he does not fit the remit of modern full-backs. But maybe he is doing this on instruction. Either way, he could put in 10 consistent performances and get little praise, so he can't win sometimes.

Benjamin Mendy – 5

Not sure what score I can give to someone who yet again rarely stepped on the pitch. The stats will tell you that he made 14 appearances over the 2018/19 season but it felt like less. Yet again, his season was wrecked by injuries, and his presence was felt more online than on a football pitch.

The news from this week heartens me though – he missed the trophy parade and cancelled his summer holiday to remain in Barcelona to deal with ongoing knee problems and to try and be ready to go for pre-season.

The down side is that he is having these problems in the first place when he tries to play football. He is in good hands, so fingers crossed. Many City fans have been scathing of his attitude whilst injured, with reports of him clubbing and being late for training. I am not here to be his apologist, but as I will repeat in the final article of this book, suffering a succession of serious injuries must be devastating to any sportsman (or woman), and it's easy for us to judge from the sides lines. Let's hope he can finally get going next season – if he cannot, this poses another serious problem for Pep Guardiola in a position that has been undermanned since the day Mendy arrived.

Danilo – 6

Another player marked down for a lack of playing time. It's a shame really, a sign of the ridiculous depth of this squad and also a sign of the problems that such depth can bring. Kyle Walker did not have a stellar season, but Pep persevered with him apart from a two week spell mid-season. Danilo therefore was rather frozen out, which was a waste as he rarely let the side down, and clearly is a top class footballer, despite his nightmare spell at Real Madrid. He filled in at left-back too before Zinchenko made the position his own, but filling in is all he was doing – it was not a natural role for him, and it never will be. Don't be surprised if he leaves this summer, and regret that we didn't see a bit more of him during his time at the club. Having said that, a recent tweet suggests he is staying, but maybe I am reading too much into it.

Zinchenko – 8

Only fails to score higher because it was the 2nd half of the season by the time he came of age and nailed down the left-back position. But what performances they were, vital to City getting 98 points and regaining their Premier League title. City really dodged numerous bullets over the past 18 months or so – not signing Fred, not signing Jorginho and not signing Alexis Sanchez. But top of the pile must be the decision whoever made it, not to sell Zinchenko. He developed superbly during the season in a position that is not natural to him. The dilemma is what to do with him in the future. In his preferred position further up the pitch, you cannot see him getting more game time. Is he prepared though to be utilised as left-back for the coming seasons? I hope so, as City have stumbled across a gem.

Eric Garcia – 6
Can't really score, as scant evidence – played three games in cup, and I liked what I saw. Barcelona were gutted to lose him to City and I can see why, even if concerns remain about his lack of physical stature for his position. One to watch.

Eliaquim Mangala - 0
Wait, what, he's still here?!!!!!
<reads Wikipedia entry>
He signed a contract extension during the season???!!!!!

David Silva - 7.5
Some of you may look at that score and think it is a tad generous. I get that. But apart from the fact that scoring a player over a season is impossible and rather futile (I've come too far to stop now though), we must remember that he was on sparkling form earlier in the season. Then there was an injury, is hair started growing back, and the rest is history. He has, admittedly, been poor in quite a few games, but in others he had been great, just not the player many of us regard as the greatest ever.
So all in all, a mixed bag, but he contributed greatly still to another record-breaking season.

Kevin De Bruyne - 6
When I looked back at the season highlights, Kevin featured more than I realised, starting 22 games, and the season was not quite the wash out I originally imagined. But it was a season that never got going. As soon as he regained fitness and form, another injury was always around the corner. Let's hope he has

a relaxing summer and comes back keen to make up for last time. It makes it even more amazing that City got 98 points without being able to call on him for most of the games.

His final shift of the season, in the cup final, reminded us not only of what he had missed, but also what an astonishing achievement the treble was without his services for much of the time.

Bernardo Silva - 9

I realised pretty quickly in his first season that Bernardo Silva was really rather good, but I could not have foreseen that he would be THIS good. My player of the season amongst the stiffest of competition, Bernardo was a revelation week after week, and I reckon City's most consistent performer too. Most of you agreed, as he was named Player Of The Season at the trophy parade too. You could list his average or poor performances on one hand. You could list them on Abu Hamza's hand. His skill set was varied, his work ethic unparalleled, his ball control mesmeric. He can also perform centrally or wide. A popular member of the squad, and speaker of four languages. He is, quite simply, magnificent.

Stat: Bernardo Silva made more tackles (79) than any other City player. Fernandinho made 77. He also won possession in the final third more than anyone else too.

Ilkay Gundogan - 8

If you're still one of those weirdos that thinks Gundogan isn't very good at football, then i would suggest that perhaps football isn't the sport for you. He is one of the unsung heroes of the season, stepping in when Fernandinho finally burned out and putting in a succession of great performances to see City through to a glorious treble. Sign that contract Ilkay right now, please.

He is not showy, his top trump stats may suggest he excels at very little, but that does not tell you the story at all. He is a great metronome, perfect at controlling midfield and keeping things ticking over. He may never master the dark arts like

Fernandinho to make that defensive midfield slot his own, and he may not want to, and that's part of the problem. I'm not convinced he is truly good enough further up the pitch, not for the biggest games anyway, but he is more than good enough to be part of this squad, and we're lucky to be able to call on such talent as him.

Stat: Gundogan made more successful passes in the opposition half (1905) than any other City player.

Fernandinho - 8

Another player that loses a mark for playing time, the worry being that the body of the 34 year old is finally beginning to show its age. When fit, he was exactly what you expect him to have been – an absolute colossus in front of the defence. As mentioned though, injuries hit him towards the end of the season, after he was substituted in the Carabao Cup final. We may not get as much football out of him from now on, which poses a problem, and above all is a sad thought, as he is two players in one and close to irreplaceable.

Stat: Fernandinho had the most interceptions of any City player – 65. Laporte was 2nd with 59.

Fabian Delph - 5

A disappointing season after he performed so admirably in an unfamiliar role last season. Injuries have followed him around like a faithful hound yet again as you would expect, to the extent that sometimes you forgot he existed. When he did play, it did not tend to go well. Think of Swansea in the cup or Spurs away in the Champions League. It's a shame, as he is the perfect squad player - English, didn't cost much, not on high wages, can play more than one position and of course an excellent footballer as shown by Gareth Southgate's inclusion of him in any England squad when he is fit. I wouldn't be surprised if he moved on to pastures new this summer. When City lost, he tended to be playing, which is rather damning.

Phil Foden - 7

I know you want me to give him a 10, and maybe considering his age I should, but I am trying to be consistent with these scores, pointless as they are, so must factor in playing time. This was the season that Phil broke through into the first team squad and then into consideration for the first team, even in big matches. Next season should see that progress further. He could not have done more, putting in assured performances that belied his age. He scored across the competitions, but his winner early on against Spurs in the league game is surely the highlight of a fledging club career. He's Phil Foden, and he's one of our own. City tied him down to a new contract mid-season too, so the future is very bright indeed.

Riyad Mahrez – 6.5
It's been a difficult season by City's high standards for the sole signing of last summer. When you actually watch back all the match highlights as I have in recent weeks the mark seems a tad unfair, but I guess highlights packages can distort. I remember at some point in September or early October commenting on a podcast that Mahrez had begun to settle in nicely. That form obviously did not last, and he flitted in and out of the team for the rest of the season. His biggest problem is not just form, but the fact that he seems to have lost the faith of fans, but it still not too late to turn that around in his second season. The other problem for me was his decision making when in attacking positions, something that Pep can definitely work on. He has frustrated for sure, but he has also scored some heavy goals – winners at Spurs and Bournemouth spring to mind, and of course the tension-removing 3rd goal at Brighton, and the what turned out to be a vital goal at Watford.
And check out the 4th goal at home to Burnley in the league, which is one of the goals of the season.

Leroy Sane – 7
I think this is a fair score considering expectations for last year's Premier League Young Player Of The Year. It's fair to say it's been a mixed bag for Leroy, and my worry is that by the time

you read these words he is no longer at the club. That really would be a shame for a player I expect to become one of the world's greatest. He started the season poorly, got his mojo back but then seemed to lose the faith of Pep in the season's final months. He has the ability, but questions will be asked once more about his attitude and determination to take on board Pep's exacting demands. By the end of the season, he had a greater impact as a substitute than as a starter. No doubt he will be sold on the cheap to Bayern Munich rather than for his actual market value, which is still surely over double the £37m City paid for his services. He still made 44 appearances this season scoring 16 goals and providing a glut of assists. Let's hope he stays.

And yes – I've given a 7/10 to a player with 17 assists for the season. I've got high standards nowadays.

Raheem Sterling - 9

What more is there left to say? He's Raheem Sterling, and he's top of the league.

The season that he came off age, on and off the pitch. He even turned around the opinions of England football fans. The sky is the limit. This was the season where the stats were off the chart, and the composure in front of goal finally arrived, most of the time. I felt, to be uber-critical, that the tense run-in did not produce the best of his form, but that could be said of many of the players, where it was about getting the job done. But Raheem Sterling is now what we would consider world-class, if we actually know a true definition of that. And with a new contract under his belt, he's here to stay. You know a City player is really, really good when they are runner up to a Liverpool player in the PFA Player of The Year awards. He got the vote of football writers though, no doubt swayed by his brave stance against racism off the field that has started a new movement that hopefully snowballs in the coming years.

Stat: Raheem had the most touches in the opposition box of any City player (and probably any Premier League player too) – 428.

David Silva was 2nd with 317. Raheem also created the most chances from open play – 102.

Sergio Aguero - 9

I think he deserves that high a score. To truly appreciate Sergio, you had to look past the statistics, and the statistics are great, with 32 goals in all competitions. Impressive indeed, as he once more got 20+ goals in the Premier League, whilst also becoming City's record goal scorer. But now more then ever, he was the player Pep wanted him to be. His game has never been more well-rounded as it is currently, so even when he was not scoring he was contributing. Working his arse off basically, the Old Trafford derby being a case in point. And whilst he still had some injuries, they were scarcer than in past seasons.
I can't deny it though - I just prefer him with dark hair.

Gabriel Jesus - 7

Another strange year in a way for a player still young, still developing. I still feel however that Gabriel did not kick on this season, but I would not be giving up on him yet. The stats suggest otherwise, but he was helped by a blitz of goals in the New Year. I wouldn't be calling him a flat-track bully just yet though, but you still feel he is not a natural goal scorer. He does not shoot enough for me, and you also wonder what his actual best position is, and what system suits him best. A team at this level is judged by the highest standards and there was plenty to enjoy from Gabriel during the season, including the first four-goal haul of his career. There were rumours towards the season end of him moving on, and a huge offer would be hard to resist, but a huge offer is unlikely as his stock has not risen, and I want to see him given more time to hopefully develop at City.
What he undoubtedly is, is a team player, and there was certainly no problem with his work-rate, and ethic. I just get this hunch that he is the one player least likely to settle in England – it was after all a huge upheaval for him to move to City. But we

will see. And I was glad to see him end on a high with a great cup final performance.

Pep Guardiola – 9.5

I could take a whole point off for his approach to the Tottenham Champions League 1st leg, but I am not in the mood to do so days after City completed an unprecedented domestic treble. Quite simply, he is the greatest manager in the world. He is not perfect, no one is, but he is the sort of man who would not be satisfied with perfection anyway. City won 50 games in a single season. City got 98 points in the league. City won both domestic cups. Hatchet jobs are being written on how football is now broken, and they are being written not because City spent loads of money, but because they have a manager who has raised the bar when we thought that wasn't possible. If English football does become uncompetitive, and it probably won't, then it is down to one man. And that man is manager of your football club.

Q & A

With the season over, I asked a few of the City podcast community their thoughts on the amazing nine months we had just witnessed. This is what they had to say on the 2018/19 season. Answers are from Mark Meadowcroft, Ste Tudor, Sam Lee, Stefan Borson, David Doodson, Leon Butler and Lloyd Scragg.

Now that the season is over, where does the domestic treble rate in the list of greatest achievements?

<u>Mark</u>: It's difficult to argue that the Cup win is not worth more than the two additional points we won last season.

<u>Ste:</u> By virtue of the fact that it's never been achieved before then it has to be right up there. Because Liverpool ran us so close then a single slip from February on – a total of 19 games across all three comps – would have made it impossible. They were brilliant for half a season then perfect for the other half. It takes a rare team to have the ability and mental fortitude to do that.

<u>Sam:</u> Well, there's a lot to go at here. Real Madrid winning three CLs in a row, the various teams to have won trebles (including the CL), unbeaten seasons, teams like Leicester and Atletico winning their leagues. The biggest successes always involve the Champions League, or those unpredictable fairy tales, because they're the ones that tend to be remember around the world - but think about the trebles that Barcelona have done (with Pep and without) that don't get *that* much coverage compared to when an English team did it in 99. That goes to show that globally the achievement has to be truly special to be remembered. What City have done is special and is a fantastic achievement - let's not forget those who doubted Guardiola could succeed here, before and after he arrived - but globally I'm not sure it will quite reach the top because that's where the really remarkable things come into play. This is an absolutely made-up and ill-considered figure but maybe it's a Top 30

achievement, perhaps, given the stats behind the Premier League win.

Stefan: The team is clearly one of the greatest ever in world football. But it's understandable that people demand a European element for the very highest accolades.

David: The domestic treble (or quadruple) is comparable with any achievement since the premier league's inception (it's when football started after all!). For me, the title race and eventual victory is the thing that puts it alongside United's treble in 1999. Context has to be given to the Premier league title race in which we gathered the 2nd highest total in Premier League history, won the league by 1 point and had to win 14 games on the spin to do so.

Leon: At the very top for me...Just a shame I was in LA! Obviously the 2011 FA cup and 93.20 will always be very special to all of us, as it had been so bloody long...

But this season, with key injuries, Liverpool on our tails and only one signing was AMAZING and thus the greatest!

Lloyd: In my lifetime it's certainly the best – and that's all I can really account for really. Winning the league in 2011/12 was incredible, overturning an eight point lead with six games to go, but this was better. To win three of the four competitions we entered into at the start of the season is frankly ridiculous. Especially when you consider that we were the length of Sergio's quiff away from progressing in the Champions League back in April. We owe so much of this season's achievements to Pep and his indomitable spirit. He's a once in a generation coach.

And where does it rate in English football's greatest achievements?

Mark: Impossible to say – and rather dull to argue about. I never saw the Preston Invincibles. And I don't know what metric could be used to compare for example the achievement of this City side and Leicester City in 2016. Put another way, it would be fun to think of Kompany and Cantona going head to head in a Derby match, prime Graeme Souness trying to disrupt the Guardiola

371

passing game or how Arsenal under George Graham (with refereeing interpretations as they were then) would manage a game against City. I am not saying one is better than the other but this gives a sense of the strengths of teams and players of earlier generations.

Sam: In terms of English football it's certainly up there with the best, perhaps only behind teams who have won the PL and CL in the same season, and of course the 99 treble would be at the top of the tree. But to win all three domestic cups speaks to City's dominance and brilliance and it deserves recognition for the achievement that it is.

Stefan: The greatest. It's the first Treble in a season where the second place team got the 3rd highest point score ever and where positions 2,3,4 and 5 are in Euro finals. The team won 14 straight, it's won something like 30 out of the last 32 (too lazy to count), it won the FA Cup Final 6-0, winning a league cup with a mix of squad and first team, which is an achievement in itself. The greatest domestic achievement, no doubt.

David: See previous answer.

Leon: If you read the press-about 10th!! I'd say it's right up there, but fucking annoyingly, until we win the champions League it won't register. In all honesty, it can't quite match 99 United, but I'd struggle to find any other achievement greater.

Lloyd: Again, in my lifetime, the greatest achievement would have to be Leicester City winning the Premier League. I think anyone reading this book will all long gone by the time something that ridiculous happens again, but City's efforts this season aren't that far behind. Despite our riches, obvious squad quality and coaching brilliance, it's still a phenomenal achievement. Hence why it hasn't been done before.

Were our performances better than last season's Centurions?

Mark: Probably about the same. In both seasons there were thrashings and narrow wins – and were masters of both styles. Weirdly, despite the huge haul of points and trophies, in both seasons we managed to lose back to back games.

Ste: Overall, possibly not but that is probably a trick of the light due to no longer having a surprise factor. In reality they probably reached the same levels but now it was against sides who were better prepared.

Sam: I genuinely think about the same. I'm tempted to say more consistent, but when you look at City's two defeats last season they were quite brutal, but then there were four this season and the last three of those were especially poor. And then of course the wins are the wins, and to get 32 in both seasons shows that the level is about the same. For the extra two defeats this season there were fewer draws, so it's swings and roundabouts. I would say that I think last season was more entertaining in terms of some of the wins. The big scores at the start of the season (7-2 v Stoke. the 6-0 at Watford in September 2017 was perhaps the best performance I've seen from them) and the fast counter-attack goals, the De Bruyne assists, were a bit more spectacular, but this season they've been every bit as effective as they were before, and given Guardiola feared they could have slacked off, that is remarkable. Overall I think the two seasons were very similar.

Stefan: More of the same I think. Can't think we were materially better or worse but the Newcastle defeat was a bad day. But one bad day in 2 years is fine. The other defeats all had extenuating circumstances (Palace a freak, Chelsea we were excellent for 40 mins, Leicester quite unfortunate to lose, Spurs a bit of a toss off).

David: Yes. Teams were more prepared for City than last season and we were without our best player for the majority of the season. The team played under much more pressure, especially during the run in. The season was much more testing mentally.

Leon: Having said all that above-not quite! Only because of a dodgy December/January and the nervy 1-0's at the end. We know why they were nervy of course, but in terms of performances not quite I'm afraid.

Lloyd: I'd probably say that some of our individual performances weren't as good, in terms of the level of football played (i.e. the 0-6 vs. Watford last season and the 7-2 vs. Stoke) but I think the season's performance taken as a whole is better. To come out on top against a Liverpool team that only lost once in the league is seriously impressive, almost logic-defying.

What impressed you most about the side during the season?
Mark: 18 wins out of 19 after Boxing Day in the League was quite exceptional. The last four league games were the equivalent of carrying a Ming vase across a polished floor while wearing socks. All four were eminently winnable. All four also had obvious dangers but the focus we showed (greatly helped by Kompany being completely on it) was outstanding.
Ste: The aforementioned mental fortitude that was needed to get over the line. Six 1-0 wins in the last two months meant it was nerve-wracking in the stands but the lads kept their composure (and more importantly their belief and trust in each other).
Sam: The complete lack of complacency from the outset, and then the determination to win every single game, in the face of all the external noise and Liverpool and, it must be said, the nerves among City fans after Liverpool beat Spurs and Newcastle during the run-in. Basically, a ridiculous level of consistency and mental strength, best demonstrated by their win against Spurs just a few days after going out of the CL, which would've wrecked a lot of teams.
Stefan: Focus, resilience, mental fortitude
David: I thought under Pellegrini and the 1st season under Guardiola the team were mentally quite weak, unable to react to adversity and generally lose their heads. We had to put up with different examples of adversity this season but came through almost all of them. Most impressive thing is how we dealt with the run in, specifically the week of Arsenal (H), Everton (A) and Chelsea (H) and after being knocked out of the CL Spurs (H) and United (A). All were must win.
Leon: Mental strength, team spirit (AGAIN!) Sergio, Razz, Bernardo and Vinny's last three games.
Lloyd: Its relentlessness – in the face of Klopp's Scouse juggernaut. To hold our nerve to win all of our last 14 Premier

League games, well, I'm not sure I've got the words to describe that to be honest.

And what didn't?

Mark: Why do we always have a wobble in early April and then recover and finish the season very strongly? Spurs and Liverpool have cost us dearly in the last two years. In 2011, we got hammered at Liverpool just before we won the United semi-final. In 2012, we lost at Arsenal and were out of it before we are back in it. In 2014, we lost at Liverpool again and then nearly cocked it up at Sunderland. I get that Christmas results can be unpredictable and see that as an inevitability, but we should be able to sort April out.

Ste: The complacency shown occasionally was nearly their undoing. It was most apparent at St James' Park. Also the controlling of games when two or three goals to the good – taking their foot off the pedal to conserve energy - could be frustrating. Really though it's like pointing out a freckle on a supermodel.

Sam: Ironically they were very unlucky to go out of the CL and I think they could have got to the final had Aguero's arse not been offside, but I don't think they were very good in Europe overall. Shakhtar away was (again, ironically) perhaps the performance most similar to 2017-18, but generally they looked too vulnerable. That's why I don't blame Guardiola for playing more defensive at Spurs, even if he also had to contend with injuries and also prioritised the PL games. He knew City had a soft centre and needed to protect it. The two Lyon games were red flags in the group stage, the start of Hoffenheim away was similar (but a good comeback all the same) and Schalke away was poor too. Something needs to change regarding Europe but I'm not sure what.

Stefan: As a team, nothing.

David: 3 defeats after being a goal up, 2 back to back, was disappointing. Also, not capitalising on a favourable Champions League draw.

Leon: Two words – Benjamin Mendy!

Lloyd: Very little. Pep's team selection for the first leg against Spurs still irks me – I still think he could've played a couple of our 'gun' players and approached it in the same way, but it's history now. I just hope he sticks to his guns in next season's Champions League and doesn't doubt his usual method.

Do you think City will dominate domestic football in the coming seasons?

Mark: Possibly, but there will be fresh challenges next season, and we'll be doing it without Kompany. We start again on zero points. It's important for everyone at the club not to expect anything more than this.

Ste: There will be several more trophies in the next decade, I'm sure of that. Reluctant to commit to 'dominate' though as things can change quickly.

Sam: They should do. My only concern at the moment is how they replace people like Otamendi and Kompany, people who have stepped into the team and ensured there's been no drop-off in quality. City need to get the transfers right again and hope they settle straight away. If they do they'll dominate as long as Guardiola is in charge, and quite possibly afterwards.

Stefan: No, especially when Pep departs.

David: If we get recruitment right this summer, yes. Really feel we have a big summer ahead, mainly based upon replacing players who want to leave/coming to the end of their careers.

Leon: 100%.

Lloyd: I think we'll be right up there as long as Pep's at the helm. Liverpool have a serious challenge on their hands trying to replicate this season's league effort, but that squad can be significantly improved. It'll be a fascinating rematch.

Does the Champions League knock out all rankle with you, or was a quadruple never really feasible?

Mark: It does in that Guardiola's selections for the first leg against Spurs and the cup semi-final that immediately preceded it were strange and wrong. It's as if the Brighton team should have played Spurs and vice-versa. Aguero taking the penalty at Spurs also upset me. Gundogan is better and should have dealt with it. However, it's a cup competition and our cup good fortune came at Swansea and also with Kepa's bizarre meltdown in the League Cup final. In the famous words of Meatloaf in the final track of Bat out of Hell, two out of the three ain't bad.

Ste: It was feasible towards the end and I really didn't mind people pointing that out. As for the defeat the manner in which it happened was only absorbed when I viewed it as compensation for the Aguero moment in 2012.

Sam: Like I say, I would have liked to have seen City against Ajax and I think they could have won, despite the issues I outlined. The annoying thing about the Spurs tie was that it was so very close in the end, and that's when you consider a missed penalty, goalkeeping mistakes and Laporte having an uncharacteristic shocker. All of that and it still came down to a falling VAR call. And also, had Sterling's goal been allowed to stand it would've been an iconic hat-trick and it may well have been the spark City need in Europe to kick on. Quadruple was feasible but it would've been even harder had they got to the semis. But I would have backed them to win anyway.

Stefan: I'm torn between the mistakes of Spurs away (the team was bizarre as was the decision to play so conservative) and thinking that a semi could have cost us 2 points and lost us the league. On balance, it was probably a blessing given how competitive the league was.

David: It does because we had a favourable draw to the final really. No complaints really with the Spurs games, especially the home game, ridiculously fine margins.

Leon: It kills it all a bit for me to be honest...If it was an Ajax v Barcelona final I'd be fine.

Lloyd: Yes, a bit. Although I would've snatched your hand off for the domestic treble before that first leg against Spurs. I think the reason it still rankles is because whilst incredibly unlikely, it was feasible and we still had a huge chance to do it – even in the second leg. But there's always next year...

What do City need to do in the transfer market in the summer?

Mark: I am not going to get many marks for originality here. Physically dominant centre back (or we are going to be playing against a target man every match), a successor for Fernandinho and a like for like upgrade for any other senior player that leaves.

Ste: A centre-back, centre-mid and centre-forward. A new spine which is somewhat concerning.

Sam: Basically a new defence! A RB, CB, LB, and then a defensive midfielder. I don't think they want all of those positions (LB for example) and they would like a new forward too, but those four would be what I would prioritise.

Stefan: I think it's a very tough summer. Delph should go as he can't be relied upon, Vinny is a real loss, good time to sell Ota and can understand Danilo wanting to go. So that's a lot to buy and I'd take at least one extra to cover any ban. Sane should stay as should Gundo but if they go that's more to buy. I'd also like an extra forward but I can't see how we can in this window.

David: A lot! Sort out Gundo and Sane either way and act accordingly to what's decided. Replace Kompany/Otamendi, probably 1 will do with Ferna dropping back. Holding midfielder a must and plan ahead re Silva/Kun.

Leon: Mbappe (dreaming there I know), a left back, holding midfielder, a centre back and LOSE NO ONE ELSE!
Delph can go actually.

Lloyd: Given the anticipated departures, we might need to do a lot. Possibly too much, to be honest. If we do lose Danilo, Kompany, Otamendi, Delph and Leroy then that is a hell of a lot of quality and experience to make up. Especially when you factor in the possibility of Gundogan not extending his contract. Our greatest strength this season has probably been our squad depth – but that could quickly become our biggest weakness if we don't absolutely nail our recruitment, which will be very difficult.

How big a blow to City is Vincent Kompany leaving? What does he mean to you?

<u>Mark</u>: We have lost a defender who proved he could still do it and a proven big match performer, but that's not the biggest thing. Since Guardiola came in, the dressing room has been very solid. But that is because Vinny is at the apex. There is absolutely no doubt who is in charge and everyone but everyone instantly defers to him. Without him there will be a vacuum and it will be very strange for the players. Who will take on the mantle? My fear is that Sergio Aguero, love him as I do, wants to do it but is not the right character for the job. Guardiola is going to need to manage that. We need to announce a new captain before the start of pre-season. After some consideration, I think City have done well with a Belgian in this role, so I would appoint another one.

<u>Ste:</u> He's been City's leader for the whole journey and in that sense he is irreplaceable. From a footballing perspective someone like De Ligt appears to be a likely successor.
What does he mean to me? I love him more than he will ever know.

<u>Sam:</u> It's a blow because like I say, City need to freshen up the squad a bit and they'll need the new players to be good straight away. I think Kompany would have had a role in that anyway, but then you have the fact that any of the new signings may well need to bring a new kind of leadership to the team. Obviously City have existing leaders of different types, whether Fernandinho, Silva or Aguero, but seeing Kompany go is a huge loss - even if there are CBs who could come in and play to a higher standard and more regularly. It's just the intangible things that'll be hardest to replace.

<u>Stefan</u>: It's a blow but we have to move on. It means a lot, he's been a big presence in the club and therefore our lives for 11 years. We've lived the highs and the injuries with him. So it's painful news.

<u>David:</u> Huge. His performances in the run in spoke for themselves but it's clear how much the players thought of him and the influence he had off the pitch. Couldn't have asked for

more from a captain, stood up for the club in the face of widespread criticism in an articulate manner. He represented the club and the region and understood what the club meant to the fans.

Leon: Not a big blow if we take our heart strings out of it. BUT he means everything and it's very sad of course! The greatest City leader and icon pretty much since the takeover, and there have been a few!

Lloyd: Huge. It's not really sunk in yet. He's more than just a footballer or a captain, he's almost an embodiment of everything that is good and right about Manchester City in 2019. He's a king amongst men and an incredible leader to boot. There will be a big hole in the dressing room I'm sure.

What will the rest of the top 6 do over the summer to try and stay competitive?

Mark: Liverpool need to focus on keeping their players – I wouldn't be shocked if Real Madrid came calling. They are very good and as long as their key players stay fit, they should keep City honest. Spurs need to reinforce but that stadium looks awfully expensive. Arsenal will improve but not dramatically so. Chelsea need a strategy. And United will play McTominay as a Trequartista , play Phil Jones in the Baresi role and focus maintaining the google review scores for their App. And Ashley Young will captain them. Aged 56. As an exciting winger. After a thrilling comeback 3-2 win over Sheffield United at OT in November with a penalty, a double deflection and the ball rolling over the line after hitting Chris Smalling on the ear in the 92nd minute, Henry Winter will tweet: "United back in the top half tonight and with Ole firmly at the wheel, they are looking up rather than down". There will be dabbing.

Ste: It will be defining seasons for Arsenal and Chelsea with Emery and Sarri in their second seasons. Liverpool will strengthen in midfield and up front. United require a huge overhaul and won't be challenging for some time to come. Spurs intrigue. Surely they need to bring players in this time.

Sam: Spend in most cases, but really there's not a lot most of them can do to be competitive with City. Chelsea won't be able to spend and are in a mess. Arsenal don't have much money and are miles off City. Spurs would be interesting but the squad could break up. I thought they would stay together but there's a suspicion that Pochettino would leave, and a lot of players are out of contract. So they're tricky. United are a mess but can at least spend a lot - whether they get that right is doubtful. Liverpool need another CB and maybe a LB, but if Keita and Fabinho progress they're quite well set. They could do with another forward but like Spurs it's kind of hard because it seems the main three are untouchable, and who wants to be signed to be a back-up? A lot depends on whether they're hungrier to win the title and therefore play out of their skins again, or if we see that they over performed hugely last season. And with VAR they will not have some of the luck they had last season.

Stefan: All have different needs and funding. Liverpool will look to find one really really good player and a couple of smart buys to maintain 97 points. They don't need much with Ox and Gomez to bolster the squad and Keita and Fabinho a further year in. Chelsea can't buy so have to craft something from what they have. Spurs are unlikely to be stronger after this Summer. Arsenal need an entire back 4 but have no budget. And United are a mess so need a few windows to correct that. In short, it's all about Liverpool.

David: United – Complete revamp.
Chelsea – Bring back loan players and sign new contracts for players who are going out of contract, eg Giroud. Losing Hazard plus transfer ban will make it difficult for them.
Spurs – Bolster squad. Players like Grealish if Villa don't come up but I don't see a huge improvement being made to their starting 11.
Arsenal – Defenders and lots of them! Also really need a quality replacement for Ramsey but I think they'll focus on the defence.
Liverpool – Don't think they'll do much, bit of creativity in centre midfield I think.

Leon: I honestly don't really care!
They need to spend a lot of money. Liverpool won't do that

again by the way. Spurs lost 13. United need a new manager and a clear out. Chelsea need a new owner and manager. Arsenal could be okay with a new defence and a leader in midfield.

Lloyd: United have too much to do, probably Arsenal too. If Chelsea lose Hazard and have this transfer ban imposed then I think they will too. And if Spurs lose Pochettino – then I think their title hopes are also over! However, if they can keep him and re-invest some of the money they'll get from outgoings (Rose, Alderweireld etc.) this summer then they could certainly compete. Liverpool undoubtedly have the least to do. They just need to strengthen their squad with genuine quality (like the signings of Gundogan and Bernardo) to ease the strain on their best XI. Klopp also needs to get that same consistency out of them again next season, which will be no mean feat.

There has obviously been numerous spats with journalists over how City have been reported in the past few months. Have City fans been overly-sensitive or has their anger been justified?

Mark: In isolation, much of the reporting can be classed as if not fair then robust and understandable and I get the point that Rob Harris isn't at the FA Cup Final to win popularity points. However, the general impression was of a media desperate for clicks in the knowledge that positivity over Liverpool and United sells as does sneering negativity about City. The demographics of newspaper readership in particular are what they are. There are exceptions and I don't want to paint everyone in a poor light but I can't help thinking that the coverage of my club – particularly from the traditional London newsrooms is as much ill-informed as anything. They don't know much about us so they are prey to some fairly obvious examples of groupthink. It's also why I don't think titles should be banned from The Etihad. The best way is to engage with them and try and get them to buy a train ticket from Euston and take a tram from Piccadilly.

Ste: The anger has been entirely justified. We are treated uniquely and unfortunately it is only worsening.

Sam: Both. I can see both sides. There are legitimate concerns about the club and City fans should be open to the idea that there's a chance the club have broken rules across the board. It's not just FFP, but signing young players, third-party ownership, all sorts. If that's proven then the punishments, and criticism, will have to be accepted. And the fans who have defended the regime in Abu Dhabi need to have a look at themselves. But I also sympathise with City because the criticism has gone overboard in some quarters, and ultimately only now that City have started winning regularly. Had they not been so good, I genuinely don't think people would care about their owners or alleged wrongdoings so much. Likewise, a lot of journalists and fans of rival clubs need to have a look at themselves and work out if they hold everything else in their lives to the same standards as they hold City.

Stefan: We can't all be imagining it. Delaney is the final straw. I can't even start breaking down where he's wrong. He belied his underlying issue with his mention of capitalism. I accept if you are a socialist, City's success is horrendous.

David: Probably somewhere in between. We're up there to be shot at and we will be by opposing fans because of jealousy and we know the big clubs get the most clicks for the press. We do need thicker skin though, accept criticism will come our way.

Leon: 100%, but it makes my blood boil so much I can't say much more...

We know the reasons, we're a relatively small club and our owners are who they are. We have none of the highest paid, we have no world record transfer fees. But we have a spine, an amazing team spirit and the best manager in the world.

Lloyd: Some fans have been – but that's natural. On the whole though, I think a decent amount of the anger has been justified. There has been a clear pattern about our recent results, performances and achievements have been caveated and that's been disappointing, but ultimately not that surprising. The club clearly has a case to answer for a number of different topics, but

383

to say that this season's footballing and coaching feat has been 'diminished' or 'denigrated' because of geo-political issues or our heavy spending (which is by no means unprecedented) is ridiculous. The latter narrative in particular is just incredibly lazy and ignores the brilliance of Guardiola and this team.

So have the team received enough praise for their achievements?

Mark: In the sense that if Liverpool had won the league, there would have been calls for church bells to ring out across the land, then no. But frankly I don't care if The Sun only covers my football club minimally. They aren't interested in us and we aren't interested in them.

Ste: Well, that depends what you mean by praise. It's easy to lavish platitudes on any team and City have had plenty of them. We're 'incredible' and 'brilliant' and even the 'best ever'. But there is zero warmth or connection, nothing like what we saw with Liverpool and United in their heyday. It's all been very detached as if praising a scientific breakthrough.

Sam: From some people yes, from some people no.

Stefan: Sort of. Ex pros recognise their brilliance and I suspect European football too. Everyone knows that City really should be in Madrid. The journalists seem to be largely left leaning politically and in that context the story is asterisked.

David: Universally, no.

Leon: You know we haven't, but like the Sterling treatment it will change. I just have to delete twitter and we get through financial fair play.

Lloyd: No. Definitely not in the last few weeks, anyway.

Does it bother you about our owners or our wealth?

Mark: Not really. I think they are good at their job and have kept their promises to me. I like the money invested in the East Manchester community and the way Womens' football is played and promoted is something every City fan should take pride in. In the 1990s when City were terrible I became a bit of an Italian football nerd. Did the ownership of AC Milan take away from my enjoyment of Maldini, Baresi, Boban, Savicevic, Massaro, Desailly and the rest of them? No – even though I didn't support them. I don't see many bien pensant Guardian hipster football journalists caveating the greatness of that team with the observation that Berlusconi was well into his FFP.

Ste: I'm not clued up on geopolitics but what I read concerns me a good deal. Regarding the wealth though...nah.

Sam: As an outsider I would say the owners should bother fans, not that I expect them to stop supporting the team. I don't expect them to go into bat for Abu Dhabi either. I would be unhappy with the owners if it were my club but ultimately I wouldn't care so much and I'd just get on with going to games and supporting the team as normal, much like other areas of my life where I probably buy clothes, eat food and use technology that has questionable origins.

Stefan: I am not responsible for my own government even if I vote for them so the idea I have some moral obligation to oppose regimes in foreign lands that I know literally nothing about via my football team is ridiculous. The emirates own many western investments - it's not relevant to the decision what I spend. Do none of these journalists fly Etihad or Emirates. Do they never holiday in Dubai? Will Delaney refuse to go to Doha for the WC? Do we really need to do a full analysis of the owners of every sponsor to assess whether it can be allowed?

Finally the idea there is one clear right answer or perspective on the gulf states or Yemen is total nonsense. And I'm confident that none of the footy press pack have a detailed understanding of the situation.

David: No

Leon: Nope-City fans deserve the world (I was there in 99 and the preceding years), and if it wasn't us they'd be benefactors to some other team.

Lloyd: Yes, I am concerned about some of the stories and allegations that have been made about our owners. But ultimately, I am able to separate that from the fact that they have been fantastic owners for my football club.

Is there a competition issue in English football now? Should we care either way?

Mark: We won the league by one point. English football has a Guardiola problem. He raises the standard and others raise their game too, just like he did at Barcelona. The rest of La Liga improved too. There was one season very like this when he won the league with 99 points but Real Madrid got 96 with Pellegrini managing them and playing what you might call the Klopp role. Matches like the Cup Final will happen in future because changes in the laws mean losing teams can't put in a few reducers a 3-nil down to in effect close down the match at that score.

Ste: There is not. Spurs knocked us out of the Champions League. Liverpool came within a point of winning title. There has always been a divide between top six and the rest of the league.

Sam: There's a competition issue cos City have Guardiola. It's more about Guardiola than it is about money, and Liverpool just got 97 points anyway. The problem is the difference in revenue between all the top clubs and the rest of the league. City have pulled away because of Guardiola and that's a sporting reason more than it is financial, in terms of how competitive the league is - because the top clubs have been the richest for years now.

Stefan: I can't seriously believe we are actually debating it when 2,3,4,5 are the Euro finalists and where that set of results at the end of the season below City and Liverpool were so mixed. The league is massively competitive. Spurs lost 13 league games - one of the toughest teams.

But even if they are right we shouldn't care. Leagues fluctuate as do teams. This is our time - soon it will be someone else's. Never forget where you've come here from, Never pretend that it's all real, Someday soon this will all be someone else's dream, This will be someone else's dream...

David: No there isn't. We won the league by 1 point and it's the first time the league has been defended in a decade. We won the League Cup on penalties.

Leon: Don't give two sh**s! We suffered for so many years when we couldn't compete, so bo**ocks to all of them.

Lloyd: There is a competition issue in English football – but it's between the Top 6 and the rest of the Premier League. We have deeper pockets than Arsenal for example, but they still have more than enough resources to compete with us as a club. In terms of caring – I do care as I remember what it was like to be a fan of 'mid-table' team – and I hope one day other teams can break the monopoly and spend their way to the upper echelons of the league. But that's more an issue with FFP than anything else…

Player of the season

Mark: Bernardo.

Ste: Bernardo is all things to all men.

Sam: Bernardo.

Stefan: Bernardo- a perfect player with a perfect personality for our club. How can we be so lucky as to have another Silva that is so similar (but likely better) to the original.

David: Bernardo Silva.

Leon: Bernardo...actually no Raz, or maybe Sergio. Can they share it? And Laporte. OK, sorry, STERLING then.

Lloyd: I'd probably say Sterling, just. But both deserve a mention. Raz built on his incredible form last season and developed a real maturity to his all-round game - akin to the manner in which he has matured into a spokesman on some of society's most troubling and pertinent issues. He's developed into a proper leader, both on and off the pitch. As for Bernardo, he might not match Sterling for stats but he's been equally as consistent in terms of his performances, if not more consistent. He stepped up to become the driving force of the team in De Bruyne's absence.

Favourite match?

Mark: The Cup Final and Schalke at home. Similar matches, come to think of it. Although it didn't turn out as we wanted it, the Spurs home CL match was just sensational and if we can't admit that, we are denying ourselves the simple joy of football.

Ste: The 6-0 dismantling of Chelsea was hilarious as Liverpool placed such emphasis on it beforehand. A Aguero hat-trick is always something to cherish.

Sam: Probably the Spurs CL game, as a spectacle and as a "that was the best match I ever went to", but I didn't feel especially happy about it! If not that then either the Arsenal game on the first weekend, or Huddersfield at home, because in both games it was like "oh! This team is evolving!" The Liverpool home game and Leicester were also satisfying but in different ways.

Stefan: Can't split Liverpool H and United A. Massive, tough games (only one tough in reality).

David: Liverpool (H) – two unbelievable teams going at it in a fantastic atmosphere.

Leon: Liverpool win at home, as it stopped them winning the title and no 100 points.

Lloyd: City 2 Liverpool 1.

And favourite moment?

Mark: Anyone who doesn't say Vinny's goal is a liar.

Ste: Sterling's winner v Spurs. For thirty seconds.

Sam: The Kompany goal probably. If I remember anything particularly mad that Ederson did I'll get back to you!

Stefan: Vinny vs Leicester.

David: Kompany's goal v Leicester.

Leon: Vinny screamer obviously.

Lloyd: It has to be Vinny's goal against Leicester.

Finally - did you (eventually) manage to enjoy the season?!

Mark: Of course. We won the treble playing amazing football. If you didn't enjoy that, you deserve to go back to watching Lee Bradbury and Ged Brannan lose at home to Oxford United.

Ste: I somehow muddled through.

Sam: No! And next season will be as bad!

Stefan: As much as I am able to. It's a body of work to look back on rather than to enjoy week by week because the minute we had achieved something the next challenge was there in 2/3 days. However, I did particularly enjoy how shite United were. Something much more immediate throughout the season.

David: Mainly yes. The stress levels were very high during the run in though!

Leon: If I'm honest not as much as I should have. And I went to a lot of games. I moved into my new house and we lost 4 in a month. I missed the League Cup final because I had to move more stuff in and me and my girlfriend split up when the Spurs dodgy handball put us out the Champions League. Then we got back together, I had to go to LA and missed all the fun!!

Lloyd: Yes. It was a corker. The pressure valve release when Mahrez bagged against Brighton was immense. It was like 9 months of tension just being released at once. It was a lovely feeling knowing we'd beaten the Scousers. Oh and the FA Cup day out was a ball too – even if it did cap-off a 'diminished' treble.

Here's To You Vincent Kompany

*"As overwhelming as it is, I feel nothing but gratefulness.
I am grateful to all those who supported me on a special
journey, at a very special club.
I remember the first day, as clear as I see the last.
I remember the boundless kindness I received from the people of
Manchester."*

The fug of a day's drinking in London hanging over me, I logged into twitter on Sunday morning to soak up the adulation of the entire UK football press at City's glorious FA Cup final victory the previous day. Suddenly something caught my attention and I got that all too familiar nauseous feeling in the pit of my stomach.

It's fair to say I wasn't expecting this on a dull Sunday morning. Manchester City's captain Vincent Kompany had announced that he was leaving the club after an 11 year spell and 360 appearances that saw him win 4 league titles, 4 League Cups and 2 FA Cups for good measure.

This day was always going to come. As a City fan, there are a number of bona fide legends whose departure will be a tough pill to swallow. But depart they must, for time waits for no man. What is galling about this departure though is the confidence many of us held that he would stay for another year. In fact, I was sure of it. I could see no reason why he would not.

But I was wrong. Rumours swirled around recently that a new contract was dependent on him being assured great playing time in future. This may or may not be true, but Pep could never promise that, nor would he if he could. The reason for the departure it seems was an offer that was too good to be true. Player/manager at Anderlecht, the club where for Vinny it all began. Now I understand the tears after the Leicester game. He will take a bit of Manchester to Belgium.

This though is truly the end of an era. Signed just before the takeover, for a meagre £6m, and envisaged as a defensive midfielder at first, few if any could have predicted the effect Vincent Kompany would have on Manchester City football club. He was soon moved back into central defence, and the rest is history. The injuries that would hamper his career throughout were perhaps more predictable, hinting at why City could purchase his services for such a small fee. When Kompany joined City from Hamburg in 2008, he was known in Germany as "The Man of Glass" because of the sequence of injuries he sustained there. This constant battle for fitness would characterise Vincent Kompany as much as his prowess on a football field. To talk about Vincent Kompany requires much talk away from the pitch. But first of all, he is a brilliant defender. We cannot focus on his qualities as a man without first dealing with the obvious. As a defender, he is one of the greatest to have graced the Premier League. Anticipation, leadership, desire, organisation and a pure defender who at times almost perfected the art. He was sublime at what he did and in leading others to do likewise. Think back to the title campaign of 2011/12. Many would argue that Joleon Lescott was the best defender that season, but he would never have achieved such levels without Vinny next to him.

And that inspiration led to key moments in our history. We all know about the goal against United, and the astonishing winner against Leicester. I don't believe in destiny or fate, but these moments make me question myself. It was if it was meant to be. When we really needed him, he always stepped up to the plate. That's what you want from a captain, my captain.

But there was always the injuries of course. Without them, what new heights could he have reached? We will never know. 17 Premier League matches this season, the same last. Just 11 the season before, and 14 the season before that. You get the idea. But what stood out above everything else was the absolute, steadfast determination not to give up and to come back and step onto that football pitch again. He changed his diet, he had a meticulous and rigorous regime to strengthen his muscles and even practiced yoga pre-match. He was utterly determined not to be beaten, and he was not. He overcame his demons. Because apart from the physical aspect of his injuries, the psychological damage must have been demoralising, and would have defeated most mere mortals. We shake our head at Benjamin Mendy acting up whilst permanently injured, but footballers just want to play football. To not be able to do so, and to return and then be struck down is devastating, and must have acute psychological effects. Surely Vincent considered many a time whether the battle was worth it?

But he persevered to finish on a high. To finish with an unprecedented domestic treble whilst playing some of the best football of his career at the age of 33. Two years ago I thought he was finished at City. One year ago I thought the same. And now I am gutted that he is not here for at least another year.

As for his final three years, I always got the feeling that Vinny provided a dichotomy for Pep's philosophy. I felt he wasn't a "Pep" player as such. His passing is hardly substandard, but he did not have the grace on the ball that someone like John Stones or Aymeric Laporte have. He is also a player that plays on the edge much of the time, something that threatens Pep's constant need for control of a football match. I thought he had little future at City after Pep arrived, especially when you factored in a body that appeared to be at breaking point by the time he hit his thirties.
But in time Pep understood that sometimes other, rare qualities can be as important as a footballer's skillset. There is after all a reason why, when the pressure hit the stratosphere during this season, Pep often turned to Vinny. Why he was picked for big games. His inclusion in the FA Cup final team was pretty much a given.

He was so much more than a great footballer though. So, so

much more. In a time when the club and its fans have had to justify their existence and their support, Vincent Kompany was the perfect representative for the club. So perfect even rival fans found it impossible to dislike him. A diplomat, public speaker, a fan representative. Yes, Vinny understood the fan base he served, and understood the problems we face. He got it. It's why I'm almost surprised that management is his next step. The opportunity was no doubt irresistible, but he could have done anything. He acquired business qualifications, he fights for the homeless and countless other good causes, and he just cares. He cares not just about the club he played for, but the city in which he lived. He would be a brilliant politician, but I am glad he remains in the game. Football would be worse for losing his services. And whilst it seems that City were desperate to keep him at the club in some role or another, I fully expect our paths to cross again at some point in the future. He will be back.

The question now is how you replace the irreplaceable. Well, you don't. City will move on, buy new players, and do just fine. But players like Vincent Kompany cannot be bought. They are a rare commodity when a player and a club form a perfect symmetry. So City will win many more games, but there will be the odd occasion, when the heat is on, when the chips are down when he won't be there to turn to, and it will hit home once more that he has gone. He won't be there to put an arm round Phil Foden, to give a stirring dressing room speech or focus the players' minds in the tunnel pre-match.

So goodbye, or au revoir, to the greatest captain I have ever seen at my football club and the greatest I will ever see. It was an absolute honour to watch you represent my club for over a decade. When City were not very good, and that was for rather a long time, players came and went at an alarming rate. Legends are rarely created in struggling sides. What the past decade has given us, apart from the amazing football, trophies and intimate knowledge of migrant workers, is the chance to hero worship and share an amazing journey with amazing players, amazing people. None will leave a bigger legacy than our departing captain. Good luck in everything you do. We'll miss you, but as Vera Lynn once crooned, I know we'll meet again, some sunny day. We get to say goodbye at the parade and at an emotional testimonial in September.

So here's to you Vincent Kompany. City loves you more than you will know.

And so we head into the summer sunset, and a welcome break. It's been a blast in the end, though it felt like hard work just being a fan. We should never forget what this team has achieved though, and what it will continue to achieve. We should feel lucky to be around to witness it. There have been many years in my City-supporting life when this sort of success, this level of football, was beyond my wildest expectations, my wildest dreams.
A summer of cricket and tedious transfer speculation awaits, before august arrives and we go through this whole crazy ride again. Make the most of the break.

So thank you Sheikh Mansour – may all your teas be chippy teas. Thank you to all the wonderful players, the background staff, the coaching team and of course thank you Pep.

Up the blues!

Thanks for reading this book. I hope you enjoyed it. I cannot take all the credit for the happy ending.

If you are interested in my other titles (mostly Season Review books), then type my name into Amazon. There's lots there, including a fun book I did with Simon Curtis looking at 10 classic City matches.

And if you are into Twitter, please follow me: I'm @howiehok3434 (until they ban me again)

Thanks once more!

46609267R00233

Printed in Poland
by Amazon Fulfillment
Poland Sp. z o.o., Wrocław